The
Spirit of
Ancient
Peru

THE SPIRIT OF

TREASURES FROM THE ANCIENT PERU

MUSEO ARQUEOLÓGICO RAFAEL LARCO HERRERA

Edited by Kathleen Berrin

With essays by

Elizabeth P. Benson

Richard L. Burger

Christopher B. Donnan

Clifford Evans

Esther Pasztory

María Rostworowski de Diez Canseco

THAMES AND HUDSON

This book has been published in conjunction with the exhibition
The Spirit of Ancient Peru:
Treasures from the Museo Arqueológico Rafael Larco Herrera

Fine Arts Museums of San Francisco
M. H. de Young Memorial Museum
17 May–10 August 1997

Knoxville Museum of Art
Knoxville, Tennessee
26 September 1997- 4 January 1998

Published with the assistance of the Andrew W. Mellon Foundation Endowment
for Publications; the National Endowment for the Arts, a Federal agency;
Mrs. Paul L. Wattis; an anonymous private donor; and Friends of Ethnic Art

First published in the United States of America in hardcover in 1997 by
Thames and Hudson Inc., 500 Fifth Avenue, New York, New York 10110.

First published in hardcover in Great Britain in 1997 by
Thames and Hudson Ltd, London.

Library of Congress Catalog Card Number 97-60322

ISBN 0-500-01802-2

British Library Cataloguing-in-Publication Data
A catalogue record for this book is available from the British Library

Printed and bound in Hong Kong

Contents

Preface

THE MUSEO ARQUEÓLOGICO RAFAEL LARCO HERRERA, the largest private collection of pre-Hispanic Peruvian art in the world, is extremely pleased to collaborate with the Fine Arts Museums of San Francisco in the important task of making the splendid archaeological legacy of ancient Peru known to a larger audience.

This exhibition and publication feature a representative selection of pieces from the civilizations that inhabited the Pacific coastal and Central Andean regions of Peru during its prehistory. Our institution lends these priceless treasures with pleasure as a symbolic invitation to those who wish to understand Peru's magnificent past and explore our country through its art.

Our museum's participation in this momentous cultural event furthers a fundamental objective: to communicate to the world in an organized and informative way the highest artistic expressions of the societies that lived in our land many hundreds of years ago, civilizations admired for their advancement and sociocultural development. This was the goal of the museum's founder, Rafael Larco Hoyle, who spent decades forming this collection and devoted much of his life to pioneering systematic research and advancing archaeological knowledge.

More than thirty years after the death of Rafael Larco Hoyle, our institution hopes that this exhibition will strongly convey the message that inspired him: to express the grandeur of Peru's ancient inhabitants as a model of the future potential that history demands of our nation.

ISABEL LARCO DE ALVAREZ-CALDERÓN
Director
Museo Arqueológico Rafael Larco Herrera

MOSAIC EARPLUG
Detail of cat. no. 148

Foreword

T HE ANDEAN REGION is a primary area in the Western Hemisphere where ancient arts and civilizations thrived from an early time. The earliest monumental architecture of Peru was roughly contemporary to the pyramids of Egypt. The work of Peru's early civilizations long has been considered among the world's great arts; the peoples of Peru associated with the names and civilizations of Cupisnique, Virú, Chavín, Moche, Nasca, Chimú, and the famed (but much later and short-lived) Inca produced magnificent pottery, precious metallurgy, stone carvings, and textiles. But while Peruvian artistry has long been admired by connoisseurs and specialists, it is much less well known and understood by the North American public.

The Museo Arqueológico Rafael Larco Herrera is one of the largest and most important world repositories of the arts of ancient Peru. Named in honor of the father of the great Peruvian archaeologist Rafael Larco Hoyle, this extraordinary private museum in Lima contains over 45,000 objects. The collection is broad and diverse, containing all media and all periods, but is especially distinctive in the spectacular ceramics of northern Peru, particularly those of the Moche culture (A.D. 50–800).

Peruvian archaeology was always a great interest of the Larco family; Rafael Larco Hoyle and his brothers grew up surrounded by his father's outstanding collection. Rafael Larco Hoyle studied agriculture and engineering in the United States and went on to become a brilliant businessman and pioneer in Peru's sugar industry as the first to introduce mechanical sugar production on the North Coast. His unique efforts in the field of economic growth were paralleled by his knowledge and passion for Peruvian archaeology. He made numerous archaeological discoveries in Peru's North Coast valleys, reshaping the thinking of Andean archaeologists (both American and Peruvian) in the 1940s. So great was his love of Peru's ancient history and his concern for its preservation that throughout his life he remained a dedicated collector, purchasing collections of Peruvian antiquities from a variety of sources.

The Museo Arqueológico Rafael Larco Herrera, repository of one of the finest and most comprehensive collections of northern Peruvian antiquities anywhere in the world, is unique because it was formed by a remarkable and charismatic Peruvian archaeologist with a great devotion to his country. Many of the works in the collection have been known to scholars for decades and have attained an almost iconological quality. Indeed, featured works in the collection frequently have been referred to as unequaled or exemplary and have significantly shaped the study of Peruvian art history. Although many of the key works have been published repeatedly, this is the most comprehensive exhibition of the Larco Collection ever to be presented outside of Lima. The Fine Arts Museums of San Francisco are honored to be the organizing institution.

Many outstanding efforts have shaped the exhibition and its accompanying publication. We are especially grateful to Isabel Larco de Alvarez-Calderón, Director of the Museo Arqueológico Rafael Larco Herrera, and her distinguished husband, Augusto Alvarez-Calderón Wells, for their friendship, generosity in lending, and hospitality to our staff while in Lima. Andrés Alvarez-Calderón, Executive Director, became a great friend and expertly facilitated all aspects of planning, whether large or small. Milagros Alvarez-Calderón could not have been more cordial or helpful, particularly during rugged travel to the North Coast. We want to thank the entire staff of the Larco Museum and especially Claudio Huarache, Keeper of the Collection since its beginnings at the Chiclin museum. Nancy Leigh Reusche was responsible for packing and transporting objects in Lima.

We are, of course, grateful to Peruvian President Alberto Fujimori for granting permission for these treasures to travel and to the Instituto Nacional de Cultura for facilitating government arrangements for all objects traveling from Lima to the United States. Beatriz Boza, Executive Secretary of PROMPERU, offered many helpful suggestions. Always enthusiastic about the project, Ricardo Luna, Peruvian Ambassador in Washington, D.C., assisted with diplomacy and planning. The San Francisco Consul-General of Peru, Jorge E. Roman-Morey, was an outstanding asset to our project; his constant help and good ideas were a major stimulus to the San Francisco presentation.

Mr. Rodney Willoughby, former trustee of the Fine Arts Museums, whose business contacts and friendships in Peru provided the initial impetus for the exhibition, was a valued friend throughout the project. We are also grateful to members of the Peru Exhibition Committee, especially Honorary Consul Isabel Wong, Eduardo Pineda, Marta Espejo, Elisa Norton-Diez, and Gail and Alec Merriam.

I am grateful to Kathleen Berrin, Curator of Africa, Oceania, and the Americas at the Fine Arts Museums, for her tireless work and creative energy as Curator of the exhibition and Editor of this publication throughout the intensive three-year period of their development. During this time, help from a number of scholars were indispensable. Foremost among them was Elizabeth P. Benson, key exhibition advisor, whose longtime experience in the museum field and expertise in the art of the Moche provided myriad insights that significantly shaped the project. The following scholars also offered vital comments, especially during the object selection period: Richard L. Burger, Lucy Salazar-Burger, Christopher B. Donnan, Susan E. Bergh, Heidi King, and Joanne Pillsbury. John W. Rick was especially generous in lending spectacular visual materials of the Peruvian landscape to provide context for the art in the exhibition. We are grateful to Heather Lechtman, Carol Mackey, Craig Morris, Gordon McEuen, Richard Townsend, and Anita Cook for comments on various aspects of the project. Esther Pasztory, long-time friend and colleague, was always available for advice and support.

Many members of the Fine Arts Museums staff worked enthusiastically on the project. Steven A. Nash, Associate Director and Chief Curator, was instrumental in laying important groundwork for the project and meeting with cultural leaders in Peru. Lesley Bone, Objects Conservator, was responsible for the physical safety of the objects as they traveled from Lima to San Francisco to Knoxville and finally back to Lima. Kathe Hodgson, Coordinator of Exhibitions, skillfully handled contracts, budgets, and internal coordination. Other key players in the exhibition planning team were Paula March in marketing, Vas Prabhu in education, Pamela Forbes in media relations, Barbara Boucke in development, and Pamela Mays McDonald in audience development. Others I would like to acknowledge are Victoria Alba, Therese Chen, Linda Katona, Connie King, Debbie Small, Bill White, and the entire technical crew. Within the Department of Africa, Oceania, and the Americas, I would also like to acknowledge NEA intern Jennifer Williams, who worked with tremendous intelligence and energy on all aspects of the project throughout her nine-month tenure. Ellen Werner and Darby Laspa assisted with many aspects of departmental planning.

Ann Karlstrom and Karen Kevorkian in publications helped guide this catalogue from beginning to end and were responsible for the editorial accuracy of all printed material connected with the exhibition. Carlos Rojas Vila of Lima provided many of the excellent photographs that appear here. Eileen Petersen provided valuable clerical support. It is always a pleasure to work with the very talented designer Dana Levy and editor Tish O'Connor of Perpetua Press, both of whom worked tirelessly to prepare this publication. It was a great pleasure for our staff to work with all of the scholars included in this volume.

Generous support for the exhibition and catalogue were made possible by a grant from the National Endowment for the Arts, a Federal agency, and by donations from Mrs. Paul L. Wattis, and an anonymous private donor. The catalogue had the additional assistance of The Andrew W. Mellon Foundation Endowment for Publications and Friends of Ethnic Art. We are grateful to Director Richard Ferrin and the entire staff of the Knoxville Museum of Art for enthusiastically joining with us to host the second venue of the exhibition in Tennessee.

HARRY S. PARKER III
Director
Fine Arts Museums of San Francisco

The Spirit of Rafael Larco Hoyle

An Introduction

Kathleen Berrin

RAFAEL LARCO HOYLE knew the importance of objects. His passion for Peru's prehistory during his lifetime (1901–1966) has hardly been surpassed by anyone before or since. His scrutiny of his collections, near-perfect memory for visual detail, and fervent belief that key objects could prove the validity of theories make him unique among archaeologists. The Museo Arqueológico Rafael Larco Herrera in Lima (Figs. 1, 2) is an eloquent testimony to the vision of this great man.

The family sugar estate, known as Hacienda Chiclin, was located in the Chicama Valley near the modern-day city of Trujillo in northern Peru. On entering the grounds of the hacienda, one first passed a grand colonnade of trees, then discovered a sweeping rectangular vista—the town square—with an elegant, covered, circular bandstand in the center. Other buildings on the hacienda included a theater, a church, several schools, and a hospital. There were also stadiums for bullfights and football.

A series of buildings aligned on one side of the town square constituted the home of the Larco family. On the opposite side was the Chiclin museum (Fig. 3), built in 1926. This elegant building, painted in the characteristic contrasting colors of Moche ceramics (terracotta and cream), featured a profusely decorated exterior with a large stepped doorway, geometric roof details, narrow relief facades of Moche scenes, and face medallions. Echoing the profile figures on Moche fineline pots, these relief scenes were repeated in decorative plaques spread throughout the town square and on the bandstand.

Although the Chiclin museum is now closed and in disrepair, and the former family home is now an agricultural collective, the splendid building, reliefs, and decor of the town square that were the powerful vision of Rafael Larco Hoyle remain as silent tributes to the rich past of Rafael Larco Hoyle's native country. For about thirty years the Chiclin museum was the repository for the Larco Collection—the foundation of many of Rafael Larco Hoyle's numerous insights and the gathering place of scholars. Inside the building, a towering arrangement of objects filled the walls from floor to ceiling, organized by subject, culture, and theme. It is likely that the storage display (Fig. 4) impressed all those who viewed it. It was, in a sense, a reflection of Rafael Larco Hoyle's powerfully intricate and orderly mind—a collector's and an archaeologist's mind—and his tireless search to fill in gaps, seize on congruencies, and establish logical sequences and phases. His aim was to define the entirety of Peruvian civilization.

It was a lofty experience for the Fine Arts Museums to prepare an exhibition of highlights from an internationally acclaimed collection that long has possessed considerable mystique and held a place of reverence in the world of Andean scholarship. In making the selection, we had the good fortune to draw upon the expertise and

Fig. 1 *Museo Arqueológico Rafael Larco Herrera, Lima, 1995*

Fig. 3 *Exterior of the former Chiclin Museum, 1995*

Fig. 2 *Study storage area of portrait vessels, Museo Arqueológico Rafael Larco Herrera, Lima, 1996*

generosity of the Larco museum and of many important scholars and specialists in Andean art and archaeology. Because Rafael Larco Hoyle is particularly associated with such cultures as Moche and Cupisnique, we emphasized these in the selection. We used Larco Hoyle's numerous publications (listed at the end of Clifford Evans's essay, this volume) as a reference, trying to select what he might have selected. Other factors were considered, chief among them the object's condition, aesthetic excellence, and appeal to the public. The latter two categories are always subjective and we have no way of knowing if Rafael Larco Hoyle would have agreed with our choices. The great care he took of his collection indicates that object condition was a category he would have valued.

We were fortunate to be given the freedom to select works both from the museum's public display collection and from Rafael Larco Hoyle's private collection. In this latter category are objects not on public view, but works which he lived with on a daily basis, wanting them close by. These objects presumably inspired him and he may well have found them essential to his soul or spirit.

Rafael Larco Hoyle believed the ceramics of the Moche (or Mochica) people A.D. 50–800) to be the most important and beautiful artworks of all the Peruvian cultures. He spent many passionate hours studying Moche iconography and making interpretations of ancient life. Larco Hoyle's scrutiny and attention to the detail of his beloved Mochica collection led him to many discoveries. His close observations of the distinctive handle shaped like an upside-down U—otherwise known as the stirrup-spout—led him to establish a chronology of Moche culture.

After noting minute changes in the lip, size, and flair of the stirrup-spout and then combing these observations with those made during his important archaeological work in the Chicama Valley (where he was evidently able to compare several hundred grave lots), Larco Hoyle established a five-phase seriation of Moche pottery based on changes in the stirrup-spout form over time. Scholars still rely on this seriation of Moche pottery (Fig. 5), at least for the southern Moche areas, and use it to distinguish five phases. What a revelation it must have been for Larco Hoyle to discover this seriation through patient observation.

Walking down row upon row of floor-to-ceiling shelves of the open storage of the Museo Arqueológico Rafael Larco Herrera today in Lima (Fig. 2), one can see hundreds of Moche pots that Rafael Larco Hoyle deliberately arranged by theme ("sea lions," "mountains," "potatoes"). These arrangements are truly a visual marvel. However, many of the stirrup-spouts on these vessels have suffered damage, while the stronger bodies of these same pots often have remained intact.

Fig. 4 *Interior Chiclin Museum, photographed in 1948.*

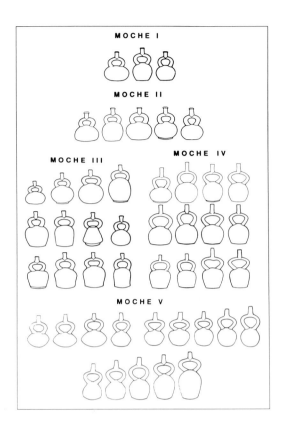

Fig. 5. *Seriation of Moche stirrup-spout bottles developed by Rafael Larco Hoyle based primarily on his sample from the Chicama Valley. Based on Figs. 50–179 in Klein 1967: 78–99 and Figs 25–28a, 29a and 30a in Donnan 1976: 45–50. Fig. 2.6 in Shimada 1994:21, Courtesy of the University of Texas Press.*

Confronted with this evidence, it is impossible not to wonder why the Moche went to such great lengths to embellish their ceramics with spouts that are complex to build, easily breakable, and essentially impractical. It is generally accepted that the stirrup-spout had strong religious significance for the earlier Cupisnique and Chavín cultures and thus was an important archaic and sanctified form for the Moche people. Other scholars (Richard L. Burger, this volume) have commented that the stirrup-spout is symbolic of the all-important cultural value of reciprocity or dualism, ultimately yielding a single linear unity. Others (Rebecca Stone-Miller) argue more utilitarian reasons — that the stirrup spout may prevent evaporation in hot climates and even allow liquids to pour better. After reading Heather Lechtman, one might wonder if the closed, rounded body of the ceramic container and its circuitous spout emphasize the cultural value of instilling "essence" (hidden contents that preserve a material essence or central core). The required spacing of the stirrup-spout handle served to link together two disparate areas; they might even have functioned as metaphors or puns. Anyone studying spouts surely ought to watch their placement and the connection of points, not only where they join but also in their relationship to the orientation of the entire vessel.

It is highly unlikely that such open-ended and essentially unprovable theories about the symbolic meaning of stirrup-spouts would have interested Rafael Larco Hoyle. His was a scientific mind and his ambition was the development of a solid base of information on which to classify the civilizations of Peru. But the vitality informing the many different types of questions posed by today's scholars mirrors the passion Raphael Larco Hoyle felt for studying archaeological questions. I like to think that no matter what questions scholars pose in their scrutiny of objects, the quest is heroic, and the spirit of Rafael Larco Hoyle lives on.

Rafael Larco Hoyle would have been amazed by the number and quality of archaeological discoveries being made in the north of his country. Just in the area near Chiclin, the sites of Sipán, Moche, and El Brujo have in recent years revealed spectacular tomb treasures and painted wall reliefs. But perseverence with work at many other sites yields important and fundamental data and such work continues. This is an exciting time in Andean studies. We are now in a position to know much more about ancient Peruvian civilizations than ever before. It is our hope that art-historical scholarship and a better understanding of the ancient arts of Peru will also flourish. It is in that spirit, too, that we offer this publication with its varying points of view that the Larco Collection has inspired.

Fig. 1 *Rafael Larco Hoyle.*

Rafael Larco Hoyle

1901–1966

Clifford Evans

Reprinted from
AMERICAN ANTIQUITY
Volume 33, Number 2, April, 1968

I N HIS BOOK *PERU* (1966), SUMMARIZING HIS IDEAS ABOUT THE ORIGIN AND SEQUENCES OF pre-Columbian Peruvian cultures, Larco paid tribute to the role of the three great pioneers in Peruvian archaeology—Max Uhle, Julio C. Tello, and Alfred Kroeber. Rafael Larco Hoyle (Fig. 1) is the fourth. The archaeology of the North Coast of Peru today is based on his contributions, including definition of such cultures as Cupisnique (the North Coastal Formative period expression of the Chavinoid horizon) and Salinar (the distinctive white-on-red Late Formative period culture with broader connections to the north in Ecuador and to the south in parts of Peru), and redefinition of Mochica into subperiods, as well as description of Mochica ethnography from the details shown on the painted and modeled pottery.

Don Rafael, or Ray as he was known to his English-speaking friends and colleagues, was born on May 18, 1901, at Hacienda Chiclin, Chicama Valley, near Trujillo, Peru, son of Don Rafael Larco Herrera and Doña Esther Hoyle de Larco. Raised on the sugar hacienda with his younger brothers, Constante and Javier (Fig. 2), he received his primary school education in Trujillo in the Instituto Moderno de Trujillo, Colegio Ntra Señora de Guadalupe, and the Barranco English Institute. In 1914, he was sent to secondary school in the United States and entered the Tome High School in Maryland. While there he was one of the outstanding high school athletes in the state of Maryland, especially in football, although he was also active in baseball, soccer, and athletics in general. In 1919 he entered Cornell University to study agriculture and then attended as a special, non-degree student New York University's School of Engineering in 1922 and the School of Commerce in 1923, where he studied business administration and finance. The primary purpose of this United States education was not to obtain formal degrees, but to study engineering with a view to mechanization of the sugar industry on the family hacienda, to become familiar with the problems of welfare, education, and organization of the sugar workers and their families, and to develop a practical understanding of business operations. To further these studies, he also traveled to Cuba, Puerto Rico, Europe, and Hawaii.

Returning to Peru in late 1923, he applied this business and engineering knowledge to the family interests in Chicama Valley and became president of the Directorio Ejecutiva de Negociación Chiclin and Hacienda Salamanca. These haciendas became famous in the north for outstanding stock raising and for breaking records in sugar production per hectare and sugar per metric ton of cut cane, the result of having been the first to introduce mechanical production on the north coast. In addition, under his direction the family developed a model sugar hacienda at Chiclin, including hospitals, clinics, and schools with advanced systems of education and modern teaching methods.

Fig. 2 *Constante Larco Hoyle, Rafael Larco Herrera, and Rafael Larco Hoyle, at Chiclin.*

Fig. 3 *Rafael Larco Hoyle chatting with Father Soriano in Huaraz, and taking notes for his fieldwork.*

Around 1924, Larco's interest in the archaeology of his country began as a result of his father's influence. On the Hacienda Chiclin, he had lived in a museum atmosphere since a few years after his birth because his famous father had begun in 1903 to assemble a collection of North Peruvian pre-Columbian pottery. While later traveling in Europe, Rafael Larco Herrera visited the Museo del Prado in Madrid and noticed that their collection of Peruvian archaeological materials was poor. He consequently donated his entire archaeological collection to Spain, and today it is on exhibit in the Museo Arqueológico in Madrid.

From this first archaeological collection, one outstanding Mochica portrait vessel was kept, and this formed the nucleus of a new archaeological collection. In 1925, Larco's father acquired 600 pottery vessels and other archaeological objects from his brother-in-law, Alfredo Hoyle, and a smaller collection from Dr. Mejía, and he gave the entire collection to his son, Don Rafael. Although the latter had shown some interest by this time in Peru's past, this collection inspired him to develop a museum and to study intensively Peru's archaeology. From this moment onward, Larco increased the collection, by buying specimens from Chicama Valley and nearby Trujillo, Virú, and Chimbote valleys in the north, and later from other parts of Peru, but always specializing in North Peru. The collection grew so rapidly that it had to be installed in a separate building on the Hacienda Chiclin, which was inaugurated as the Museo Rafael Larco Herrera on July 1926, to protect the archaeological riches of Peru and as a monument to his father, who was still living.

In 1933, two large private collections were acquired, one of over 3,000 pieces from Mr. Carranza in Trujillo, and the other with 8,000 pieces of pottery, metal, and textiles from Carlos A. Roa of the Hacienda Clara in the Santa Valley. Transferal of the Roa collection without breakage from Santa Valley to Chicama Valley was a major operation, since the Pan American Highway did not yet exist. After two weeks everything was packed with straw in wooden boxes and was loaded into trucks which drove along the beach at low tide. Everything arrived in good condition, but then the job of removing the salt impregnated in the pottery had to be undertaken, since this had never before been done. One of the largest swimming pools on Hacienda Chiclin was commandeered for archaeology. The pots were submerged, and they soaked over a period of two months, during which 15 boys kept the water changed as it became contaminated with dissolved salt. After this treatment, the vessels could be stored and exhibited free of the damaging salt crystals.

At the same time Don Rafael was buying collections, he also began extensive explorations and excavations in the desolate foothills, valleys, and talus slopes of the Virú Valley and its branches, such as Cupisnique Quebrada. This field work became a family affair, with everyone showing the same enthusiasm and love of the work in developing the collections of the Museum. Don Rafael and his brothers, Constante and Javier, his wife Isolina, their close friend Enrique Jacobs, of Trujillo, spent considerable time together in the field (Fig. 3). Much valuable data on grave-lot association were recorded, information which would be of great help to scholars if it could be published. From this continued activity, the Museum grew until at his death in 1966 it contained some 40,000 complete pottery vessels and thousands of metal, textile, wood, and other artifacts. On the Hacienda Chiclin, it filled 17 rooms, and the overflow was so great that a provisional roof had been built between two buildings to house specimens in long rows, out of the weather.

Fig. 4 Rafael Larco Hoyle (right) with Dr. Alfred Kinsey working with ceramics for the book Checan: Essay on Erotic Elements in Peruvian Art.

In 1949, family business interest took Don Rafael from the north coast to Lima. To be separated from his collections would have meant cessation of his archaeological research, as well as "un duro golpe para mi espiritu" (1964: 20). He also felt that the collections would be more accessible to scholars, scientists, and interested persons if located in the capital. Therefore, a decision was made to move the entire collection to Lima, to construct a new Museum, and to create a Foundation to guarantee the permanence of the Museum and the maintenance of the collections. The new Museo Rafael Larco Herrera was not only constructed in the architectural style of Trujillo of the early 1700s, but it incorporates grills, doors, columns, beams, and brackets from the manor house of the Marqueses de Herrera y Villahermosa in Trujillo. When he was mayor of Trujillo, Don Rafael had tried to protect the house as a national historical monument, since it was one of the best surviving examples of Colonial architecture. Later, political interests, however, allowed the house to be destroyed. Although these few salvaged items give the Museum in Lima a colonial flavor, in all other aspects it is modern. It contains 6 exhibit halls plus a vault for exhibition of the gold and silver, 11 storage rooms, 4 offices serving as library, laboratory and work room, and a garden, patio, and terrace where the largest stone objects are displayed. Plans at the time of Larco's death included the addition of a conference room. Don Rafael was particularly proud of the fact that the Museo Rafael Larco Herrera, with all its collections, publications of the Museum, the staff, and the buildings, had all been developed privately, without any direct or indirect governmental assistance.

The move to Lima did permit Don Rafael to continue his archaeological studies, and in recent years he began to publish again after a lapse of 12 years (1948–1960), during which he was deeply involved in family business interests and handicapped by poor health. He was an active member of the Boards of Directors of various companies, including the Banco Comercial del Peru, Rayon Peruana, Rayon Celanese, Quimica El Pacífico, Cia. De Seguros El Sol, Cia. Pesquera Consa, and Amial del Peru. Earlier he had founded the newspaper, Diario "La Nación," in Trujillo, and then succeeded his father as president of the Board of Directors of the Diario "La Crónica" in Lima. All of these activities detracted from the time he could spend on archaeology.

Ray was a strong-willed person with a positive personality. Beneath a highly dignified manner, he was outstandingly generous. Always delighted to help qualified scholars, he would willingly put his materials at their disposal. He could be equally negative to those whom he felt were wasting his time, being motivated by curiosity or seeking a special favor. As a young graduate student assistant of William Duncan Strong on the 1946 Virú Valley Project, I remember many a pleasant Sunday at Hacienda Chiclin when Don Rafael favored the group (including Strong, Bennett, Willey, Ford, Bird, and Collier) with his ideas about Peruvian archaeology. Afterwards, we always enjoyed the magnificent hospitality of the entire Larco family at a sumptuous and delicious midday meal. Then we would retire to the study with an offer of high-quality imported cigars and brandy or some special aged "chicha" made on the Hacienda for pleasant

Fig. 5 *Members of the Chiclin Round Table, 1946. Left to right, back: M. Dingwall, (Administrative), D. Collier, C. Evans. Middle: F. W. McBryde, W. C. Bennett. G. Willey, W.D. Strong, J. Ford. Front: J. Bird, R. Larco Herrera, R. Larco Hoyle, J. Larco Hoyle.*

conversations on economics, politics, and the problems of sugar plantations. But always sooner or later the conversation would return to Peruvian archaeology. During these sessions, I was always amazed how, although at times he had not had time to read the latest article or monograph on archaeology in his excellent library, Larco exhibited an intimate knowledge of the tens of thousands of objects in his Museum. He had such a photographic memory of the collections and the ethnographic details shown on some of the pottery that he could often settle arguments by bringing out a specimen that proved his point.

This intimate knowledge of the thousands of objects in the Museum collections was reflected in Larco's outstanding contributions to mythology and socio-political structure of the Mochica, based on scenes on the painted and modeled vessels; his analysis of modification of the spout forms of Mochica vessels, which permitted subdivisions into subperiods; and the detailed studies of the erotic pre-Columbian pottery (Fig. 4), to mention just a few publications. He always undertook each project with intensity and thoroughness, documenting the argument with a large number of specimens. His major professional fault was his failure to document fully the basis for his conclusions, which stemmed in part from the multiple demands on his time. His last books were produced under great pressure and haste. Shortly before his death from a heart attack in Lima on October 23, 1966, he was working on a new well-illustrated monograph on wooden keros, based on what is probably the largest kero collection assembled in any one museum.

Through his drive and determination to let nothing get in his way, Don Rafael Larco Hoyle not only managed well the properties of the family but advanced North Coastal Peruvian archaeology at a time when little was known of the sequential development of the pre-Columbian cultures of that region. His classic contributions to the Formative period have withstood the test of time. He directed and hosted so well the 1946 Chiclin Conference on North Peruvian Archaeology (Fig. 5), at the close of the Virú Valley Project, that it is unfortunate that other such conferences could not have been organized to facilitate the exchange of ideas. Tragically, his poor health over the past decade, his pre-occupation with family business, and his limited time for archaeology isolated him from the international scientific community to which he had contributed so much. However, his publications, the collections of the Museo Rafael Larco Herrera, and their perpetuation to manage and direct the Museum, have assured for Rafael Larco Hoyle the position as the fourth great pioneer in Peruvian archaeology.

1938   *Los Mochica,* Tomo I. Casa Editora, Lima. 140 pp.

1939   *Los Mochicas,* Tomo II. Empresa Editorial "Rimac," Lima. 165 pp.

1941   *Los Cupisniques: Trabajo presentado al Congreso Internacional de Americanistas de Lima XXVII Sesion.* Casa Editora "La Cronica" y "Variedades," Lima. 259 pp.

1942   La Escritura Mochica sobre Pallares. *Revista Geográfica Americana,* Año IX, Vol. 18, pp. 93–103. Buenos Aires.

1944   La Escritura Peruana Pre-Inca. *El Mexico Antiguo,* Vol. 6, Nos. 7–8, pp. 219–38. Mexico.

1945   *La Cultura Virú.* Buenos Aires. 28 pp.

        Los Cupisniques. Buenos Aires. 25 pp.

        Los Mochicas. Buenos Aires. 42 pp.

        La Cultura Salinar. Una civilización remota del Peru pre-incaico. *Revista Geográfica Americana,* Vol. 23, No. 141, p. 327–36. Buenos Aires.

1946   A Culture Sequence for the North Coast of Peru. In "Handbook of South American Indians," edited by Julian H. Steward, Vol. 2, pp. 149–75. *Bureau of American Ethnology, Bulletin 143.* Washington.

1948   Cronología arqueológica del norte del Perú. *Sociedad Geográfica Americana.* Buenos Aires. 87 pp.

1960   La Cultura Santa. In *Antiguo Perú, Espacio y Tiempo,* pp. 235–9. Lima.

1962   *La Cultura Santa.* Lima. 28 pp.

        La Divinidad Felínica de Lambayeque. Lima. 14 pp.

1963   *Las Epocas Peruanas.* Lima. 83 pp.

1964   *Museo "Rafael Larco Herrera."* Lima. 39 pp.

1965   *La Cerámica de Vicús.* Lima. 46 pp.

        Escultura litica del Peru pre-Colombino. *Instituto de Arte Contemporaneo, Seri: Origines del arte Peruano—No. 2: Escultura litica.* Lima. 34 pp.

        Checan: Essay on Erotic Elements in Peruvian Art. Nagel Publishers, Geneva. 146 pp.

1966   *Archaeologia Mundi: Peru.* Nagel Publishers, Geneva. Also in French and German editions. 243 pp.

1967   *La Cerámica de Vicús y sus nexus con las demas culturas,* No. 2. Lima. 111 pp.

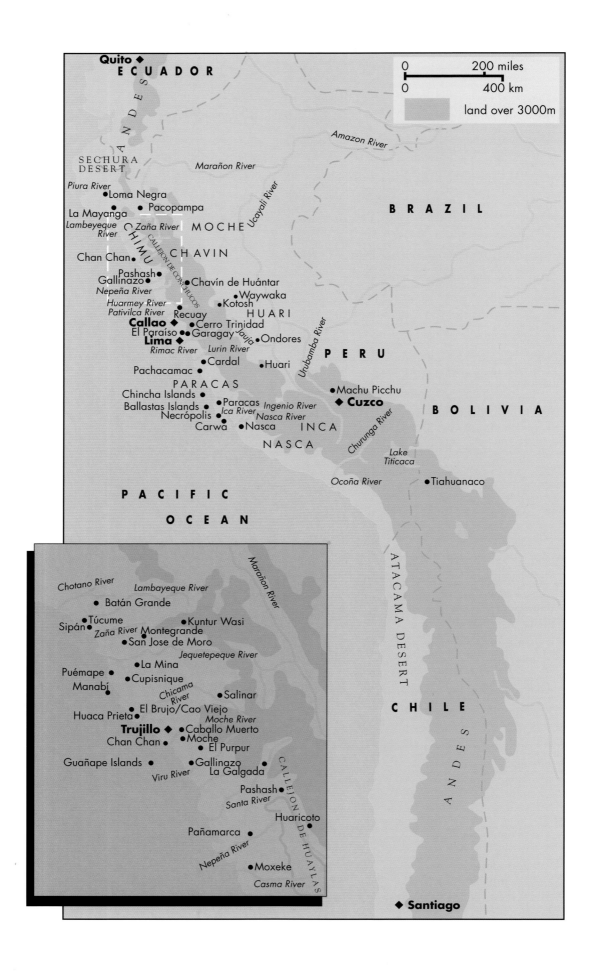

Quito ◆
E C U A D O R

SECHURA
DESERT

Piura River
● Loma Negra
● Pacopampa
La Mayanga ●
Lambeyeque
River ○ Zaña River **M O C H E**
Marañon River
Amazon River

B R A Z I L

Chan Chan ●
Pashash **C H A V I N**
● Chavín de Huántar
Gallinazo ●
Nepeña River ● Waywaka
Huarmey River ● Kotosh
Pativilca River **H U A R I**
Recuay
Callao ◆ ● Cerro Trinidad
El Paraíso ●● Garagay
Lima ◆
Rimac River Lurin River
● Cardal ● Huari
Pachacamac ●
P A R A C A S
Chincha Islands ●
Ballastas Islands ● Paracas
Necrópolis ● Ica River Ingenio River
Carwa ● ● Nasca Nasca River **I N C A**
N A S C A

Ucayali River

Urubamba River

P E R U

● Machu Picchu
◆ **Cuzco**

Churunga River

B O L I V I A

Lake
Titicaca

Ocoña River ● Tiahuanaco

P A C I F I C

O C E A N

A T A C A M A   D E S E R T

C H I L E

A N D E S

◆ **Santiago**

Chotano River Lambayeque River Marañon River
● Batán Grande
Túcume ● ● Kuntur Wasi
Sipán ● Zaña River ● Montegrande
● San Jose de Moro
Jequetepeque River
Puémape ● ● La Mina
Manabí ● ● Cupisnique
Chicama
River ● Salinar
El Brujo/Cao Viejo
Huaca Prieta ● ● Moche River
Trujillo ◆ ● Caballo Muerto
Chan Chan ● ● Moche
● El Purpur
Guañape Islands ● ● Gallinazo
Viru River La Galgada
Pashash ●
Santa River
Huaricoto ●
Pañamarca ●
Nepeña River
● Moxeke
Casma River

C A L L E J O N   D E   H U A Y L A S

Life and Afterlife in Pre-Hispanic Peru

CONTEXTUALIZING THE MASTERWORKS OF THE MUSEO ARQUEOLÓGICO RAFAEL LARCO HERRERA

Richard L. Burger

T HESE OBJECTS FROM THE MUSEO ARQUEOLÓGICO RAFAEL LARCO HERRERA were made by peoples who lived in the Central Andes (today's Peru) before the Inca civilization was established. Ancient and remarkable in their own right, they can be appreciated aesthetically without a deeper understanding of the ways in which they were utilized or the meanings they held for those who created them. Nevertheless, the unfamiliar forms and symbols that make these products of the past so exotic and attractive can illuminate ancient cultural traditions established many centuries or even millennia ago on another continent. The ostensibly realistic depictions on some specimens may tempt some viewers to assume that these are scenes of everyday life, but studies have shown that even these are in fact episodes from a mythical narrative.[1] Because most objects in the Larco Museum Collection were interred in tombs to accompany the dead, they probably reveal as much about that culture's ideas on afterlife as they do about the life of the deceased. So charged with meaning for their creators, these objects need to be understood within the systems of meanings they embody.

Because a conventional writing system was not developed in the Andes prior to the Spanish conquest, archaeological evidence and historical records and reports compiled by the Spanish colonial government are the primary sources for reconstructing these cultures. Investigators have also studied rural indigenous communities that still maintain cultural as well as linguistic continuities with the societies of the pre-Hispanic past. Yet with the collapse of the Inca empire in 1532 under Pizarro's onslaught, Andean culture was profoundly disrupted and transformed, and only those traditional behaviors and ideas that continue to be relevant and viable in the modern world have survived over the last four centuries. Ethnographic analogy—extrapolating from contemporary data what may have existed in the past—is a difficult and even dangerous approach, but it can be an effective tool for penetrating the alien and often mysterious world of the ancient Andes, when linked with critical archaeological and historic evidence.[2]

DIVERSITY, CHRONOLOGY, AND CHANGE

Some general Andean cosmological principles and ritual practices were widely shared across time and space, but enormous cultural diversity characterized the Central Andes throughout prehistory. Those beliefs and practices that Central Andean cultures shared can be traced both to their common ancestors and to long-term historical contact between centers. The first links between groups were limited to social and economic ties, but during the first millennium B.C., the religious cult associated with the site of

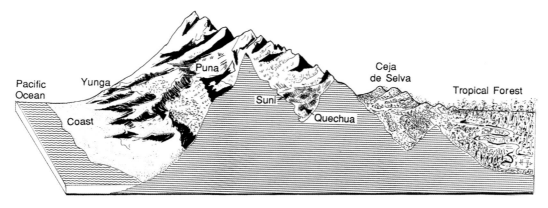

Fig. 1 *Schematic diagram illustrating the position of the major life zones in the Central Andes. The terms, in the Quechua language, correspond to zones of agricultural production, defined by altitude:*
puna: 4,000–4,800 m,
suni: 3,200–4,000 m,
quechua: 2,300–3,200 m,
ceja de selva: 2,000–3,000 m,
yunga: 1,000–2,300 m
After Pulgar Vidal, 1972.

Chavín de Huántar spread to other areas during the florescence of the Chavín civilization (900–200 B.C.), and alliances intensified. The increase in inter-regional exchange and tribute, in the form of gifts, to the religious center contributed to the evolving sociocultural complexity and led to the rapid spread of similar artifact styles over a vast area. Scholars call the phenomenon of an art style that attains sudden and widespread popularity an archaeological horizon and use the term as a convenient marker of rough contemporaneity between distant sites.

Archaeologists have identified three such horizons in the prehistory of the Central Andes, which linked groups spread from the northern highlands to the South Coast. Between each of these horizons are intermediate periods, when linkages became more limited in scope and diversity intensified.[3] In the chronology of the Central Andes (see chart, p. 23) periods of unity and diversity alternate; preceding these blocks of time is the stage known as the Preceramic, during which ceramics had yet to be adopted, and the Initial Period, during which ceramics were being used but preceding the appearance of Chavín influence in the Ica Valley of Peru's South Coast.

The Early Horizon (900–200 B.C.) encompasses coastal Cupisnique culture and the highland Chavín, both of which already existed in the Initial Period, and coincides exactly with the Paracas culture. During some periods, like the Early Intermediate Period, which follows the demise of Chavín de Huántar (ca. 200 B.C) and the collapse of its sphere of interaction, groups—including Salinar (200 B.C –A.D. 100) and Gallinazo (A.D. 1–100) on the North Coast—seemed to be creating styles that intentionally contrasted with those of their neighbors, perhaps as part of the process of reinforcing ethnic and/or political identity. The diverse styles associated with the Early Intermediate Period include Recuay (A.D. 1–650) in the northern highlands, and Moche (A.D. 50–800), Lima (350–450), and Nasca (1–700), along the coast from north to south.

This pattern of stylistic diversity was reversed by the military and economic expansion of competing states centered in Huari and Tiahuanaco, which are identified with the Middle Horizon (A.D. 650–1000). The Huari empire proved to be short-lived (A.D. 650–800), and throughout the Late Intermediate Period (A.D. 1000–1450) most of the Central Andes reverted to smaller-scale cultural units, including the Lambayeque (800–1350) and Chimú (1100–1550) cultures on the North Coast. The greater stylistic homogeneity of the Late Horizon (1450–1532) is identified with the expansion of Tawantinsuyu, the Inca empire, in the fifteenth century.

Chronologies like that proposed by Rowe have been essential to the appreciation of cultural and social change during Andean prehistory. Some subsistence and ideological features span many centuries or even millennia, but most political units lasted only a few centuries or fewer. The cultures of late Andean prehistory differed radically in many respects from those of the Initial Period or Early Horizon. The widespread representations of social hierarchy and inequality in later styles like Moche, Lambayeque, or Chimú attest to profound sociopolitical transformations. Nevertheless, the three horizons and interaction between the multiplicity of distinctive independent groups during the intervening Early Intermediate and Late Intermediate Periods produced enough shared cultural features that one can meaningfully speak of Central Andean civilization.

The chronology of cultures and art styles:

Time	NORTH HIGHLANDS	CENTRAL HIGHLANDS	SOUTH HIGHLANDS	NORTH COAST	CENTRAL COAST	SOUTH COAST	RELATIVE CHRONOLOGY
A.D. 1600–1400	Inca 1450–1550	Inca 1450–1550	Inca 1450–1550	Inca 1450–1550	Inca 1450–1550	Inca 1450–1550	LATE HORIZON 1450–1532
1300–1000				Chimú 1100–1550 / Lambayeque 800–1350			LATE INTERMEDIATE PERIOD 1000–1450
900–700	Huari 650–800	Huari 650–800	Huari 650–800		Huari 650–800	Huari 650–800	MIDDLE HORIZON 650–1000
600–100	Recuay 1–650			Moche 50–800	Lima 200–600	Nasca 1–700	EARLY INTERMEDIATE PERIOD 1–650
A.D. 100 / 0				Gallinazo 1–100 / Salinar 200 B.C.–A.D. 100			
B.C. 200–700						Paracas 700 B.C.–1	EARLY HORIZON 700 B.C.–1
600–900	Chavín 900–200 B.C.			Cupisnique 1200 B.C.–200 B.C.			
1000–1200	Pacopampa 1100–1300 B.C.						INITIAL PERIOD
B.C.							

The chronology of cultures and art styles is relevant to the text. This chart was adapted from *Andean Art at Dumbarton Oaks*, 1996.

Fig. 2 *The high-altitude grasslands (called* puna *in Figure 1), located in the Ondores area of Junín, central Peru highlands.*

Fig. 3 *The Mosna Valley, which is identified as the* quechua *life zone in Figure 1, is located in the northern highlands of Peru. The site of Chavín de Huántar is visible on the valley floor.*

BACKGROUND

The sophistication and complexity of Central Andean societies in the early sixteenth century greatly impressed the European invaders: admiration for Inca statecraft pervades Colonial Spanish accounts. Its ability to sustain a dense, well-organized population of some twelve million people in circumstances relatively free of crime and famine compared favorably to situations in western Europe at that time. Although the Incas lacked some of the technological features that we tend to associate with advanced civilizations—wheeled vehicles, writing, and iron tools, for instance—the Andean peoples not only developed a stable subsistence system but also eventually created the Inca empire, known as Tawantinsuyu, that stretched 3000 miles from the borders of what is now Colombia south to what is now central Chile. The Inca empire was a multicultural world in which many languages were spoken, many styles of dress were maintained, and many different burial customs were followed. Crisscrossed by an elaborate state road system and administered by a hierarchy of formally trained bureaucrats, who kept knotted-string records, known as *quipus*, Tawantinsuyu was larger than any existing European state at the time of the Spanish conquest. Yet the empire of the Incas, which lasted less than a century, was merely an episode in the long and remarkable history of the Central Andes. The Incas drew upon thousands of years of cultural experiments and accomplishments of its preceding cultures, whose artworks now form the majority of objects in the Larco Museum Collection.

The earliest human inhabitants of the Andes arrived by 13,000 years ago, some time after their ancestors had crossed the Bering Land Bridge from eastern Asia and migrated south through North America in search of more attractive resources. The Andean landscape they encountered was unlike that seen today. The Pacific Ocean was significantly lower and broad coastal plains, now submerged, were found along the shore. The offshore currents that now dictate contemporary weather patterns did not then dominate: what is now desert along the northern coastline of Peru was then a moist tropical environment. The climate was colder and glaciers covered some of the Andes' most productive high-altitude meadows and slopes. Savannahs rather than rainforests dominated the eastern lowlands of Amazonia. Over the following millennia, the initial inhabitants of Peru learned to exploit and manipulate the unique resources of these varied environments, previously unoccupied by humans. The original settlers of the Andes carried with them cultural systems from eastern Asia, which may explains similarities between later Andean cultures and other prehistoric groups in the Americas.

Early attempts to explain the existence and development of civilization in the Central Andes by Max Uhle and other pioneering investigators often relied on claims

Fig. 4 *The Pativilca Valley on Peru's central coast, which corresponds to the* yunga *zone in Figure 1.*

of diffusion or influence from other parts of the world, and the Near East, China, and Central America were all put forward as possible donors. Such explanations have been largely refuted by scientific evidence accumulated by research into Andean prehistory. The autochthonous character of these developments is now widely acknowledged, and the Central Andes is recognized as one of five or six areas of the globe where civilizations evolved in situ, without major input from complex cultures in other parts of the world. Indeed, archaeologists can now trace local Andean trajectories spanning millennia in which subsistence systems, monumental architecture, metallurgy, cities, states and other cultural achievements appear and are transformed again and again.[4]

This does not mean that the Andes were completely isolated in prehistory. There is ample evidence of contact with the tropical lowlands to the east, and there were apparently terrestrial and maritime links between the Central Andean region and what is now Ecuador. The ancient cultures of Ecuador, which had intermittent contact with western Mexico during much of prehistory, may have indirectly linked the Central Andes and Mesoamerica, but such contact appears to have relatively little impact on the structure and cultural trajectory of Central Andean cultures.[5]

As Julio C. Tello, Peru's first great archaeologist, observed in 1929, Andean civilization begins when the indigenous people master the challenges of these diverse environments—mountains, desert coasts, and forested lowlands—and create unique systems from these resources, which provide a stable productive basis for increasingly complex and elaborate cultures.[6] For Tello, the accomplishments of ancient Peru were a testament to the creative genius of the Andean people, and the impoverishment of Peru that followed the Spanish conquest reflected the failure of European invaders to produce a viable alternative system to replace the one that they toppled.

THE ANDEAN ENVIRONMENT

The achievements of Andean civilization are all the more impressive when one considers the difficult environments in which they occurred. The Central Andes includes some of the world's highest mountains, driest deserts, and densest tropical forests. These landscapes are compressed into a relatively small area, so that in some places a traveler moving east from the Pacific can encounter twenty of the world's thirty-four life zones in 200 km or less (see Fig. 1).[7]

The core of the Central Andes is the highlands with its intermontane valleys, high grasslands, and rocky or glaciated peaks, the highest of which reaches 6768 meters. In prehistory and until very recently, most of the population lived in the

highlands, with the greatest demographic density between 2800 meters and 3900 meters. No other part of the world has sustained so many people for so long at such high elevations. Two of the largest and most important pre-Hispanic cities in the ancient Andes, Tiahuanaco and Cuzco, were located at 3845 meters and 3250 meters above sea level.

Early inhabitants of the Andes discovered plants and animals that had evolved in highland habitats, and they genetically modified them through breeding to meet the special needs of human populations. From numerous wild plants that had developed fleshy tubers, early Andean people developed a host of productive crops that could survive the steep slopes, poorly developed soils, and cold temperatures of the sierra. Many of these multicolored and flavorful tubers, like the *oca* (*Oxalis tuberosa*), *ullucu* (*Ullucus tuberosus*), *mashua* (*Trapaeolum tuberosum*) and *maca* (*Ledpidium meyenii*) are generally unknown outside the Andes, but the potato (*Solanum tuberosum*) attracted the attention of Spanish sailors and went on to revolutionize the diet of the Old World. Some two hundred named varieties of potato were developed in the Central Andes, including five distinct species. The rich variety of domesticated tubers was complemented by high-altitude grains such as quinoa (*Chenopodium quinoa*) and *kiwicha* (*Amaranthus* sp.), lupines such as *tarwi* (*Lupinus mutabilis*), and beans (*Phaseolus lunatus* and *Phaseolus vulgaris*).

The vast high-altitude grasslands known as the *puna* (Fig. 2) were converted from a marginal zone to an important resource through the domestication of llamas and alpacas by five thousand years ago. Bred by the high-altitude hunter-gatherers from their wild relatives, these animals yielded fiber for textiles, leather and bone for tools, and meat; in addition, llamas served as pack animals moving bulky subsistence and craft items between the varied mountain environments and beyond.

The frequent frosts of the high altitudes (Fig. 3) were harnessed by ancient Andean peoples: they discovered how to freeze-dry potatoes (known as *chuño*) and meat (known as *charqui*), which could then be stored without spoilage for years and could be easily transported to lower zones because of their reduced volume and weight. On the steep Andean slopes, a combination of terracing and irrigation made it possible to grow such fragile crops as maize; on the cold high plain surrounding Lake Titicaca, ridged field systems were created to reduce flooding and resist frosts. Virtually all these technologies and domesticated plants and animals mentioned had been developed long before the appearance of complex cultures during the first millennium.

The coast of Peru, where much of the modern agricultural and industrial efforts occur, is actually one of the driest regions in the world. On most of the coast, no significant precipitation occurs most years, and the fifty-seven tiny rivers that cross the coast to drain into the Pacific are fed by rains that fall at 1600 meters or higher. The majority of these watercourses are dry for at least part of the year.

While the extreme aridity makes rainfall-based cultivation on the coast impossible on all but a few small patches of land watered by river overflow, irrigation can turn the coastal valleys into natural greenhouses (Fig. 4). With rich, unleached soils and moderate climate throughout the year, almost any crop, whether native to the Amazon or the highlands, can thrive along the coast if enough water can be provided. Experiments in irrigation technology were well under way over four thousand years ago, and by three thousand years ago, coastal valleys were filling up with communities of hydraulic agriculturists and their massive public centers. The coastal plain is virtually nonexistent in southern Peru, but it gradually widens to about 100 kilometers across in northern valleys. The broadening of the coastal plain along the North Coast and the greater highland precipitation above these drainages resulted in a concentration of high-quality agricultural land, a pattern magnified by multivalley canal systems built before the Spanish conquest. The abundant agricultural resources of the northern coastal valleys supported a series of remarkable civilizations, all of which are particularly well represented in the Larco Herrera Collection.

The frigid Humboldt Current runs from the Antarctic up the coast of western South America, cools the ocean air and thereby prevents precipitation along the coast. Fortunately for the ancient inhabitants of Peru, this deep upwelling current supports the globe's richest concentration of marine fauna and, until recently, it supplied one-fifth of the world's fish catch. These maritime resources, available year-round, provided the main source of protein for most of the pre-Hispanic cultures all along the coast. The ability to supplement the agricultural yields with protein-rich ocean products enabled dense populations to exist in arid coastal areas, despite only limited hunting and herding resources.

This stable arrangement, however, was disrupted without warning, however, in those years when the warmer northern current running along the coast of Ecuador shifted to the south, provoking a phenomenon known as El Niño. The unpredictable intrusion of warmer waters leads to massive loss of marine life, as well as torrential rains. In the deserts of coastal Peru, El Niño events resulted in landslides, floods, and the destruction of agricultural infrastructure (canals, roads, and so on) as well as extensive damage to housing and other perishable constructions. The scars of floods triggered by ancient El Niño's are still visible on many of Peru's most impressive mud-brick pyramids.[8]

On the other side of the mountains, water-laden winds carried from the Atlantic over the Amazon collided with the steep face of Andes, producing heavy rains for much of the year. Thick montane forests punctuated with more arid pockets of land (known as rain shadows) covered the eastern slopes up to elevations above 3000 meters (Fig. 5). These montane forest environments (or *ceja de selva*) were a source of such tropical products as coca leaf and a bridge to the more extensive eastern lowlands occupied by riverine-oriented tropical-forest groups. For most of Andean prehistory, the forested eastern slopes were integrated into the Andean world, and contact with the tropical-forest cultures further to the east was maintained. In fact, many of the most important crops in prehistoric Andean agricultural systems were introduced from these Amazonian societies.

The subduction of the Nazca Oceanic Plate beneath South America makes the Peruvian area subject to serious earthquakes and, on occasion, accompanying tidal waves. In 1746 Peru's main port, Callao, was obliterated by an 18 meter tidal wave. As recently as 1970 an earthquake measuring 7.7 on the Richter scale killed some 75,000 people in the Callejon de Huaylas. These same tectonic forces have made what is now southern Peru and northern Ecuador the victim of repeated major volcanic eruptions. The geologic causes of these disasters have existed for millions of years, and so the archaeological record shows ample evidence of natural disasters in prehistoric as well as historic times. As these examples suggest, environments in the Andes offer severe challenges, not only for developing reliable subsistence systems but also for coping with unpredictable crises triggered by tectonic or climatic oscillations. Moreover, recent studies of ice cores and other data demonstrate that there have been significant fluctuations in temperature and rainfall over the last four thousand years, and that ancient societies in the Andes had to confront climatic stress that

Fig. 6 *Rollout of the Lanzón sculpture at Chavín de Huántar, depicting the supreme deity. Drawing by Richard L. Burger and Luis Caballero.*

resulted in prolonged droughts and loss of productive high altitude farmland because of lower temperatures.[9]

IDEOLOGY AND ADAPTATION IN THE CENTRAL ANDES

While the success of Central Andean cultures was made possible by the remarkable subsistence systems developed before the emergence of complex societies three millennia ago, the potential of these systems could, however, only be realized by concomitant breakthroughs in the sociopolitical organization of Andean peoples. The construction of canals and terracing systems exceed the capabilities of single families: the labor of many family units needs to be pooled to build and maintain such systems. Group cooperation was also essential to confront unpredictable and disruptive environmental crises. One of the distinctive features of the Andean prehistory is that such substantial cooperative endeavors appear long before the existence of states and stratified societies. In fact, archaeologists have found evidence that by five thousand years ago, groups were engaged in collective efforts on a monumental scale along the coast and in the highlands.

Ruins of large public buildings at sites like El Paraíso, La Galgada, and Kotosh, are some of the most conspicuous vestiges of these cooperative social units. El Paraíso, which was completed by circa 2,000 B.C., is a massive masory complex covering more than 100 acres (58 hectares) and involving over 100,000 tons of stone. It consists of a series of terraced platforms surrounding a large open space; buildings for public and religious activities have been found on their summit. At highland Preceramic sites like Kotosh and La Galgada, stone-faced pyramids, rising to the height of a four-story building, had a series of small windowless ritual chambers for making burnt offerings on their flat-topped summits. These centers usually lasted many centuries, longevity that, like the formal continuity in their construction, suggests great stability. Excavation has revealed that monumental architecture of the Late Preceramic and Initial Period was used for worship and public gatherings. Walls decorated with painted and sculpted supernatural images have been found in some buildings at Garagay and Moxeke, as well as on Huaca de los Reyes at Caballo Muerto, the late Initial Period complex that epitomizes Cupisnique public architecture. Interior spaces in these complexes sometimes feature altars, as at Cardal, or ceremonial hearths, as at Huaricoto. Viewing these finds, it is difficult to escape the conclusion that religious ideology played a central role in the formation and maintenance of these early social groups. Ethnohistoric and ethnographic evidence attests that this pattern has endured throughout Andean history.

Indigenous Andean peoples were profoundly religious and their beliefs pervaded all aspects of their lives. The mythical history of a group provided the basis for its claims to land and water, and membership in such a group was based on both relation to a common ancestor and on participation in religious ceremonies devoted to these ancestors or sacred places in the landscape associated with the group's mythical past. Cooperative labor in public projects, whether construction of canals or temples, were carried out as part of the community's ritual cycle. Failure of a family to participate raised questions about group membership and, by extension, rights to resources. Similarly, the proper completion of religious rituals were seen as essential to maintaining a community's relationship with the supernatural which, in turn, determined whether the community would be provided sufficient water for cultivation and continue to be spared the stochastic disasters to which the Andes is so vulnerable. In a world in which land and water were communally controlled, the pressure to be involved in the community and share in its cosmology and rituals was substantial, even before state-based governments exerted more organized coercion.[10]

These religious beliefs remained of critical importance to everyday life under state-based governments and expansionist empires, but the exercise of ritual became more narrowly associated with society's elites. By later Andean prehistory, leaders claimed special links to the supernatural and even wore the costumes of mythical figures. Inca rulers, who claimed descent from the sun, are the best-known example of this trend, but a millennium earlier Moche elite interred at Sipán and San Jose de Moro were buried with the distinctive garb of the mythological characters known from the murals and fineline decorations on food and drinking vessels. Scientific excavation at Kuntur Wasi revealed the most ancient unequivocally elite burials in the Andes: early leaders at the height of the Chavín civilization were interred wearing gold crowns and ear ornaments with religious symbolism.[11] The gold crown in the Larco Museum Collection (cat. no. 137), which depicts the principal deity of Chavín cosmology and its supernatural avian attendants, lacks provenance, but it probably came from a similar Early Horizon elite tomb somewhere on the North Coast.

While the religious systems of the ancient Andes varied regionally and through time, some general cosmological principles were held in common by many. The universe, both in this world and beyond, was conceived as a dynamic balance of complementary forces. Male and female gender categories are perhaps the most obvious example of this principle, which can be recognized at all levels of experience, from coordinating the left and right arms and legs of an individual to the division of a polity into moiety-like divisions of hanan (upper) and hurin (lower). It was axiomatic that both distinct components were necessary to form an organic whole and could not meaningfully exist in isolation. The notion that balancing opposing forces was essential to community well-being is manifested in the stance of the principle deity of Chavín de Huántar on the Lanzón, a 4.5-meter high granite sculpture that served as the cult object for the Old Temple around 800 B.C. With its right arm raised and its left arm lowered, the deity's pose reveals its role in mediating between opposing forces. This personification of the principle of balance and order is reinforced by the depiction of the deity's palm on the right hand, but the back of the hand on its left. The Cupisnique bottle with its dual division into feline and human elements is a vivid enunciation of this principle, but it is more subtly reflected in decorative schemes that contrast red- and black-painted zones or undecorated, polished elements with textured matte zones. Even the long-term fascination with the idiosyncratic stirrup-spout bottle, popular for 2,500 years on the North Coast, may derive from its resonance with dual organizational principles. The role of dual organization can be traced at least as far back as the Temple of the Crossed Hands, which dates to the Late Preceramic, at Kotosh, where in a roughly square building with a circular firepit in the center of the floor, a low-relief frieze of crossed hands was sculpted beneath pairs of niches on either side of the large central niche. Such duality continues through Inca times into contemporary Quechua and Aymara communities in Peru and Bolivia.[12]

Supernatural power and transformation is a theme in ancient thought that persists in some modern Quechua communities. From her research at Sonqo in Cuzco, Catherine Allen described a belief in an animating spirit or energy known as sami that is unevenly distributed throughout the landscape not only among the living plants and animals but also among inorganic matter.[13] This animating force is concentrated in portions of the landscape that therefore have special power, and sami continually circulates through the world in the form of water and light. This modern Quechua concept is germane because it enunciates pre-Hispanic ideas about the power of certain places, like natural springs and mountain peaks, and conforms to the general willingness to accept the mutability of one substance into another. Andean myths and folklore are filled with stories of heroes transforming into mountains and stars and of mountains fighting with each other. Priests and shamans claimed the power, sometimes with the assistance of psychoactive drugs, to transform themselves into jaguars or raptorial birds, and wild animals were alter egos who assisted leaders and their communities. Animals and plants possessing human traits are shown frequently in prehistoric Andean art, which suggests that a thin line separates humans from the surrounding nonhuman world.

The concern with the flow of energy or spirit underlies the making of offerings to the supernatural, whether by "blowing" the spirit from coca leaves to the mountain peaks, by pouring corn beer (*chicha*) into "mother earth" (known as *pachamana* in Quechua), or by turning special items into smoke through burnt offerings. All such ceremonial activities express the hope that by accepting the spirit or essence of the special items being offered, the otherworldly powers—whether supernaturals or ancestors—will reciprocate by maintaining the health of the community. This sacrifice of an energetically rich material to gain supernatural favors pervades Andean myths, which often feature the death of a mythical hero in order to acquire critical cultigens or to guarantee agricultural fertility. The sacrifice scenes of the Moche are obvious illustrations of such themes, but depictions of decapitated heads among the Cupisnique or prisoners awaiting sacrifice among the Moche likewise relate to such concerns. The significance of these deaths is compounded when they occur in places redolent with supernatural power, such as mountain peaks or offshore islands.

Such spots were seen as linked to each other as nodes within the pathway of moisture circulating through the universe, passing from the sky to the mountains and then ultimately to the sea. The offerings of shells or other marine materials on mountain peaks, or the combination of mountain and wave symbolism, seems to relate to this perceived pattern and the desire to manipulate rainfall and water for irrigation through religious offerings and other rituals.[14]

Early in Andean prehistory, coca leaves became crucial elements of such rituals. Similarly, the distinctive red-colored shell of the *Spondylus* came to be viewed as a particularly potent offering: its acquisition for use in ceremonial presentations can be documented from Late Preceramic times and continued until after the Spanish conquest in diverse Central Andean cultures. Many basic cosmological principles and rituals of the Andes appeared by the time of the so-called formative cultures like Cupisnique and Chavín and endured through three millennia of considerable social and cultural upheavals.

DEATH, AFTERLIFE, AND THE LARCO MUSEUM COLLECTION

The people of ancient Peru rarely parted with unbroken items that could still fulfill their intended function, yet intact tools, jewelry, and other artifacts were routinely included in burials. As a consequence, most pre-Hispanic Andean objects in museums come from looted or scientifically excavated tombs. Interring personal items, rather than destroying them or passing them on to friends or relatives, reflects the society's ideas about death and the afterlife. Although such concepts vary, there are enough commonalties to suggest why these precious items were left as grave goods among the cultures of the North Coast and elsewhere in the Central Andes.

In the Andes, death was considered a process during which the deceased gradually changed from a soft substance to a hard one and transformed from a relative to an ancestor. At the time of the initial burial, the deceased still retained his or her social identity, and drinking and banqueting with the dead was a common component of mourning rituals throughout the Andes. Under such circumstances, it was essential for the deceased to wear the clothing and jewelry that were emblematic of social status and individual identity. The prone burial position preferred during most of North Coast prehistory was selected to suggest that the deceased was merely resting, while the seated position favored during the Middle Horizon suggested that the deceased was still in some sense awake and in attendance. Because ancestors were viewed as linked to fertility and community well-being after death, tombs and cemeteries served as the focus of community ritual, as well as being tangible evidence of the history and resource rights of a social group.[15]

One common idea in the Andes was that burial marked the beginning of a journey by the soul to the next world. The dead, like the living, required nourishment and it is likely that the corn beer and food filling the bottles and plates buried with the dead were designed to sustain the deceased during this journey to the afterlife. These vessels, like the clothing and jewelry worn by the deceased, often show traces of wear or break-age, suggesting that they were personal possessions rather than offerings specially produced for the burial ritual. Notions of the afterlife were apparently varied and often unclear, but frequently the next world was imagined as a more benign version of this one. It was assumed that normal work activities basic to sustaining and structuring daily life would continue, and so tools and other utilitarian items were routinely buried with the dead. Moche iconography, in particular, suggests that the dead were imagined as having an afterlife that involved pleasure as well as hard work. It is also probably significant that many ancient Peruvian cultures buried pairs of eating and drinking vessels, thereby preparing the deceased for the reciprocal entertaining that lay at the core of Andean social life. Naturally, the treatment of the dead had an important role in the re-establishment of the social and moral order that had been disrupted by death. Consequently the inclusion of the grave goods to reaffirm the status of the deceased and, by extension, of his or her kin, had significance in this world for the survivors, above and beyond particular cultural notions of death and afterlife.

As we contemplate the pieces in the Larco Museum Collection, we can begin to imagine the women and men who once used these items and the world in which they lived. While these objects offer only a partial and admittedly biased perspective on the Andean past, they also provide a glimpse of ancient realms often inaccessible using other types of archaeological evidence. It is mainly through objects such as these that we can penetrate domains such as religious cosmology, humor, sexuality, and the texture of interpersonal relations. Like the fine stone masonry at Machu Picchu and the monumental mud-brick pyramids at Tucume, the remarkable specimens collected by Rafael Larco Hoyle and his father offer a vivid testament to the complexity and variety of ancient Andean civilization and its remarkable artistic and technological achievements.

NOTES

1. This theme has been most fully explored by Christopher Donnan and his collaborators in their study of Moche art: Christopher Donnan, *Moche Art and Iconography* (Los Angeles: UCLA Latin American Center Publications, 1976) and *Moche Art of Peru* (Los Angeles: Museum of Cultural History, University of California, 1978); Christopher Donnan and Donna McClelland, *The Burial Theme in Moche Iconography*, Studies in Pre-Columbian Art and Archaeology, no. 21 (Washington, D.C.: Dumbarton Oaks, 1979); compare Luis Jaime Castillo, *Personajes Míticos, Escenas y Narraciones en la Iconografía Mochica.* (Lima: Fondo Editorial de la Pontificia Universidad Catolica del Perú, 1989); Anne Marie Hocquenghem, *Iconografia Mochica* (Lima: Fondo Editorial de la Universidad Católica del Perú, 1987).

2. The power of ethnographic analogy has been vividly illustrated by Christopher Donnan and Douglas Sharon, "Shamanism in Moche Iconography," in *Ethnoarchaeology*, ed. C. Donnan and W. Clewlow, Monograph 4 (Los Angeles: Institute of Archaeology, University of California), 51–77, and its misuse has been critiqued by William Isbell, "Constructing the Andean Past or 'As You Like It'," *Journal of the Julian Steward Anthropological Society* 23 (1995), vol. l/2: 1–12.

3. Rowe's terminology, defined in "Stages and Periods in Archaeological Interpretations," *Southwestern Journal of Anthropology* 18(1962), vol. l: 40–54, was designed to maximize precision and minimize ambiguity when used by scholars. To achieve this end, the horizons were defined as beginning when they can be detected in Ica, consequently each horizon actually begins in the intermediate period (or initial period) preceding it.

4. See Max Uhle, "Civilizaciones Mayoides de la Costa Pacifica de Sudamerica," *Boletín de la Academia Nacional de Historia* VI (1923), vols. 15–17: 87–92, Quito, and "Desarrollo y Origein de las Civilizaciones Americanas," in *Proceedings of the 23rd International Congress of Americanists* (New York, 1930), 247–258, for examples of early diffusionary explanations of Andean civilization. The evidence for the autochthonous development of Andean civilization has recently been summarized by Richard L. Burger, *Chavin and the Origins of Andean Civilization* (London: Thames and Hudson Ltd., 1992).

5. For an introduction to the evidence for Andean-Mesoamerican contacts see Donald Lathrap, "Relationships between Mesoamerica and the Andean Area," in *Handbook of Middle American Indians* (vol. 4), ed. Gordon Eckholm and Gordon Willey (Austin: University of Texas Press, 1966), 265–275, and the exhibition catalogue Donald Lathrap, D. Collier, and H. Chandra, *Ancient Ecuador: Culture, Clay and Creativity. 3000–300 B.C.* (Chicago: Field Museum of Natural History, 1975), and Jorge Marcos and Presley Norton, *Primer Simposio de*

Correlaciones Antropológicas Andino-Mesoamericano. (Guayaquil: Escuela Técnica de Arqueología, 1982). Hosler and Lechtman have recently presented compelling evidence for the introduction of Andean metallurgy into Mesoamerica from the Ande: Dorothy Hosler, "Ancient West Mexican Metallurgy: South and Central American Origins and West Mexican Transformations," *American Anthropologist* 90 (1988): 832–855, Hosler, *The Sounds and Colors of Power* (Cambridge: MIT Press, 1994), and Hosler, Heather Lechtman, and Olaf Holm, *Axe Monies and Their Relatives* (Washington, D.C.: Dumbarton Oaks, 1990).

6. Julio C. Tello, *Antiguo Peru: Primera Epoca* (Lima, 1929). See also Tello, "Origen y Desarrollo de la Civilizaciones Prehistóricas Andinas," in *Actas y trabajos científicos del XVII Congreso Interanacional de Americanista 1939*, vol. 1 (1942): 589–720, Lima, for a summary of his broad vision of Andean prehistory.

7. Javier Pulgar Vidal, *Las Ocho Regiones Naturales del Perú* (Lima: Editorial Universo, 1972) and *Geo-ecology of the mountainous regions of the tropical Americas*, ed. Carl Troll (Bonn: Colloquium Geographicum Band 9, Dummlers Velag, 1968) offer excellent overviews of Andean geography. Joseph Tosi,"Zonas de vida natural en el Perú: Memoria explicativa sobre el mapa ecológica del Peru," *Boletín Tecnico* 5 (1960) provides a comprehensive description of environments in Peru using the Holdridge system.

8. Evidence of radical environmental crises in the Andes has been summarized by Michael Moseley, Robert Feldman, and Charles Ortloff, "Living with Crises: Human perception of process and time," in *Biotic Crises in Ecological and Evolutionary Times*, ed. M. Nitecki (New York: Academic Press, l981), 231–267, and F. Nials, E.Deeds, M. Moseley, S. Pozorski, T. Pozorski and R. Feldman, "El Niño: the catastrophic flooding of coastal Peru," *Field Museum of Natural History Bulletin* 50 (1979), vol. 7: 4–14 and vol. 8: 4–10. Daniel Sandweiss, "El Niño, Past and Present," *Reviews of Geophysics* 27 (1990), no. 2: 159–187, and others have traced the history of the El Niño phenomenon and its impact on Andean prehistory.

9. Recent ice-core evidence on Holocene climatic oscillations in the Central Andes has been published by L. Thompson, E. Mosley-Thompson, J.F. Bolzan and B.R.Koci, "A 1500-year record of tropical precipitation in ice cores from the Quelcaya ice cap, Peru," *Science* 229 (1985): 971–973.

10. Descriptions of Andean prehistoric terracing systems are offered in Robin Donkin, *Agricultural Terracing in the Aboriginal New World*. Viking Fund Publications in Anthropology, vol. 56 (Tucson: University of Arizona Press, 1979) and *Pre-Hispanic Agricltural Fields in the Andean Region*, ed. William Denevan, K. Mathewson, and G. Knapp, BAR International Series 359 (Oxford: British Archaeological Reports, 1987), and Michael Moseley and Eric Deeds, "The land in front of Chan Chan: Agrarian expansion, reform, and collapse in the Moche valley," in *Chan Chan: Andean Desert City* (Albuquerque: University of New Mexico Press, 1982) provide an overview of changing prehistoric hydraulic systems in one north coast valley. Good illustrations of the intimate relationship of hydraulic and religious systems among the Inca and modern Quechua communities is provided by Jeanette Sherbondy, "Organización hidraúlica y poder en el Cuzco de los Incas," *Revista Española de Antropología Americana* 17 (1987): 117–153, and Billie Jean Isbell, *To Defend Ourselves* (Austin: University of Texas Press, 1978).

11. Walter Alva and Christopher Donnan, *Royal Tombs of Sipán* (Los Angeles: Fowler Museum of Cultural History, 1993); Christopher Donnan, "Moche funerary practice," in *Tombs for the Living: Andean Mortuary Practice* (Washington, D.C.: Dumbarton Oaks, 1995); Christopher Donnan and Luis Jaime Castillo, "Excavaciones de tumbas de sacerdotisas Moche en San José de Moro, Jequetepeque," in *Moche: Propuestas y Perspectivas*, ed. Santiago Uceda and Elías Mujica (Lima: Universidad Nacional de La Libertad, 1994), 415–424; and Yasutake Kato, "Resultados de las Excavaciones en Kuntur Wasi, Cajamarca," in *El Mundo Ceremonial Andino*, compiled by Luis Millones and Yoshio Onuki (Lima: Editorial Horizonte, 1994), 199–224.

12. Richard L. Burger and Lucy Salazar-Burger, "La Organización Dual en el Ceremonial Andino Temprano: Un Repaso Comparativo," in *El Mundo Ceremonial Andino*, compiled by Luis Millones and Yoshio Onuki (Lima: Editorial Horizonte, 1994), 97–116.

13. Catherine Allen, *The Hold Life Has: Coca and Cultural Identity in an Andean Community* (Washington, D.C.: Smithsonian Institution Press, 1988).

14. Johan Rheinhard, "Sacred Mountains: an Ethno-Archaeological Study of High Andean Ruin," *Mountain Research and Development* 5 (1985), vol. 4: 299–317.

15. See John H. Rowe, "Behavior and Belief in Ancient Peruvian Mortuary Practice," in *Tombs for the Living: Andean Mortuary Practices*, ed. Tom Dillehay (Washington, D.C.: Dumbarton Oaks, 1995), 27–42, and Frank Salamon, "'The Beautiful Grandparents': Andean Ancestor Shrines and Mortuary Ritual as Seen through Colonial Records," 315–354, in *Tombs for the Living: Andean Mortuary Practices*, 315–354.

The Coastal Islands of Peru

MYTHS AND NATURAL RESOURCES

María Rostworowski de Diez Canseco

THE ISLANDS SCATTERED ALONG THE COAST OF PERU are arid, inhospitable, and unfit for year-round habitation. These rocky outcrops, buffeted by winds and surrounded by currents, countercurrents, and strong waves, are the domains of sea lions and seabirds. Ancient Peruvians, however, perceived the islands as extensions of the mainland, important not only for the guano of seabirds but also for their religious and mythical significance. The inhabitants of the coast perceived the beauty of the islands—with their hidden coves, deep caves, and whimsical shapes emerging from choppy seas—and saw in these harsh and rocky islets enchanted beings, lords, and divinities. The clouds of birds that nest on the islands and whirl around sun-drenched and precipitous cliffs add to the feeling of mystery that pervades the locale.

Although there have been numerous studies on guano production and mining, there has been no historical research on the islands. Accounts contained in Spanish chronicles and unpublished documents reveal a world full of life, rich in the traditions and legends that form part of the Andean cultural legacy.

GUANO: A RENEWABLE NATURAL RESOURCE

Even before the Spanish invasion, ancient Peruvians considered guano an important resource and used it and other fertilizers to increase crop yields. There are references to guano use scattered among the chronicles and archives and illustrations of maize plants sprouting from small fish on ancient murals. Our understanding of the pre-Hispanic use of fertilizers is limited largely to the habits of coastal peoples, although we know that some highland peoples also used guano. The *Señoríos* of the southern highlands, for instance, acquired guano through their enclaves of colonists located on the coast. (*Señorío* is a Spanish term that describes pre-Hispanic societies of varying political complexity and territorial extent, ruled by a series of greater and lesser chiefs, or *curacas*. Their domains are known as *curacazgos*.) There is no information currently on what occurred in other parts of ancient Peru.[1]

Coastal farmers used three types of fertilizer. Pedro de Cieza de León, a Spanish soldier who traveled throughout the Andes in the 1540s, described how farmers placed one or two sardine heads next to each maize grain, remarking "But the seed of the corn in no wise sprout nor yield if they did not put with each a head of two of the sardines which they take in their nets."[2] The seventeenth-century Jesuit priest Bernabé Cobo noted that this was practiced all along the coast.[3]

The murals of the Painted Temple at the coastal sanctuary of Pachacamac, one of the most revered oracles in ancient Peru, include painted images of maize plants sprouting from small fish, which indicate that Pachacamac farmers used these fish in the cultivation of this important grain.[4]

Farmers also used the decomposed leaves of *algarrobo* and *guarango*, trees native to Peru, which once flourished in almost all the coastal valleys. Decomposed leaves piled up below the trees in layers of several *codos* ("elbows," a Spanish measurement equivalent to the distance between the elbow and the hand).[5] They used these leaves to fertilize their crops, especially maize.

The third type of fertilizer used by ancient Peruvians was the guano of seabirds, which nest by the thousands on offshore islands and outcrops. The cold waters of the Peruvian, or Humboldt, Current support one of the world's richest concentrations of fish—and the birds that feed on them. The leading guano producer is the Guanay cormorant (*Phalocrocorax bougainvillii*), which feeds on anchovy (*Engraultis ringens*). Next in importance is the Peruvian booby (*Sula variegata*), followed by the Peruvian pelican (*Pelecanus thagus*), a species endemic to the Peruvian coast.[6]

In their travelogues, chroniclers such as Cieza de León mention the use of guano by the native inhabitants, and in 1575,[7] the *curaca* of Guamán "in the valley of Chimo," near modern-day Trujillo in northern Peru told the Crown inspector, González de Cuenca, that he and his Indians made a habit of going to the islands to extract guano "because from them we carry out exchange and barter and use, with which we are able to pay our tribute and sustain ourselves." [8] This reference is important not only because it underscores the natives' understanding and use of the resource but also because it demonstrates that it was extracted and used for barter.

In addition to making offerings and sacrifices before going to sea, the fishermen also fasted for two days, abstaining from *aji* (chili pepper; *Capsicum* sp.), salt, and sex. Then, before they boarded their boats, they poured a little *chicha* (fermented maize beer) onto the sands of the beach. When they came back, their boats filled with guano, they again fasted for two days. Only later did they celebrate their return with dances and feasting.

Several documents refer to the inhabitants of the small *curacazgo* of Guamán as fishermen who were familiar with the ocean and who came and went to the islands. The Inca imposed the name Guamán, which means hawk in their language, after they conquered this part of the Peruvian coast sometime in the 1470s. Before the Inca conquests the *curacazgo* of Guamán was known as Chichi.[9]

Myths about the Islands

Historian Catherine Julien points out that there are only limited references to the use of guano as fertilizer in the south and they are scattered among a few chronicles. She also notes that there is no information about the mining of guano in pre-Hispanic times. The myths that underscore the beliefs surrounding the acquisition of this resource partially fill this void.

The Spanish chroniclers Antonio de la Calancha and Pablo José de Arriaga noted that it was customary among fishermen to offer sacrifices to the guano god, whom one of the authors calls *Guamancantac* and the other refers to as *Guamancanfac*. They wrote that before going to sea, the natives would pray to the guano god, asking his permission to embark on the mission that they were about to undertake.[10]

We do not know what this god looked like, although he may have had avian features. How did the fishermen envision *Guamancanfac* or *Guamancantac*? The first part of this deity's name, *guamán*, means hawk in Quechua, the language spoken by the Inca, which suggests that he was not a guano-producing bird but may have taken the guise of a bird of prey.[11]

Evidently, the deity's name is a translation into Quechua from Muchic, the language spoken by people on parts of the North Coast before the Spanish invasion. *Canfac* or *cantac*, the second part of the name, is impossible to translate because there

Fig. 1 *Natural stone arch, Ballastas Island near the Paracas coast, southern Peru.*

is no Muchic dictionary. Scholars demonstrated the importance of the osprey (*Pandion haliaetus carolinensis*), a large fish-eating hawk, in Moche iconography.[12] This imagery and the linguistic association between *guamán* and related birds suggest that the fishermen may have envisioned their god as an osprey.

Gods with avian features were prominent in the mythology of the Moche people who inhabited the North Coast of Peru from A.D. 50 to 800. Christopher Donnan has identified a basic subject in Moche art called the Presentation Theme, in which a goblet containing sacrificial blood is presented to a major figure by another individual (known as figure B) who appears in the guise of an osprey with human and warrior attributes. It is possible that figure B in the Presentation Theme was the god called Guamancanfac. The osprey, a migratory bird who visits the Peruvian coast during the southern hemisphere's summer, may have impressed the Moche, who likened its comings and goings to those of a divine messenger.[13]

In another myth reported by Calancha, the god Pachacamac struggles with his brother Vichama.[14] Vichama, along with his father, the sun, killed all the inhabitants of the coast in reprisal because they had failed to prevent the death of Vichama's mother. It was not long, however, before the gods regretted what they had wrought, for they had killed all those who worshipped them and made sacrifices. Thus, Vichama decided to honor the old *curacas* and lords by transforming them into coastal islands so that a new generation of inhabitants would worship them as their *huacas* (Quechua word for place, person, or object considered sacred).

The myth demonstrates that the native peoples did not regard the islands merely as arid and lifeless rocky formations; rather, they represented important persons from

Fig. 2 *Sea Lions, Ballastas Island near the Paracas coast, southern Peru.*

their past, divinities, and enchanted lords who had to be venerated with offerings and celebrations.

Arriaga also describes how coastal peoples believed that the dead would be taken to the islands by sea lions, which they called *tumi*. In the *Lexicón* of Fray Domingo de Santo Tomás, a word, *thome*, describes these marine mammals.[15] This word relates the islands to burial places. These references confer singular importance on the islands.

For pre-Hispanic peoples, the natural world pulsated with life. Where our eyes may see only sterile and desolate islands, *yunga* (coastal) mythology taught the ancient peoples that these were their old lords and gods transformed. For this reason, coastal peoples went to the islands to celebrate their *huacas* and their dead during the time of year that coincided with the mining of guano.

THE NORTHERN ISLANDS

As a result of the devastating demographic collapse suffered by coastal peoples in the wake of the Spanish invasion, only very small quantities of guano were exploited on the northern islands, in contrast to southern Peru, where the resource continued to be mined. Many archaeological remains were found on the islands once guano began to be extracted again after 1821 (the year Peru gained independence from Spain). Between 1869 and 1872, the administrator González la Rosa distributed questionnaires on archaeological matters to the various governors of the guano islands. Among the layers of guano, according to the governor of Manabí's report, prospectors found pottery vessels, some in the shape of birds, as well as gold figurines, gold masks, and great quantities of cotton textiles, along with many headless female mummies. The crews took the gold objects and threw the mummies overboard.[16]

The island of Guañape, distant from Manabí, was also exploited for guano. Miners found vessels and sheets of silver and gold, very thin and decorated with animals in relief, as well as tools, weaving instruments, pottery, maize, textiles, petrified eggs, and bird and sea-lion skeletons.[17]

Guano production varies according to climatic and oceanographic conditions, making it difficult to determine the age of the buried objects. One example of the delicate balance of several variables that affects colonies of guano birds is the relationship of water temperature and location of fish, on which the birds feed. Ocean temperatures are affected periodically by El Niño, which pushes warm currents southward, displacing the cold Peruvian Current and the anchovy shoals offshore. Trade winds that blow from the south-southwest help maintain the stability of the cold current, but a change in wind direction affects the climate and triggers a chain reaction.[18]

Thanks to the archives we know that during the sixteenth and seventeenth centuries, gold fever spurred the Spaniards to search for treasure in the ancient platform mounds made of sun-dried adobe bricks that often contained burial offerings. Treasure seekers were particularly active in the Trujillo region. For example, a man by the name of Luis Rodrigués borrowed a small boat from Alonso Losano, the *encomendero* (head of a Spanish land grant) of Guañape, to "go to the islands of Malabrigo of Macabí to open up a *guaca*."[19]

According to one document, the Corregidor (an official of the Colonial administration) of the Santa Valley, a certain Cristóbal de Santillán, began to excavate on Guañape in search of the treasures contained in its *huaca*. Santillán needed laborers to carry out his mission and resolved the problem by forcing the men from the village of Guañape to go to the island, located two leagues—a Spanish league is roughly equivalent to five kilometers or three miles—offshore, and excavate the sanctuary. Like other Spaniards, Santillán probably signed a "mining" license to excavate the *huaca*, for the archives abound with many documents of this nature. In the document studied, the Corregidor is not accused of having searched for treasure. The *Procurador de los Naturales*, who protected the rights of the natives, gathered their protests, but simply pointed out that the Corregidor had failed to pay the natives for their work and that he was obliged to pay them the salary that he had offered.

Working for the Corregidor gave the native peoples less time to carry out their other jobs, which they undertook in order to pay their tribute. The fishermen of Guañape, for instance, were obliged to serve as *chaski* runners, taking and delivering official mail along determined routes. According to the testimonies of the natives who presented their complaints against the Corregidor, even their *curacas* were forced to go to the islands. Women and girls, they also contended, had to gather water and firewood and bring it to the islands while the men dug for treasure.[20] The document does not mention whether they discovered gold in the *huaca*; we know only that the work was arduous and took several months. The document also does not indicate where the sanctuary was located. The existence of a sanctuary on the island of Guañape, to be investigated in the seventeenth century, indicates that in ancient times coastal peoples had embarked on pilgrimages to the island to worship.

During the guano boom of the nineteenth century, prospectors discovered many archaeological artifacts on the islands, which were covered in thick layers of guano. No doubt, most prospectors failed to record the majority of the objects they found, as much the result of ignorance as their desire to keep the treasures for themselves. Their activity followed concerted efforts by the Spanish during the Colonial period to locate treasure in cemeteries as well as *huaca*, including the guano islands.[21]

The oscillations of guano production and the disturbances caused by the activities of treasure hunters make it risky to use the depths of the guano layers to date the artifacts found.[22] The majority of objects identified as found on the islands have since disappeared, but in his 1948 article, art historian George Kubler listed various objects found in the guano. Kubler dates artifacts found on the Chincha Islands (a group of islands off the south coast) to the thirteenth and fourteenth centuries A.D. and those from the islands of Guañape and Manabí from the seventh to ninth centuries A.D. According to the author, pottery vessels found on the Chincha Islands representing nude men with ropes around their necks indicate that Moche peoples, who lived on the North Coast, were present in southern Peru.

González la Rosa, the administrator who surveyed the archaeological record of the guano islands in 1869–72, discovered that most of the artifacts came from the Chincha Islands off the south coast. These islands, where guano deposits reached depths of 100 to 200 feet, revealed artifacts that González la Rosa identified as "Chimú" and "Chincha." Chimú, a large kingdom on the North Coast, and the *señorío* of Chincha, in the south, both date to around A.D. 1100–1450. In the nineteenth century, nothing was known of the Moche and scientific archaeology did not exist.

The varying depths at which the objects reported by Kubler and González la Rosa were found among the layers of *guano* and the conflicting accounts and contradictions make it difficult to date the objects without seeing them. This is further complicated by the fact that we cannot date the systematic production of guano, which, as we saw, fluctuates according to climatic and oceanographic conditions.

The coastal islands formed part of the cultural legacy of Peru's ancient inhabitants. In myths and legends the islands were transformed into divinities, and even enchanted lords were disguised as rocky outcrops. Tutelary beings to whom sacrifices were made, and the islands also served as resting places for the dead.

Today, the islands have lost their magic and sorcery. Lonely rocky outcrops, battered by waves and swept by the winds, they are inhabited by sea lions and seabirds and are perhaps only of interest to the occasional naturalist, adventurer, or photographer. While it is sad that so much archaeology has been lost, perhaps clues about the past importance of these islands can be gleaned by studying historic documents and by careful examination of artifacts.

NOTES

1. Catherine J. Julien, "Guano and resource control in sixteenth century Arequipa," in *Andean Ecology And Civilization: An Interdisciplinary Perspective on Andean Ecological Complementarity*, edited by Shozo Masuda, Izumi Shimada and Craig Morris (Tokyo: University of Tokyo Press, 1985).

2. Pedro Cieza de León, *The Incas* [1553], translated by Harriet de Onis (Norman: University of Oklahoma Press, 1959), 337.

3. Bernabé Cobo, *Inca Religion and Customs* [1653], translated and edited by Roland Hamilton (Austin: University of Texas Press, 1990); Antonio Vasquez de Espinoza, *Compendium and Description of the West Indes* [1629] (Washington D.C.: Smithsonian Miscellaneous Collection, 1948), paragraph 1332.

4. Jorge Muelle and Robert Wells, "Las Pinturas Del Templo de Pachacamac," *Revista Del Museo Nacional* VIII (Lima), no. 3 (1939); Duccio Bonavia, *Mural Painting in Ancient Peru*, translated by Patricia J. Lyon (Bloomington: University of Indiana Press, 1985)

5. Cobo, *Inca Religion And Customs*.

6. Maria Koepcke, *The Birds of the Department of Lima, Peru*, translated by Erma J. Fisk (Newtown Square, Pennsylvania: Harrowood Books, 1983).

7. Cieza de León, *The Incas*.

8. AGI-Justicia 456, folio 1871.

9. María Rostworowski, *Costa Peruana Prehispánica*. Revised edition of *Etnía y Sociedad* (1977; Lima: Instituto de Estudios Peruanos, 1989).

10. Fray Antonio de La Calancha, *Crónica Moralizadora* [1638], chapter XI, vol. 3 (privately published by Ignacio Prado Pastor, Lima, 1977); Pablo Joseph de Arriaga, *Extirpación de la idolatría del Pirú* [1621], chapter V (Madrid: Biblioteca de Autores Españoles, vol. 209, atlas, 1968).

11. Diego Gonzalez Holguin, *Vocabulario de la Lengua General de Todo el Peru Llamada Quechua* [1608] (Lima: Instituto de Historia, Universidad Nacional Mayor de San Marcos, 1952).

12. Eugenio Yacovleff, La deidad primitiva de los Nasca. *Revista del Museo Nacional* (Lima) 1, no. 2 (1932).

13. Christopher B. Donnan and Donna McClelland, *The Burial Theme in Moche Iconography*. Studies in Pre-Columbian Art and Archaeology, No. 21 (Dumbarton Oaks, Washington, D.C.: Trustees for Harvard University, 1979). Donnan, who interpreted what he called the Presentation Theme, assigned letters (A–D) to the principal figures featured in the sacrifice ceremony, an elaborate blood-letting ritual portrayed on Moche ceramics and murals. One of the most complete scenes of the final episode in the sacrifice narrative portrays attendants slitting the throats of naked prisoners; the attendants then present the captives' blood in goblets to the four individuals presiding over the ceremony. Figure A wears a warrior's helmet and all the paraphernalia of a god, figure B is a bird with warrior attributes. Figure C is an important priestess and, finally, figure D, whom we assume is a dual divinity, is the pair of figure A. In another portrayal, the sacrifice ceremony is carried out between the priestess, figure C, and figure D, to whom she offers a goblet containing the blood of a victim.

Looking at the Chimú myths we find in Fernando de la Carrera's *Arte de la Lengua Yunga de los valles del Obispado de Truxillo del Peru, con un confessionario y todas las oraciones traducidas en la lengua y otras cosas* (Lima:

José Contreras, 1644) the names of two creator gods: Aiapaec and Chicopaec. We do not know why Rafael Larco, who pioneered the study of Moche iconography, only mentions one of these gods and disregarded the other; perhaps he didn't believe that there were two creators.

We are not certain whether these creator gods were known by these two names in Moche times, but the concept must have been the same as that of Guamancanfac, the guano god, who may have been represented by a different name, but embodied the same idea and the same beliefs (on the duality of masculine gods, see Rostworowski, *Estructuras Andinas del Poder. Ideología religiosa y politica* (Lima: Instituto de Estudios Peruanos, 1983).

14. María Rostworowski, *Pachacamac y el Señor de los Milagros* (Lima: Instituto de Estudios Peruanos, 1992).

15. Fray Domingo de Santo Tomas, *Lexicon* [1563]. Facsimile edition (Lima: Instituto de Historia, Universidad Nacional Mayor de San Marcos, 1951).

16. M. González La Rosa, Estudio de las antiguedades peruanas halladas bajo el guano. *Revista Historica* (Lima), no. 3 (1908).

17. M. Gonzalez La Rosa, Estudio de Las Antiguedades...

18. For many years, the Compañia Administradora del Guano, which administered the guano islands, kept records on the numbers of birds and guano production. Bulletins published by the company reflect the fluctuations in guano yields. These statistics show us, for instance, that production increased notably between 1909 and 1939, when a record 169,000 metric tons were produced. But after that period, there is a marked drop in production as a consequence of high mortality rates among birds (Carlos Llosa Belaunde, *Boletín de La Compañia Administradora Del Guano* (Lima) XXI (1949), no. 7: 200.

19. ADL-Protocolos Notariales-Juan de La Mata, 1570, Folios 12 and 13.

20. ADL-Corregimiento-Legajo 268-Exp 3159.

21. Llosa Belaunde, *Boletín de La Compañía Administradora Del Guano* (Lima) XXI (1949), no. 7

22. George Kubler, Towards Absolute Time: Guano Archaeology. *Memoirs of the Society for American Archaeology* (Salt Lake City), no. 4 (1948).

Moche Art

MYTH, HISTORY
AND RITE

Elizabeth P. Benson

THE MOCHE PEOPLE lived from approximately A.D. 50 to 800 in a narrow strip of desert on the North Coast of Peru, just south of the equator (see map, p. 20). Rain rarely falls on the coast. The Andes mountains—some of the highest in the world – block moist, warm winds from the east. The deep, cold, fish-laden waters of the Humboldt (or Peru) Current, flowing up from Antarctica, condense moisture offshore to the west. Where rivers come down from the high, snow-capped mountains, the desert is irrigated for agriculture. The need to control water for irrigation led to the development of extensive canalization and perhaps to battles with mountain peoples for water rights. In the coastal valleys, the Moche farmed and hunted or performed religious, administrative, or artistic work in the centers. Some people went up the valleys and through the mountain passes to exchange coastal goods for products of the various heights and climates of the Andes and the Amazon forests beyond. Others went to sea for fish, and probably for sea lions and guano from offshore islands (Fig. 1).

Recent archaeological work indicates the existence of southern and northern Moche regions, which had many similarities but also sociopolitical and artistic differences.[1] Their relationships are not fully understood. In the northern region, objects of Moche IV style—in the ceramic sequence established by Rafael Larco Hoyle—are rare, suggesting a lack of political unity for the whole Moche area and seemingly some lack of trade within it. Both regions had ceremonial and administrative centers with impressive pyramids and other structures made of adobe bricks. The northern region extends to the Piura River in the far north, where the site of Loma Negra has yielded burials rich with gold and gilt-copper offerings. The sites of Sipán in the Lambayeque Valley and La Mina in the Jequetepeque Valley also had rich burials from the early stages of the Moche development. The southern region—from the Chicama Valley down to at least as far as the impressive site of Pañamarca in the Nepeña Valley—has long been better known. The most explored and surely the most important site is Moche, in the valley of the same name (derived from Muchic, the language spoken there in early times). Its two immense structures are called today the Huaca de la Luna and the Huaca del Sol; the latter was probably the largest adobe structure in the Americas. The southern region was the area that Rafael Larco Hoyle knew best and described in the early days of Moche studies.[2] (It is his collection now housed in the Museo Arqueológico Rafael Larco Herrera in Lima that this catalogue documents and on which most of the observations of this essay are based.)

Fig. 1 *Present-day tule (reed) boats at Huanchaco Beach, standing upright to dry. Modern examples are nearly identical to boats represented in Moche art 1,500 years ago.*

Fig. 2 *Huaca de la Luna at Moche, with the sacred mountain Cerro Blanco.*

Larco Hoyle not only formed a superb collection of Moche artifacts, he published a fine corpus of material for study, wrote the earliest body of iconographic studies, and established a ceramic seriation that is still in use for the southern region: Moche I pottery (A.D. 50–100) has a compact vessel form and a short spout with a thickened lip; Moche II (A.D. 100–200) has a longer spout with a less thick lip; Moche III (A.D. 200–450) has a slightly flared spout; Moche IV (A.D. 450–550) has a long, straight-sided spout; and Moche V (A.D. 550–800) has a stirrup with sides that curve inward so that they almost meet. No provenances are listed for objects in this catalogue, but most probably come from the south, especially the Chicama Valley.

Art

Moche art reflects the extraordinarily varied environment and the beliefs, customs, adaptations, and organization of life that it inspired. Undoubtedly, the higher status of the individual, the more and finer the grave goods. Some burials were remarkably rich. Grave goods also tell of the duties and accomplishments of the deceased and of the rituals he or she engaged in. In seeking the meaning of Moche art, one must keep in mind the questions: what would these ancient people have wanted to put into a grave and why?

Artists and artisans expressed themselves in many media. Massive adobe architecture marked the desert landscape; most notable were the Huaca de la Luna and the Huaca del Sol at the site of Moche (Fig. 2). The walls of Moche structures often bore painted murals (Fig. 3).[3] Stone architecture and sculpture were lacking, but small objects were carved from stone, wood, bone, and shell. Cloth was of great importance in the Andes, which produced some of the world's finest preindustrial weavings; however, because of preservation conditions on the North Coast, few Moche textiles remain in good condition.[4] A splendid Moche achievement was metallurgy, with complex work created in gold, silver, and copper, often adorned with inlay of stone and shell.[5] A remarkable sample of this survives, considering that quantities of gold were melted down by early Spanish invaders.

Ceramic art in distinctive shapes was a major art form. The most prestigious shape was the stirrup-spout bottle. An ancient form, it presumably was thought of as a link with the sacred ancestors, for it was an important Cupisnique form earlier on the

Fig. 3 *Modeled and painted mural in Huaca de la Luna at Moche, depicting the head of a supernatural being. Uncovered recently by the Proyecto Arqueológico Huaca de la Luna de la Universidad Nacional de Trujillo.*

coast (1200–200 B.C.) and it was also an early highland form. These bottles were often globular and decorated with scenes or designs; bottles could also be shaped as boxes. Both forms might have a full-round "deck figure" on top. Frequently, the bottle itself took effigy form. A few other shapes carried important subject matter —the *florero* or flaring bowl, and the spout-and-handle or cruet-shaped bottle—but these are relatively rare.

Most Moche pottery was basically made in two-piece molds, which produced the two halves of the finished product. When the clay began to dry and the molds were removed, coils of clay were added to finish the top; the stirrup spout was modeled by using three tapered wooden rods as forms.[6] Details could be applied by hand. Sometimes a design was press-molded or stamped on the surface. Occasionally, inlay of shell or stone was used, or metal jewelry was added to a figure. Often scenes and motifs were painted with broad brush strokes or a very fine line using slip; these scenes have all come to be called "fineline." In earlier times, Moche artists sometimes painted details in light-colored slip on a red-slip figure, or they might cut into red-slip figures to create detail by revealing the light-slip background. In later times, detail was added with lines. In the last phase (Moche V), surfaces are often a maze of fine lines that seem driven by a *horror vacuui*.

Fineline composition schemes vary. A single figure or scene may be repeated almost identically on both sides of a vessel, or there may be a pairing of figures. There are also multiple figures in scenes, sometimes performing sequential actions. Scenes that roll out around a globular bottle have two focal areas, one at either side of the vessel. Each may define the realms of the deities or show, for example, the presentation of captives on one side and sacrifice on the other (cat. no. 99). Some vessels have horizontal scene divisions; some spiral up. Single effigy figures may be parts of a sequence or narrative for which it might have been possible to put many effigy bottles together to compose a whole scene.

The Moche surely told more about themselves on their ceramics than any culture in the world, possibly excepting Maya and Greek civilizations. Interpreting information on Moche pots is not easy, however, given the absence of written texts and survival of few traditions. A series of scholars have been intrigued, however, by this rich subject matter.[7]

The "realism" of Moche art has been noted; indeed, species of birds, mammals, or plants often can be identified (Larco Hoyle named many of them), and portraits, clothing, and objects are convincingly represented. Yet it is evident that realism was not the purpose of these depictions; mixtures of species frequently appear and other variations on reality – a peanut playing a flute, a god head emerging from maize ears (cat. nos. 61, 63), for example – suggest other goals. Weapons and accouterments of warriors have human faces, arms, and legs, picturing a belief that *things* had life that was related to the Moche way of life (cat. no. 95).[8] The animism of weapons, which imbued them with power to aid Moche warriors, expressed the concept of sacred or power objects. In the past, such beliefs were surely held much more widely and strongly than they are today. The basic Moche belief in the life of things may have been intensified through the ritual use of psychoactive drugs, for example, the San Pedro cactus, with which the shaman reached the other world.

In fineline scenes, snakes may be poised in the air near a house; sacrificial offerings of arms and legs float, tied with cord; plants, frequent components of fineline scenes, are usually shown with roots, drifting in the air. Pottery also can be suspended in space. A stirrup-spout vessel floating in a house or over someone's head seems to mark a sacred, charged space or person. All of these depictions are glosses, parts of symbolic language that describe the meaning of the scene rather than being parts of the setting. They also may refer to the other world.

The other world was a widespread concept in the past. It was understood that here things were alive and species mixed. It was a world of inexplicable things that cosmology sought to define. It was the world the shaman visited or communicated with in order to understand it. It was the world of the dead and of the sacred ancestors, who were thought to be still alive in that world. It was the other side of the so-called real world.

Human beings were close to animals. Animals symbolized human attributes and ambitions; moreover, humans and animals were thought to have the same kinds of minds and souls; animals even knew things that human beings did not know. Anthropozoomorphs—creatures with human bodies and limbs, and animal heads and tails and other attributes—appear frequently in Moche ceramic art. In some cases, there are exact equivalencies between Moche depictions of human roles and those of creatures that are part man and part animals. A man may sit with a bag in his lap; an anthropomorphic deer or fox can sit in the same way, wearing the same garments. A man sits surrounded by his curing remedies; an owl can appear in the same role. Anthropozoomorphs routinely have human hands, which allows them to hold bags or knives or other objects, or make gestures.

Running warriors and lightly clad runners, holding bags, move through vegetated landscapes. They are depicted as men in some scenes but in others as anthropozoomorphs; foxes, deer, falcons, hummingbirds, and snakes are common. Warriors and runners may have been the same people—or the same animal-people— at different moments in a rite. In two runner scenes, the destination is shown. In one, a pyramid is adorned with step motifs and war clubs on the roof; in the other, a pyramid features a god enthroned and in front of him an owl in the soft, white garments of a priest, two *ulluchu* fruits, and an unfolded bag with two beans.[9] The bags probably held shamanic/divinatory equipment, including beans (or other seeds) for this purpose or for a planting ritual. The ulluchu depictions indicate blood sacrifice; this fruit, related to the papaya, contains an anticoagulant.[10] There is a rough parallel between the last scene described above and a scene in which the running captives approach a house with an enthroned figure and a man in priestly dress (cat. no. 99).

In all of these images, the Moche presented their physical world and their attitudes or beliefs about it. The practical, political world, the military world, and the ritual, supernatural world were interrelated parts of the same whole. The art indicates those interrelationships. None of the decorated vessels seems to have been made purely to satisfy the potter's artistic urges, although many vessels are extraordinary works of art. Whatever was depicted was shown for a purpose, following certain conventions of what had meaning in the society. Dress is a critical source of information about the identity of the wearer, his status, and the rite enacted. Everything had a place within the scheme of things; it was a highly structured world. Cosmology is reflected everywhere. Quadripartite designs, for example, demonstrate a cosmic scheme based on the four world corners or directions. Effigy vessels show vegetables in fours (cat. nos. 58, 59). Captors or captives are shown in groups of four (cat. nos. 98, 99).

Houses are depicted, both as effigy vessels (cat. nos. 25, 26) and as elements in painted scenes. In a fineline portrayal of the arrival, presentation, and demise of captives, the ruler sits in a house, a defined and probably sacred space that defines and separates him from the scene and also establishes his role and status (cat. no. 99). Such houses often have glossing elements on the roof—foxes, a jaguar, war clubs, or a step motif. Simpler houses with lesser figures still outline special space, essential to the meaning of the scene. Certain scenes are marked as ritual by the presence of a simple structure.

A very high percentage of the pottery presents sea scenes: rafts, both natural and supernatural; fish and fish monsters; humans and deities fishing; sea birds, sea lions, and shell, realistic or anthropomorphized.

Made from earth, water, and fire, pottery was a sacred substance, formed in significant shapes and used to present important themes. Pottery also appears as symbolic language in scenes depicting ritual or the other world.

DEITIES

The language of the later Incas offers no word for "god," only a word for "sacred," *huaca*.[11] Apparent gods are depicted, however, in Moche art, although they are not well understood. They can be recognized by a mouth with fangs and arrow-shaped corners, a face surely inherited from earlier Chavín art and religion in the mountains to the east. Occasionally, this mouth appears on lesser creatures, sacred beings, or even human beings, perhaps as a sign of the sacredness of a particular moment or of a rite that has sacralized the person.

What can be called the major god has round, staring eyes (cat. nos. 84, 92). In his active aspect, bent knees give him an air of intensity and movement. His attributes may vary but are generally recognizable—a headdress with jaguar head and limbs, often with a large semicircle and sometimes smaller ornaments, all probably feathered; pendant snake-head ear ornaments and snake extensions on his belt; and usually a short tunic or shirt with a step motif, a symbol of important status and perhaps sacredness, which may derive from mountain forms. The active version of this god is likely the culture hero of the Moche people. He is shown fighting and beheading a fish or crab monster, or making love to a woman (an act that perhaps originated the Moche people). He may be the son of or an aspect of an old god shown seated in the mountains, who might be a creator, sky, and mountain god. The active god probably possessed a solar identity as one who comes every day to the coast from the east, going into the sea in the west. Deities surely had astronomical identities.

The god may be one god with varying aspects, or a passive-active, father-son dyad, or twins or brothers, or some combination of these. Such questions arise when the active major god is depicted with another supernatural who shares some of his godly attributes.[12] Questions also arise when the god wears different garments, or when a crab or a centipede, for example, shows some of his traits. The major god may change garments or guise for a particular purpose (cat. no. 91). Recent folk literature is full of accounts of a god who becomes a hummingbird, deer, or fish in order to accomplish a

Fig. 4 *Drawing by Gerdt Kutscher from a stirrup-spout vessel depicting a probable moon goddess with snake-headed radiances, riding in a supernatural balsa raft propelled by human legs. (Kutscher 1983: Abb. 316B)*

certain task; it is also peopled with many supernatural twins, brothers, or father-son combinations.

A frequent figure, who sometimes has a god's mouth or sometimes a bird's, is an anthropomorphic owl in warrior garments (cat. nos. 83, 84, 107). He seems to be the war god or the idealized Moche warrior. He also appears as a sacrificer with a knife in one hand, a human head in the other. Again, the warrior and the sacrificer may be one or two deities. An anthropomorphic bat with a snarling arrow mouth is also a supernatural sacrificer of human beings (cat. no. 88), but the bat does not seem to be a deity.

A radiant-warrior god, who appears in Moche IV, was likely a solar deity, perhaps introduced for political reasons at a time when serious changes were occurring, because of influences from the south and/or because of natural phenomena and other possible events. In pre-Hispanic religions it is not uncommon to have more than one god who is related to the sun.

A likely moon goddess appeared at the same time (Fig. 4).[13] She seems to be the only important supernatural woman present in Moche art. Female portrait heads and portrayals of women in top-status positions are rare or nonexistent. Women do play an important role in sacrifice scenes, however, and they sometimes are seen in roles peripheral to a ritual in which coca leaves were chewed. It is also true that an actual burial of an important woman has been found.[14]

The owl warrior, the radiant warrior, and sometimes the female goddess appear in various scenes: the Presentation Theme, which is a sacrifice scene (cat. no. 107); the top level of a scene of gods with beans and sticks (cat. no. 83); and a scene with active anthropomorphized weaponry, among others.[15] The woman and the owl are seen with the major god but the radiant warrior apparently never confronts him.

A fish monster (opinions vary as to the species of fish), who normally has a human leg and an arm holding a knife, is another supernatural being. It appears alone (cat. no. 85), with a crab monster, or with the major god. A crab monster or god is probably a separate being, although it may be an aspect of the major god (cat. no. 92).

RITUALS

Myth, history, ritual, and power symbols are major motifs on Moche ceramics. Myth and history are intermixed, and ritual reenacts their events. Many rites have to do with warfare and the presentation and sacrifice of captives. War was a ritual affair, and purely ritual warfare may have been conducted. However, as the Moche expanded from the principal site of Moche into valleys to the south, they maintained a *modus vivendi* with the more independent valleys to the north as well as with the highland groups who controlled the sources of water and other resources. All this could not have been accomplished without serious military incursions.

The capture of sacrificial victims was undoubtedly a major part of war. "Trophy heads," a prevalent motif in much pre-Hispanic art, are not battle trophies, but heads decapitated as offerings in sacrificial ritual. War, sacrifice, and fertility are intimately connected. Sacrifices are often offerings to the controllers of nature. Even in societies with more generous landscapes, religion and ritual are often dominated by concepts of fertility and sustenance. Rulers who do not provide food—who do not contract with the spirits of nature to provide food for the people—are not rulers for long. Many pre-Hispanic objects and accessories have a knife or blade shape that probably refers both to agriculture—clearing and harvesting—and to human and animal sacrifice. A very high percentage of Moche supernaturals hold a knife in one hand. Vegetation appears in many Moche scenes.

In one group of scenes, Moche warriors battle men in dress identified with the coca-chewing rite; they often have bags in which the leaves of the sacred plant were carried. A ritual reenacting a historical battle for control of the fields where coca grew would have a force like that of ritual that reenacted myth. A battle may even be a part of the coca ritual.

Christopher Donnan, having published the Presentation Theme some years ago,[16] more recently calls it the Sacrifice Ceremony. Sacrifice is part of other ritual complexes, however, and so the original name is used here. The Presentation Theme, with its warrior gods, belongs to a larger complex, in which the same major characters appear. These deities surely possess astronomical identities, and depictions of them must refer to sky events. Rulers or priests undoubtedly imitated the gods in ritual (cat. nos. 107, 108).

Some high-relief stirrup-spout vessels show sacrifices in the mountains, rituals that seem to relate to requests to the mountains for water (Fig. 5). A complex scene with captives falling into a crevasse might be related to those scenes (cat. no. 99).

The sacrificial rites on guano islands that are depicted on pottery are sea-lion hunts (cat. no. 47), but evidence exists on the islands of ritual activity with military connotations, and one island scene shows animated weapons and a captive figure.[17] Not only was the sea a great resource and symbol of vast significance, the very idea of water was precious to these desert-dwelling people.

Deer hunters are richly dressed, more or less like warriors, but they sometimes wear elements of priestly dress or are accompanied by people in the soft, white garments of priests. Both elements are present: war and sacrifice. On effigy vases, the deer is depicted like a human captive because, as a hunted creature, it was a sacrificial victim.

PORTRAITS

The Moche IV phase produced many recognizable portraits. The common official Moche portrait was a ceramic head, usually a stirrup-spout bottle. Portrait heads normally show men in soft cloth headdresses, very like those worn by curers and men who arrange offerings and perform other priestly activities.[18] Because the portrait heads are individualized and presented as important, repeated motifs, they seem to represent the most important people, perhaps rulers, and yet they are modestly dressed. Usually, in full-figure depictions the portrait-head men wear dress slightly more elaborate than that of the figures engaged in priestly occupations. (cat. no. 68).

Other prominent full-figure human effigies wear a headdress with a knife and/or jaguar head and/or two "rosettes"; this is essentially warrior dress – it is also a costume that the radiant-warrior god sometimes wears (cat. no. 82).[19] Some of the seated, enthroned figures dressed in this fashion might be portraits, but they are more prototypical.

Fig. 5 *Drawing by Adolf Baessler. The bottle shows a mountain sacrifice scene in the presence of a deity. (Baessler 1902–1903, pl. 93)*

The relationship between these two types of figures, the priestly and the military, is not understood. Generally, a figure seated on a throne or receiving prisoners wears the more worldly headdress, although soft headdresses appear in scenes with captives. Two different sets of people in different kinds of roles seem to be shown. Was there perhaps dual rulership? There may have been a spiritual leader and a military leader. It is conceivable but unlikely that one leader wore different headgear on different occasions. If this were so, why is the man given individual portraiture only in priestly headgear? When the two types appear together in fineline scenes, the non-priestly man is usually bigger or has a more prominent place. The effigy depiction of the man in warrior garments perhaps means to suggest the incarnation of the god, or if not quite the god, the god's double, avatar, or companion. The ruler's personal portrait is set in priestly dress, not in a god's.

Another puzzling aspect of the portrait heads is their occasional disfigurement. Some faces have scars. (cat. no. 67) and a few are diseased (cat. no. 69) or blind. The scars may be battle scars, but could also be scars from a shamanic initiation. Larco Hoyle suggested that people were deliberately disfigured as a form of punishment.[20] This might account for some of the injuries on less high-status faces, although disfigurement might also have been caused by tropical diseases. Captives who are blind in one eye (cat. no. 78) might have received injury from a war club in battle, although there could be many other causes.

Several prominent, well-dressed figures, seated for the presentation of prisoners, are pictured with a missing arm.[21] A quite well-dressed, standing figure with a portrait face has a missing foot (cat. no. 73). [22] The foot might have been offered in sacrifice, lost in battle, amputated for medical reasons, or removed as punishment or to limit movement. Although probably of lesser status than chieftains and portrait figures, one-footed figures are well dressed and shown playing important roles. Other afflictions – loss of both feet, for example – are of even lower status.

If people with illnesses were believed to have special powers – a belief that has prevailed in many cultures – it is possible that people were deliberately disfigured to give them those powers. Do the blind have special ability to see into the other world because they are blind? Was their blinding an offering or a sacrifice? The Moche apparently both honored and respected natural and diseased disfigurement and, for whatever reasons, created deformation.

These are some of the elements of Moche iconography with which one can work to try to approach interpretation of Moche belief, cosmology, and social structure. It is tantalizing to explore the tremendously rich imagery left to us by the Moche. We can identify many of the basic themes and patterns, yet the details of what they signify and how they relate remain elusive, so complex is the legacy of the Moche people.

NOTES

1. Izumi Shimada, *Pampa Grande and the Mochica Culture* (Austin: University of Texas Press, 1994); Santiago Uceda and Elias Mujica, eds. *Moche: Propuestas y perspectivas* (Trujillo: Universidad Nacional de La Libertad, 1994).

2. Rafael Larco Hoyle, *Los Mochicas*, I (Lima: La Crónica" y "Variedades", S.A, 1938); *Los Mochicas*, II (Lima: Empresa Editorial "RIMAC" S.A., 1939); *Los Mochicas* (Lima, 1945); *Cronología arqueológica del norte del Peru* (Buenos Aires: Sociedad Geográfica Américana, 1948); *Las épocas peruanas* (Lima, 1963).

3. Duccio Bonavia, *Mural Painting in Ancient Peru*. trans. Patricia J. Lyon (Bloomington: Indiana University Press, 1985); Uceda and Mujica, eds. *Moche: Propuestas y perspectivas*.

4. William J. Conklin, "Moche Textile Structures," *The Junius B. Bird Pre-Columbian Textile Conference*, eds. A. P. Rowe, E. P. Benson, and A.-L. Schaffer (Washington, D.C.: The Textile Museum and Dumbarton Oaks, 1979), 165–184.

5. Walter Alva, *Sipán* (Lima: Backus y Johnston en la cultura y artes del Peru, 1994); Walter Alva and Christopher B. Donnan, *Royal Tombs of Sipán* (Los Angeles: University of California, Fowler Museum of Cultural

History, 1993); Julie Jones, "Mochica Works of Art in Metal: A Review." *Pre-Columbian Metallurgy of South America*, ed. Elizabeth P. Benson (Washington, D.C.: Dumbarton Oaks Research Library and Collections, Washington, D.C., 1979), 53-104.

6. Christopher B. Donnan, "Moche Ceramic Technology." *Nawpa Pacha* 3 (1965):115-135; *Ceramics of Ancient Peru* (Los Angeles: University of California, Fowler Museum of Cultural History, 1992), 56–65.

7. Luis Jaime Castillo Butters, *Personajes míticos, escenas y narraciones en la iconografía mochica* (Lima: Pontificia Universidad Catolica del Peru, 1989); Christopher B. Donnan, *Moche Art and Iconography* (Los Angeles: University of California Latin American Center Publications, 1976); Donnan, *Moche Art of Peru* (Los Angeles: Fowler Museum of Cultural History, UCLA, 1978) Anne Marie Hocquenghem, *Iconografía Mochica* (Lima: Pontificia Universidad Católica del Perú, 1987); Gerdt Kutscher, *Chimu: Eine altindianische Hochkultur* (Berlin: Verlag Gebr. Mann, 1950); Kutscher, Nordperuanische Keramik: Figürlich verzierte Gefässe der Früh-Chimu/Cerámica del Peru septentrional: Figuras ornamentales en vasijas de los chimúes antiguos, *Monumental Americana*, I (Berlin: Der Ibero-Amerikanische Bibliothek zu Berlin and Gebr. Mann, 1954); Larco Hoyle 1938 and 1939.

8. Bonavia, .*Mural Painting in Ancient Peru*, figs. 54–61, 73–74; Gerdt Kutscher, *Nordperuanische Gefässmalereien des Moche-Stils*, Materialien zur Allgemeinen und Vergleichenden Archäologie 18, ed. Ulf Bankmann (Munich: Verlag C. H. Beck, 1983)

9. Kutscher 1983, Abbn. 295, 296.

10. S. Henry Wassén, "Ulluchu in Moche Iconography and Blood Ceremonies: The Search for Identification." *Göteborgs Etnografiska Museum Arstryck Annals* (1985/86): 50–85. Göteborg.

11. María Rostworowski de Diez Canseco, *Estructuras Andinas del Poder: Ideología religiosa y política*. 4th ed. (Lima: Instituto de Estudios Peruanos, 1996), 9–10.

12. Yuri Berezkin, "An identification of anthropomorphic mythological personages in Moche representations." *Nawpa Pacha* 18 (1980 [1981]): 1–26.

13. Elizabeth P. Benson, "The Moche Moon." *Recent Studies in Andean Prehistory and Protohistory*, eds. D. P. Kvietok and D. H. Sandweiss (Ithaca: Cornell University, Latin American Studies Program, 1985), 121–135l; Benson, "Women in Mochica Art." *The Role of Gender in Pre-Columbian Art and Archaeology*, ed. Virginia E. Miller (Lanham, MD: University Press of America, 1988) 63–74.

14. Christopher B. Donnan and Luis Jaime Castillo, "Finding the tomb of a Moche priestess." *Archaeology* (1992) 45 (6):38–42.

15. Kutscher 1983, Abbn. 267.

16. Donnan 1976, 117–129; Donnan 1978, 158–173.

17. Elizabeth P. Benson, "Art, Agriculture, Warfare and the Guano Islands," *Andean Art: Visual Expression and its Relation to Andean Beliefs and Values*, ed. Penny Dransart, Worldwide Archaeology Series 13 (Avebury, Aldershot, England, 1995), 245–264; George Kubler, "Towards Absolute Time: Guano Archeology." *A Reappraisal of Peruvian Archaeology*, ed. Wendell C. Bennett. Memoirs of the Society for American Archaeology 4. (Menasha, WI, 1948), 29–50; Gerdt Kutscher, "Nordperuanische Gefässmalereien des Moche-Stils." ed. Ulf Bankmann, *Materialien zur Allgemeinen und Vergleichenden Archäologie* 18 (Munich: Verlag C. H. Beck, 1983), Abb. 270.

18. Elizabeth P. Benson, "Death-associated Figures on Mochica Pottery," *Death and the Afterlife in Pre-Columbian America*, ed. E. P. Benson (Washington, D.C.: Dumbarton Oaks Research Library and Collections, 1975), 105–144.

19. Elizabeth P. Benson, "The Well-Dressed Captives: Some Observations on Moche Iconography." *Baessler-Archiv* N.F. XXX (1982):181–222.

20. Larco Hoyle 1939, 153–165.

21. Benson, 1982, figs. 16,17.

22. See Daniel Arsenault, "El personaje del pie amputado en la cultura mochica del Peru: Un ensayo sobre la arqueología del poder." *Latin American Antiquity* 4, no. 3 (1993): 225–245. Donnan and Castillo 1992.

Deer Hunting and Combat

Parallel Activities
in the
Moche World

Christopher B. Donnan

LTHOUGH IT IS USUALLY POSSIBLE to recognize what is being depicted in pre-Hispanic Peruvian art, it is far more difficult to understand why it is depicted and what it would have meant to the ancient people who created it. Often the meaning can only be reconstructed by deriving subtle clues from various sources and carefully piecing the clues together until the meaning is revealed. The beautifully sculpted deer in the Larco collection (Fig. 1) seems to be an enigmatic combination of human and animal characteristics. Yet by combining insights from a variety of sources it is possible to understand not only the various elements of what is being depicted but also why it was depicted and what it may have meant in the people who created it.

The bottle was made by the Moche people, whose civilization flourished in a series of river valleys along the North Coast of Peru between approximately A.D. 50 and 800. Although the Moche had no writing system, they left a vivid artistic record of their activities, environment, and beliefs in thousands of sculpted and painted ceramic vessels.

Deer were frequently depicted by Moche artists. Some were shown in a fully natural state, while others combine deer and human characteristics. The deer in Figure 1 is seated in human fashion, with its legs crossed. Its genitals are showing, and it has human hands. Around its neck is a ropelike object, with the end extending down across the chest.

Humans were sometimes depicted by Moche artists in a very similar fashion (cat. no. 96). Like the deer, these figures are seated, with their genitals showing, and have ropes around their necks with the ends extending down across their chests. It is curious that Moche artists depicted only deer and humans seated with ropes around their necks. To understand why, we must reconstruct the activities of warriors and deer hunters in Moche culture.

Many warriors are shown in Moche art. An excellent example is the kneeling warrior in cat. no. 94, who has a square shield on his left wrist, and whose right hand originally grasped a war club. Many painted scenes depict warriors engaged in combat (Figs. 2, 3). Although slings and spear-throwers with spears were often used, the club was the most frequently shown weapon. The hills and plants shown in some scenes indicate that combat took place away from Moche settlements, religious structures, canals, or even cultivated fields — presumably in the barren expanses of desert terrain that lie between fertile river valleys. There are no depictions of warriors attacking a

Fig. 1 *Seated Anthropomorphic Stag Captive. Museo Arqueológico Rafael Larco Herrera, XSC-000-194.*

Fig. 2 *Warriors in Combat.*
Drawing by Robert Easley from a
Moche ceramic bottle in a private
collection, Buenos Aires.

castle or fortified settlement, nor any showing the killing, capturing, or mistreatment of noncombatant personnel. The combat seen in Moche art appears to have nothing to do with conquest of an enemy group, but rather to have been a ceremonial activity of high-status Moche males.

There are a few depictions of two warriors fighting a single opponent, but the essence of Moche combat appears to have been the expression of individual valor in which the warriors engaged one-on-one. In rare instances, one or more were actually killed, but it is clear that the real objective was to capture rather than kill the opponent.

Once captured, some or all of the opponent's clothing was removed, a rope was placed around his neck, and his hands were sometimes tied behind his back. The victor then held the rope tied to the prisoner's neck and marched him off the field of battle (Fig. 4). The prisoners were taken to a place where they were formally arraigned

Fig. 3 *Warriors in Combat.*
Drawing by Donna McClelland
from a Moche ceramic bottle in the
Museo Nacional de Antropología,
Arqueología y Historia, Lima.

52

Fig. 4 *Warriors in Combat. Drawing by Donna McClelland from a Moche ceramic bottle in a private collection, Buenos Aires.*

(Fig. 5). One scene shows them being brought into a ceremonial precinct, defined by large pyramids with temple structures at their summits (Fig. 6). Following arraignment, there was a ceremony in which the prisoners were sacrificed. Their throats were cut, and their blood was consumed in tall goblets (cat. no. 107).

The paisley-shaped elements that appear to float in the background of sacrifice scenes (e.g., cat. no. 107) are plants called *ulluchus*. Wassén suggested that they were related to the papaya family, which has anticoagulant properties well known to the native people in the tropical forest of South America. If *ulluchus* have similar properties, the Moche may have used them to keep the blood from coagulating during the sacrifice ceremony.[1]

Nude males with ropes around their necks, like those in cat. no. 96, are clearly prisoners who have been captured in combat. They are destined to be sacrificed and their blood consumed as part of a religious ceremony. But why were deer depicted in

Fig. 5 *Arraignment of Prisoners. Drawing from a Moche ceramic bottle in the Museum für Völkerkunde, Berlin. After Kutscher 1954: 23.*

Fig. 7 *Deer Hunt. Drawing by Donna McClelland from a Moche ceramic bottle in the Bowers Museum, Santa Ana, CA*

this manner? Could it be that deer were seen as analogous to warriors, to be captured as part of a religious practice in order to be sacrificed for their blood? Evidence from various sources strongly suggests that this was the case.

All deer depicted by Moche artists are white-tailed deer (*Odocoileus virginianus*), a species that is native to the North Coast of Peru.[2] It is curious that they are almost always depicted with their tongues hanging out the sides of their mouths. No other animal in Moche art is shown in this way. Deer are known to run with their tongues out when they are winded or tired, and the artists may have intended to show them in this state. Moreover, when a deer is killed, the tongue will often drop out the side of the mouth through a gap that exists between the deer's incisor and molar teeth.[3]

In Moche deer hunting scenes, hunters consistently wear elaborate clothing, headdresses, and ornaments — attire that is altogether unsuited to the stalking and killing of deer (Figs. 7-9, cat. no. 106). To understand why they are dressed this way,

Fig. 6 *Arraignment of Prisoners. Drawing by Donna McClelland from a Moche ceramic bottle in the American Museum of Natural History, New York.*

Fig. 8 *Deer Hunt. Drawing by Donna McClelland from a Moche ceramic bottle in the Dallas Museum of Art.*

it is useful to consider the ethnohistoric records describing the great hunts practiced by the Inca. The best account is of a hunt held by the Inca ruler, Manco Inca, near the valley of Jauja in honor of Francisco Pizarro around 1536. On that occasion, 10,000 Indians formed a ring around an area 30 to 60 miles in circumference. They then closed toward the center, driving all the animals in the area before them, and forming several concentric rings as their circle grew smaller. When the circle was small enough, designated hunters entered it and killed as many animals as was desired.[4]

The elaborately dressed individuals in Moche deer-hunting scenes are undoubtedly killing animals that have previously been surrounded or driven into net enclosures. The nets are indicated with a crosshatch pattern, often shown along the bottom or border areas of the scene. Some representations show the nets being held together by plainly dressed individuals (Fig. 7), or propped up by long staffs.

Hunting and killing of deer were so commonly depicted in Moche art that one might assume that deer provided a large portion of the Moche diet. When archaeologists excavate Moche habitation sites, however, they find almost no deer bone in the refuse.[5] The most plausible explanation for this is that the deer were ritually killed, and their remains were treated with great ceremony—including a special process of disposal.

Ritual disposal of the remains of sacrificed animals was widely practiced in the Andean area at the time of European contact. Llamas and alpacas were the principal animals ritually sacrificed in the Inca Empire. Most of the early Spanish writers indicate that the carcasses of sacrificed animals were burned. Some state that the meat was consumed by the public on occasions or that the blood was utilized for the blood communion of the Inca religion. The disposal of the bones, however, involved a specific ceremony which was conducted annually:

> ...they brought out the ashes and charcoal which had been kept from what was left over from the bones of the sacrifices of the past years. They ground these up with two baskets of coca, many flowers of a variety of colors, aji [chile pepper], salt, and roasted peanuts. Ground up together in this manner they took out a small amount, and carried the rest to the [river].[6]

The mixture was put in the river, along with cloth, feathers, gold, and silver. Two hundred people followed the floating sacrifice downstream, where they offered more baskets of coca.

The ceremonial disposal of sacrificial bones appears to have been a widespread

Fig. 9 *Deer Hunt. Drawing by Donna McClelland from a Moche ceramic bottle in a private collection, New Hampshire.*

practice in Peru centuries before it was first recorded by the Spanish writers; it is still practiced by people living in the southern sierra of Peru today.[7] The scarcity of deer bone in Moche refuse is probably because the deer were seen as sacrificial animals rather than animals killed for secular purposes.

Among white-tailed deer, body spots are only characteristic of fawns. It is curious, therefore, that the deer shown by Moche artists frequently have body spots, even though antlers on many of the individuals clearly identify them as adults. On about five percent of the animals, however, spots appear for a few weeks in the fall of the year, when they are changing from their summer to winter coat.[8]

It is also curious that body spots occur on approximately two-thirds of the deer depicted by Moche artists. More than 60 percent of the scenes with deer have at least one deer with body spots, and more than half of the scenes only illustrate deer with body spots.

Two explanations could account for the high frequency of adult deer with body spots in Moche art. One is that there may have been a greater frequency of adult deer with body spots inhabiting the North Coast of Peru 1,500 years ago than among white-tailed deer populations that have been observed in recent times. The other

Fig. 10 *Deer Hunt. Drawing by Donna McClelland from a Moche cup in the American Museum of Natural History, New York.*

possibility is that spotted adult deer were rare, but had a special significance to the Moche and thus were depicted more frequently than they occurred in nature. Since the spots occur on adult deer only during the fall of the year, it may be that the deer hunting shown in Moche art was restricted to that season.

As noted above, only elaborately dressed individuals are shown killing deer. They wear ornate clothing, headdresses, and jewelry, and generally have face and leg paint, all of which are nearly identical to those of warriors. The only notable difference is that most warriors wear conical helmets and have a trapezoidal object suspended from the back of their belts, while most deer hunters wear soft turbans and a sash with the ends hanging from the back. There are, however, some scenes in which the deer hunters wear the trapezoidal object suspended from their belts (Fig. 9), and others where some warriors wear soft turbans that are almost identical to those worn by deer hunters (Figs. 2, 3). One deer hunt (Fig. 10) even shows a hunter wearing the conical helmet.

Only two implements are normally used in killing the deer: a spear and a club. The spear is identical to that used in combat by Moche warriors. With a long barbed point and a fairly short shaft, it is thrown with the aid of a spear-thrower. The club

Fig. 11 Reed boats carrying prisoners and jars. Drawing by Donna McClelland from a Moche ceramic bottle in the Art Institute of Chicago.

Fig. 12 Deer Hunt. Drawing by Donna McClelland from a Moche ceramic bottle in the M.H. de Young Memorial Museum, San Francisco

normally has a round or elliptical shaped club head at one end and a point at the other. In a few instances, however, the club used in hunting deer is identical to the club most often used in combat (Fig. 10).

Another element linking combat and deer hunting is the fact that females shown in some deer hunting scenes (e.g., Fig. 8 right) are identical to females who participate in human sacrifice (Fig. 6). These women are always shown with long hair, wearing dresses of dark color, and either carry or stand adjacent to large jars. The jars normally have domed lids and branches or rope tied around their necks. They may have contained blood and been conceptualized as the equivalent of prisoners with ropes around their necks. Jars and prisoners are frequently shown together in the holds of large reed boats (Fig. 11). Perhaps both were considered simply as containers of blood.

Fig. 13 Anthropomorphized deer warrior. British Museum, London

Ulluchus are sometimes associated with deer hunting in Moche art (Fig. 12). As noted above, their possible anticoagulant property may be the reason for their frequent occurrence in scenes of the human sacrifice.[9] Their occurrence in deer-hunting scenes strongly implies that the blood of the deer was an essential element of this activity.

Finally, it should be noted that when deer are anthropomorphized in Moche art, they are often shown as warriors (Fig. 13). Like their human counterparts, they are frequently engaged in combat (Fig. 14).

Fig. 14 Anthropomorphized deer warriors in combat. Drawing by Donna McClelland from a Moche ceramic bottle in a private collection, Buenos Aires.

Interpreting the illustrations of both deer hunting and combat as ritual rather than secular events is in keeping with the essence of Moche art and iconography, which seemingly does not illustrate the secular, mundane aspects of Moche life.[10] The many parallels between deer hunting and warfare strongly suggest that these were related activities in the Moche world. The similarities in dress, ornament, body paint,

and weapons used in these two activities indicate that the same class of adult males, and perhaps even the same individuals, were participating in both. The purpose of combat was not the conquest of enemy territory, but the capture of opponents for ritual sacrifice. Similarly, the purpose of deer hunting was not to obtain food but to capture deer for ritual sacrifice. By participating in these two activities, high-status adult males could both demonstrate and augment their prestige in Moche society.

NOTES

1. Henry Wassén, "Ulluchu in Moche Iconography and Blood Ceremonies: the Search for Identification," *Etnografisca Museum Arstryck Annals* (1985/86): 59–85. Goteborg.

2. William Monypeny Newsom, *Whitetailed Deer* (New York: Scribner's, 1926).

3. Raymond E. Chaplin, *Deer* (Pool: Blanford Press Ltd., 1977).

4. Bernabé Cobo, *Historia del Nuevo Mundo.* 4 vols. Edited by Marcos Jimenez de la Espada (Seville: Sociedad de Bibliofilos Andaluces, 1890-1895), bk. 14, ch. 16; Garcilaso de la Vega, *Primera Parte de los Commentarios Reales.* 2nd edition (Madrid: Ediciones Atlas, 1923), pt. 1, bk. 6. ch. 6.

5. Melody Shimada, Paleoethnozoological/botanical Analysis of Moche V Economy at Pampa Grande, Peru. Ms. thesis, Princeton University, 1979; Shelia Griffis Pozorski, Prehistoric Subsistence Patterns and Site Economics in the Moche Valley, Peru. Ph.D. dissertation. Department of Anthropology, University of Texas, Austin, 1976.

6. Cobo, *Historia del Nuevo Mundo.* bk. 13, ch. 26

7. George Robert Miller, An Introduction to the Ethnoarchaeology of Andean Camelids. Ph.D. dissertation, Department of Anthropology, University of California, Berkeley, 1979.

8. John Dean Caton, *The Antelope and Deer of America* (New York: Forest and Stream Publishing Company, 1877), 156–157.

9. Wassén, "Ulluchu in Moche Iconography and Blood Ceremonies."

10. Christopher B. Donnan, *Moche Art of Peru* (Los Angeles: Museum of Cultural History, University of California, 1978), 174–189.

Acknowledgments

I am grateful to Donna McClelland for preparing the drawings that illustrate this report and to the following individuals for their assistance with different aspects of the text: Donna and Don McClelland, Sheila Pozorski, Elizabeth Wing, Ed McGuire, George Miller, and John Rowe.

Fig. 1 *Natural rock shrine, Machu Picchu.*

Andean Aesthetics

Esther Pasztory

The ancient Peruvians erected no Parthenons or Colosseums, they carved no Venus di Milo, they painted no masterpiece. Their architecture was characterized by massiveness rather than by beauty, remarkable for its stupendous masonry rather than for its art. Stone sculptures are rare on the coast, ponderous and severe in the highlands. It was on the smaller objects, the pottery vessels, the textiles and the metal-work that the Peruvian artist lavished his skill and his creative art. Art was a constant element of his daily life, not an interest apart from it. However, it was as a craftsman—or craftswoman rather than as an artist, that the Peruvian was pre-eminent. As weavers, potters, and goldsmiths they could hold their heads proudly among their peers anywhere in the world. And in the textile industry the Peruvian woman is considered by many technical experts to have been the foremost weaver of all time.

— J. Alden Mason, The Ancient Civilizations of Peru (Harmondsworth, England: Penguin Books, 1957), p. 235.

IT HAS TAKEN A LONG TIME for Andean objects to be admired as works of art by Westerners. As late as 1957, the distinguished historian J. Alden Mason felt the need to apologize for the lack of monumental sculpture and architecture and praised mainly the crafts and techniques in the smaller media. Peru did not have ruins like Palenque in Mexico to draw the nineteenth-century explorer and artist. No early drawings or photographs made the area famous. There were no writing systems to decipher, as in Mexico and Egypt. At best, turn-of-the-century books on ornament—which was considered by many at the time to be secondary to real art—included bits of Andean textile designs as examples of primitive designs.[1]

Then two discoveries in the early twentieth century altered Peru's status in the world of art and antiquities. In 1911 Hiram Bingham found the ruins of Machu Picchu and Peru was added to the map of great ancient cultures for tourist pilgrimage. The other major discovery, in 1908, was the find in a Copenhagen library of Guaman Poma de Ayala's lengthy illustrated letter to the King of Spain. Unpublished until 1936, the letter, in which the author complained that the Spanish governed Peru worse than the Inca, was written in the seventeenth century but never reached the king.[2] Its four hundred illustrations are unique in the colonial texts of the Andes. No pictorial codices like those in Mexico exist and the Spanish made no illustrated texts either. Without the drawings of Guaman Poma—who was probably taught to write and draw in a Christian school—reconstructing Andean life would be impossible. His authentic depictions of life in the Inca empire provide images to go along with sixteenth-century chronicles and documents.

Only at the beginning of the twentieth century then did the art of the Andes begin to emerge from obscurity and Mason's assessment indicates the generally apologetic attitude typical still at mid-century. Although the Museum of Modern Art put Peruvian objects on display in 1954, asserting thereby that they were "art," the text of the catalogue was strictly anthropological and not aesthetic. Based on the choice of objects, the general theme was evidently "abstraction." In his introduction Rene D'Harnoncourt wrote that he found Peruvian art puzzling and lacking in spontaneity.[3]

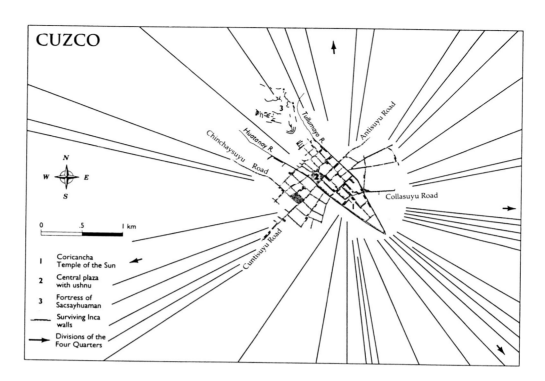

Fig. 2 *Cuzco and the* ceque *(sight-line) system. Peru, Inca. Drawing: Mapping Specialists Limited.*

It was not surprising to him that modern artists were not influenced by Andean art as they were by African.

Andean artistic traditions also suffered from a lack of definition: what exactly was the nature of Andean art and what was its relationship to the Andean worldview? Was there an Andean worldview? In the second half of the twentieth century, Andean art and culture have been extensively studied and certain specific Andean characteristics in aesthetics, culture, and thought patterns have been identified.

Andean concepts of art were clearly very different from those of Mesoamerica and of Europe and the U.S., and it is precisely because of this difference that recognition came so slowly. So well preserved that one could put the thatched roofs back and move in, Machu Picchu has a surprising lack of the figurative arts. With not one image anywhere, it is all stone masonry, rock, and scenic views. Instead of elaborately carved stone monuments such as the Aztec Coatlicue or the Calendar Stone, the Inca set up or modified natural stones with abstract carvings. [4] These stones range from the partly modified to the entirely natural (Fig. 1). Beautiful, precisely fitted masonry encircles them or provides a platform. Springs, caves, geological faults, ice-age striations are incorporated into shrines. The idea that nature is alive and all aspects of it are interconnected is expressed purely abstractly, rather than through the animal/human/plant combinations of earlier Andean cultures. The various gradations between the human and the natural suggest that the Inca saw a continuum between those two realms.

Reminiscent in their aesthetic of Japanese rock gardens and of the Earth Art created in the U.S. by such artists as Robert Smithson and Michael Heizer in the 1970s, the Inca shrines are are now much appreciated in the West. [5] Often we value the art of another time in so far as it relates to our own aesthetic ideas. Many of us now find meanings in those aspects of Andean art that were perhaps difficult to understand by some in the early part of the century.

In their book *The Code of the Quipu*, Marcia and Robert Ascher outline an ideology that helps give a context for the famed Inca stones. Inca thought, they suggested, is exemplified by the sophisticated yet abstract *quipu*, a knotted-string recording device (see cat. no. 136). Made of yarn, the primary symbolic material in the Andes, information is encoded not in pictures, glyphs, or narratives—as in the codices of Mesoamerica—but in the decimal placement of knots on various colored strings.[6] The spatial placement of elements was emphasized in this highly intellectual and cerebral system. Tom Zuidema has studied the stones in the Cuzco area and how they fit into the social and religious system known as *ceque*, which was well described in the sixteenth century.[7] All shrines in the Cuzco area were conceptually aligned on forty-one imaginary lines radiating from the Coricancha, or Sun Temple of Cuzco (Fig. 2). The shrines numbered close to 365 and were cared for in daily rotation by various families. Like an imaginary *quipu* spread out over the land, the *ceque* system linked together the calendar, the social system, and the shrines. Shrines could be temples, springs, rocks, or even views. The last view of Cuzco from a given spot was often a shrine in itself. The idea that a view could be a shrine indicates the extent to which mental concepts were as important as material things to Andeans.

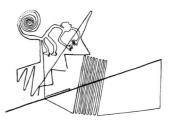

Fig. 3 Nasca geoglyphs. Drawing by Janice Robertson

The preoccupation with spatial relations, mental patterns, and the lack of interest in visibility place the famous Nasca geoglyphs (Fig. 3) squarely into this Andean system. An entire plateau, barren except for lines and figures created by the placement of surface rocks into paths, was a huge sacred area.[8] Visible only from a nearby hill or from the air, the lines were probably laid out with ropes and may be ceremonial paths. Because it could not be seen, the shape needed to be imagined and experienced. The same can be said of the Inca road system, which has been considered as much an imperial symbol and ceremonial construction as a practical road.[9] No one person was likely to traverse the entire 4800-km length of it—it existed as much as a spatial concept as a reality.

The habit of thinking in networks and invisible lines might derive, according to many Andeanists, from the textile arts because designs on textiles must be planned before the weaver begins to move the yarns. Among the most ancient Andean art forms, textiles are found in Preceramic contexts, as early as the third millennium B.C. All known techniques in the pre-industrial world—plus a few incredibly cumbersome types unique to the Andes—have been identified among the Andean repertoire.

One of these unique types is the discontinuous warp technique. In most textiles a set of warp threads are held in place and various colored weft threads are passed over and under the warp threads. The warp gives shape and tension to the textile in the process of being woven. In the weaving of a discontinuous warp textile, there is no set of warp threads. Instead, a set of temporary yarns are put in place (known as scaffolding) because neither the warp nor the weft threads go all the way through the textile. When the piece is finished, the scaffolding threads are removed. Although the actual reason for using such a complex technique is unknown, Elena Phipps has theorized that the goal may have been to have the same color in both weft and warp for each color area, resulting in rich color and light weight—because the weft threads need not cover the warp as densely as in the more usual type of weaving.[10] Some of the most amazing textiles in Peru represent complex figures woven in such discontinuous sections. The special qualities of these textiles are not necessarily apparent—some technical knowledge is required for their appreciation. These textiles reveal other aesthetic values, which are not readily apparent to the eye. Weight and texture, for example are as important in fabrics as appearance. Because they are usually seen behind museum glass, one rarely discerns the delicacy and lightness of Andean textiles.

As indicated by the saturated color areas found in the discontinuous warp textiles, Andeans may have also had a belief in the importance of essences. Heather Lechtman has argued for the concept of essences in the use of alloys and depletion gilding in Andean metalwork.[11] In depletion gilding the surface of a copper and gold alloy object is made to look all gold by the removal of the copper by an acid. If saving the metal had been the primary interest, Lechtman argues, a copper object could have been given a gold-foil cover. The gold inside the alloy is therefore seen as superfluous technically but necessary ideologically for the object to have significance. Techniques in weaving and metalwork are interesting because they provide insights unavailable from other sources. The concept of essences would seem to indicate that to Andeans materials were more aesthetically and religiously powerful if they were somehow pure and solid throughout. They were as interested, it would seem, in the material itself—like stone—as in the processes that transformed it. In architecture this notion is evident in their use of colored stones and in their practice of not covering walls in plaster and paint.

Visibility is one of the major issues in Andean art, not just in what cannot be seen from the ground but in the importance of the burial cults and objects made for burial. Huge amounts of textiles, gold and pottery were buried with the dead and thereby removed from view. These burial cults may have been facilitated by the desert sands of Peru and the remarkable preservation of bodies as well as things. While these cults removed things from currency, they also preserved them. New graves often cut into old ones and resulted in the discovery of older styles, which were often copied. We are quite familiar with the Moche copies of Chavín-style vessels, as well as with the Chimú copying and revival of Moche vessels. [12] Archaism is deeply embedded in the Andean tradition. Besides the imitation of forms or subjects, techniques were also revived. Even after the introduction of redware pottery, the earlier blackware continues. This archaism is such that in the case of some designs, they could be perfectly at home in later periods. For example the Preceramic textile designs of Huaca Prieta (a ca. 2500 B.C. site on the North Coast) would not be inappropriate among the Chimú more than three thousand years later.

The idea we now have of Andean art is of a tradition that was not, for the most part, based on picturing or reproducing the world, but on constructing mental diagrams of it. In this system the actual objects or places are nodes within larger networks. It is no accident that we come to understand this aspect of Andean art in the last twenty years when our own art has become minimal, conceptual, and philosophical. Mel Bochner, Sol LeWitt, and Barry Le Va all created conceptual systems rather than works of art in a mimetic sense. Sol LeWitt's work was praised by one author because of its systemic quality: "there is always a system, thus rather stressing the mental process than the finished product." [13]

Try as we might to get at the Andean view of things, we keep discovering that we can see best those aspects of the Andes that relate to our own views. This does not mean that our understanding of the conceptual aspect of Andean art is incorrect, it merely

Fig. 4 *Adolescent by Chaim Gross. Philadelphia Museum of Art, gift of David A. Teichman*

Fig. 5 *Drawing by George Grosz from* The Berlin Years *showing military figures in front and skull-faced women in the rear.* © *1997 Estate of George Grosz/Licensed by VAGA, New York, NY*

means that currently we have a tendency to focus on these aspects. In fact, much of Andean art fits well into this schema, and I would argue that only through it have we been able to see some of the unique aspects of this art that had not been discerned before.

The aesthetic we currently see as Andean was not the one Larco Hoyle is likely to have imagined, given that he was more interested in anthropological questions—chronology, for example, and the meaning of the various designs. Nevertheless, he had an aesthetic view based on the arts of his time. Writing from the 1930s to 1960s he is likely to have seen Andean art through a Classical and Modernist lens.

Connoisseurs in Larco Hoyle's time were interested in objects that could fit more readily into existing traditions of European art. This meant modeled and painted objects, which in Peru are usually in the form of ceramic vessels. While some of these—such as the Moche portrait heads—are remarkable for their naturalism, most, when compared to European art, are schematic and conventionalized. Images of animals, plants, humans, and scenes in their liveliness and simplicity are, however, very similar to sculptural styles then popular in Europe or seen in the works of Chaim Gross (Fig. 4) in the U.S.[14] At the time these styles were seen as radical departures from European tradition in their avoidance of realistic form. Moreover the more abstract styles had been inspired by so-called primitive art. Still maintaining the traditional types and subjects of European art, sculptures of figures, nudes, mothers and children, Modernism's combination of a clear subject with the stylization of form gives it much in common with Moche and other art of the North Coast of Peru. The abbreviation of the seated man in cat. no. 71 or the exquisite lines of the simplification of the cormorant in cat. no. 49 are the sort of things that appealed to writers and collectors in mid-century.

Some Andean objects—such as the Huari figures in cat. nos. 118, 119, and 122—are so geometric and abstract that they bring Cubism or the works of Mondrian to mind. Nor should the Chimú wooden figures (cat. nos. 128 and 129) be left out of such a catalogue of images appreciated through the lens of Modernism. Their Brancusi-like geometric perfection found an audience in its time. All these types of objects were brought together in the Museum of Modern Art exhibition of 1954.

In the late 1950s the Peruvian tradition of modeled figures was compared to the ceramics of western Mexico, which were also extremely popular. Miguel Covarrubias, as an artist as well as collector, expressed most vividly what was appreciated about them.[15] Because Modernists also disliked the complex art of organized religions with its elaborate iconography to be decoded, the art of Moche and western Mexico were popular partly because they appeared not to have a complex iconographic system but to be representations of things of daily life. Potatoes, gourds, fish, frogs, and birds were immediately recognizable. Until the work of Benson and Donnan, Moche iconography was given a simple interpretation. Art lovers like D'Harnoncourt could imagine that the objects could be experienced unmediated. At their best, their appeal lay in their presumed directness and spontaneity.

Fig. 6 Stirrup-spout vessel in the form of a woman lying on her back. Museo Arqueológico Rafael Larco Herrera

Fig. 7 *Drawing of beans and bean warriors from a Moche vessel. Drawing by Janice Robertson*

What was most evident to the Modernist collector was the aesthetic choices the artists made in order to stylize and yet to add vivid lifelike detail to forms. The pleasure of the viewer was translated into the pleasure of the artist. Writers imagined that the artists responsible for these modeled and painted traditions were free from the usual artistic constraints and could experiment with forms and explore the wide world of abstraction. Clearly, the model here in this joy of formal exploration was the post-Cubist Western artist liberated from the Classical tradition. Despite the many elaborate iconographic studies undertaken since, aesthetically it is almost impossible to see these modeled arts outside of the conceptual visual categories of Modernism.

An exception to this are the famous Moche portrait heads (cat. nos. 64–67), which were appreciated for their realism as early as the turn of the century and which fit easily within the European Classical aesthetic. Larco Hoyle liked them the best. The first European writer on art to mention them is H. Reed, who in 1911 considers all the rest of Moche and Peruvian art "rude" but finds the portrait heads fine and in particular similar to a representation of Jean, Duc de Berry, on his tomb at Bruges, as drawn by Holbein![16] The West is so wedded to the Classical heritage in art that wherever Westerners see something similar—as in the art of the Maya of Mesoamerica or the Ife in Africa—they are amazed, impressed, and appreciative.

Curiously, however, these European aesthetic visions are mutually exclusive: the Modernists developed in opposition to the Classical. Moreover, they are assumed to be consistent but contradictory ways of seeing the world that therefore cannot coexist at one time or one place (except for Picasso who bridged the times and places in his own life).[17] In the case of the Moche, realistic and conventionalized forms coexist in a way that makes little sense to the European view of art. Some images, the heads and a few figures or the details of a figure are seen, as if in a close-up realistically, while the rest is schematized. We may see Moche art through various lenses derived from European tradition, but we may find the Moche view in the various aspects that appear most contradictory to us.

The same can be said of the painting style—some of it is reminiscent of the Classical Greek style of vase painting in its elegance and purity of line, others are reminiscent of cartoonlike styles like those of the artist George Grosz (Fig. 5). This is particularly true of scenes with surrealistic elements such as those of the women with skull heads.[18] It is Western art of this sort that makes us appreciate the simplicity, the stylization, and the preoccupation with detail that characterizes the Moche. Perhaps Moche art throws a new light on Grosz as well.

Fig. 8 *Drawing of vessels with feet from a Moche vessel (after Larco 1939 Tomo II, Lamina XXXI)*

Moche studies have been so involved with issues of chronology and thematic interpretation that the formal aspect of the objects has been left unexamined. The question is not only what do these objects tell us about the Moche but what they tell us about the processes of art that might add to art theory? First of all, they tell us that the notion of the integrity of a style based on a particular type of vision is a European construct, valid only in its own context and useful only for discussion. If anything, the Moche example shows that naturalism can develop in almost any context and does not require anything more specific than the desire to achieve verisimilitude. It need not take centuries to develop, and it need not affect all of the arts or all of a figure. Evidently able to create realistic images, artists often do not. So the really interesting question is, Why do they select the styles, or combination of styles, that they do? Would the Moche have selected the same pieces that that the museum has for this exhibition?

The answers emerge in the examination of the objects. The paintings, for example, are more involved in conveying scenes with many levels of meaning—formal invention, iconographic complexity, or humor—rather than just the recreation of appearances. In fact this combination is very similar to the combination of elements in a Grosz drawing. A good line in the drawing of arms and legs is necessary but is not the primary emphasis of the artist. Abstraction and conventionalization is always a better matrix for a multiplicity of contradictory tasks than realism, which is in some ways an artistic straitjacket.[19]

It is impossible to talk about Moche art without talking about its humor. Much of the humor is sexual humor, which always cuts deep into the psyche, religion, and social behavior. Without written texts, it frequently difficult to see humor in another culture, according to Bergh.[20] Sexual humor, in its most basic forms, certainly has evocations that defy barriers of time and place. Whatever specific meanings the vessel of a woman lying on her back with a stirrup emerging from her vagina (Fig. 6) may have meant to a Moche, it is amusing as a Bergsonian unexpected juxtaposition. One can also see it as frightening, however, as if she were pinned by the stirrup.

One doesn't know where humor starts and where it ends. A great deal of what the Moche do with beans—bean warriors, beans turning into warriors—is humorous on a level to which a child can relate. The famous mural from the Pyramid of the Moon of the battle gear rising up and fighting humans (Fig. 7) is amusing even if the makers believed that these armaments had souls of their own and were beings in their own right. Little feet indicate the aliveness of inanimate things such as bowls (Fig. 8), who

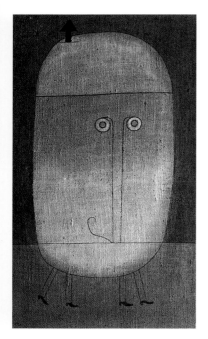

Fig. 9 Mask of Fear, *oil on burlap by Paul Klee, 1932, Nelson A. Rockefeller Fund © The Museum of Modern Art, New York.*

manage to walk on their own—a little like the Paul Klee painting called *Mask of Fear* (Fig. 9) that walks on four little legs.[21] Details less obvious than these in the rendering of plants and dogs and the details of bodily parts bring forth our delight and amusement. It is hard to imagine that they left the Moche cold. Although it is not possible to be certain in the matter of humor, its very possibility is significant. The issue does not come up with the reliefs of Chavín de Huántar or Chan Chan, for example. Moche humor may be close to that of Bosch or Brueghel in spirit and could have been based on proverbs and well-known elements. It could have been collectively understood, yet personal, ribald or naive, positive or full of darker meanings.

With its exuberant subject matter and naturalism, Moche art is something of an anomaly in the art of Peru. Most Andean art is conventionalized and abstract in form and there is little narrative or figural interaction. Although the art of the North Coast was always more human and lively, Moche art is still a surprise. Ascher and Ascher have used the term "insistence" to describe the predominant style of a culture. Every culture has its own style that affects everything from its concept of time to its art objects. The Andean insistence appears to have been a focus on conceptual networks, which include kinship ties, the procurement of goods from different ecological zones, the *quipu* recordkeeping device, and the various arts, especially textiles. Such a conceptual tradition dominated Peru from Huaca Prieta in Preceramic times to Inca Cuzco (A.D. 1450–1550). Whether its causes are environmental or social and political is very difficult to determine. It may be based on early initial choices that were felt to be viable in later times and became a "tradition." This insistence remained the Andean lens as late as the seventeenth century when Guaman Poma made his illustrations.[22] As Rolena Adorno has shown, the structure of Guaman Poma's Europeanized drawings continue to be based on the Andean system.

Moche art indicates that it is possible for a culture to go against the prevailing traditions of its time and place and develop in another direction. Taking the existing tradition of modeling and human subject matter, the Moche explored naturalism and narrative in addition to conventionalization and the conceptual. Curiously, in the art of Mesoamerica, which is predominantly based on the human figure, glyphs, and narratives, one culture, that of Teotihuacan, goes against the grain in the direction of abstraction and the systemic.[23] These two examples, Teotihuacan and Moche, indicate that an "insistence" within a tradition is not an absolute necessity, but primarily a tendency that subsequent cultures reaffirm or not. They indicate not necessarily the freedom of the artist to escape convention, but the freedom of the culture to select its own emphases over time. Evidently, however, this does not happen often. In the case of Teotihuacan, I have shown that the reason for its style may have been the collective nature of Teotihuacan culture, quite unlike that of its Mesoamerican neighbors. In the case of the Moche, I would suggest that the opposite might have been the case. The individualized heads, the individualized exploits of human and gods, the glorification of conflict in war and in mythology in Moche art suggest a culture in which these values were preferred over those of harmony, order, and the collective.

Moche art could fit comfortably into Mesoamerica, while Teotihuacan art could fit in the Andes. What's fascinating about them is that they are where they are. It's their opposition to the prevailing traditions that makes one ask why they should have developed in such different directions. The answers to this lie in history that may be hard to recover archaeologically. Anomalies in their own traditions, they are proof of the vitality of cultures and their artistic experiments. As exciting as the Moche experiments in art were, in our eyes, they were not imitated by other Andean cultures. Despite their admiration and copying of things Moche, the Chimú never imitated the most radical innovations of the Moche: the portrait heads and the fineline drawing scenes. These belonged to a social context that existed only for a short time on the North Coast of Peru.

NOTES

1. Alexander Speltz, *The History of Ornament* [Leipzig, 1915] (New York: Portland House, 1989), plates 1–2.

2. John V. Murra y Rolena Adorno, *El primer nueva cronica y buen gobierno por Felipe Guaman Poma de Ayala*, 3 vols. (Mexico City: Siglo Veintiuno, 1980).

3. "While it would be difficult to find anywhere in the world standards of technical excellence to match those of Peruvian ceramics and textiles, in certain types of work such as the quantity production of elaborately decorated ceramics typical of the later phases of Peruvian art standardization of skill seems to have produced a conflict between quality of execution and quality of design. Looking at a large number of such vessels one is often struck by their monotony in spite of the great variety of subject matter in their decoration. The designs seem to have been put together according to established formulas rather than by spontaneous reaction to an artistic problem." Rene D'Harnonourt, "Introduction," in Wendell C. Bennett, *Ancient Arts of the Andes* (New York: The Museum of Modern Art, 1954), 12.

4. Esther Pasztory, "Presences and absences in Inca stonework," paper presented at the Douglas Fraser Memorial Symposium on Primitive and Pre-Columbian Art, Columbia University, 15 April 1983. Cesar Paternosto, *Piedra abstracta, la escultura Inca: una vision contemporana* (México: Fondo de Cultura Economica, 1989).

5. For a discussion of Earth Art in comparison to the art of the Andes, see Lucy Lippard, *Overlay, Contemporary Art and the Art of Prehistory* (New York: Pantheon Books, 1983), 135–141. For Earth Art, see also Julia Brown, *Michael Heizer:Sculpture in Reverse* (Los Angeles: Museum of Contemporary Art, 1984) and Robert Hobbs, *Robert Smithson:Sculpture* (Ithaca: Cornell University Press, 1981).

6. Marcia and Robert Ascher, *The Code of the Quipu* (Ann Arbor: University of Michigan Press, 1981).

7. R.Tom Zuidema, *The Ceque System of Cuzco* (Leyden: E. J. Brill, 1964) and *Inca Civilization in Cuzco* (Austin: University of Texas Press, 1990).

8. Marilyn Bridges, *Planet Peru: An Aerial Journey through a Timeless Land* (Photography Division of Eastman Kodak, 1991); Tony Morrison, *Pathways to the Gods: The Mystery of the Andes Lines* (New York; Harper and Row, 1978)

9. John Hyslop, *The Inka Road System* (New York: Academic Press, 1984).

10. Elena Phipps, Discontinuous Warp Textiles in Pre-Columbian Weaving Tradition, MA thesis, Columbia University, 1982; Rebecca Stone-Miller, *To Weave for the Sun: Andean Textiles in the Museum of Fine Arts, Boston* (Boston: Museum of Fine Arts, 1992).

11. Heather Lechtman, "Issues in Andean metallurgy," in *Pre-Columbian Metallurgy of South America*, edited by E.P.Benson (Washington D.C.: Dumbarton Oaks, 1979),1–41.

12. John H.Rowe, "The Influence of Chavin Art on Later Styles", in *Dumbarton Oaks Conference on Chavin*, edited by E.P.Benson (Washington D.C.: Dumbarton Oaks, 1971), 101–123.

13. Enno Develing, quoted in *Sol LeWitt*, (The Hague: Haags Gemeentmuseum, 1969), 21. For conceptual artists, see also Richard S. Field, ed., *Mel Bochner:Thought Made Visible 1966–1973* (Yale University Gallery, 1973) and *Barry Le Va 1966–1988* (Pittsburgh: Carnegie Mellon University Press, 1988). See also Ann Goldstein, *Reconsidering the Object of Art: 1955–1975* (Los Angeles: Museum of Contemporary Art and MIT Press, 1995).

14. Fran Getlein, *Chaim Gross* (New York: Harry N. Abrams, 1974).

15. Miguel Covarrubias, *Indian Art of Mexico and Central America* (New York: A.Knopf, 1966).

16. Esther Pasztory, "Still Invisible: The Problem of the Aesthetics of Abstraction in Pre-Columbian art and its Implications for Other Traditions," *RES* (1990–91): 110

17. Ernst Gombrich, *Art and Illusion* (Princeton University Press, 1960).

18. *George Grosz, Obra Grafica, Los Anos de Berlin* (Valencia, Spain: Ivam Centre Julio Gonzalez, Institut Valencia d'Arte Moderna, 1992) pl. 127.

19. Esther Pasztory "Still Invisible..."

20. Susan E. Bergh, "Death and Renewal in Moche Phallic-Spouted Vessels," *RES* (1993): 78–94.

21. Enric Jardi, *Paul Klee* (New York: Rizzoli, 1991), pl. 75.

22. Rolena Adorno, *Writing and Resistance in Colonial Peru* (Austin: University of Texas Press, 1986), 80–114.

23. Esther Pasztory, *Teotihuacan, An Experiment in Living* (Norman, Okla.: University of Oklahoma Press, 1997).

Catalogue of
Objects

1

PLAIN BOTTLE
Cupisnique, Late Initial Period,
1200–200 B.C.
Ceramic
25.5 cm x 13.2 cm (10 x 5¼ in.)
XXC-000-046

In pre-Hispanic Peru, acts of generosity and reciprocity—whether between people or between humans and ancestral or other supernatural forces—played a central role in daily life. Because serving food and drink, particularly maize beer (*chicha*), was a critical component in both political and religious activities, considerable effort was channeled to producing vessels for food consumption. Pottery appropriate in different contexts and for use by individuals of varying socioeconomic status was produced in the Central Andes from the beginning of second millennium B.C. Most of the earliest pottery styles feature poorly made ceramics imitating plant forms, particularly the bottle gourds used to serve food before ceramic vessels were produced. With the development of greater control over the pottery medium and the increasing complexity of society, however, more elaborate pottery vessels were created embodying religious and aesthetic concepts. Not surprisingly, artisans devoted their greatest efforts to vessels that were used in public settings where their symbolic and artistic messages could be appreciated. Cooking vessels, by contrast, were often coarse and undecorated.

One of the most refined ceramic styles produced in early Peru was that of the Cupisnique culture, which inhabited Peru's North Coast from 1200 to 200 B.C. The quality of Cupisnique ceramics has long suggested the involvement of highly skilled specialized potters, and recent excavations in the Lambayeque drainage has documented an extensive zone of subsurface kilns for firing Cupisnique pottery in well-controlled environments. Classic Cupisnique pottery only begins to be produced during the late Initial period, probably no earlier than around 1100 B.C., and the immediately preceding styles, known from sites like Monte Grande and Puemape, share some of the features but little of the artistic merit of classic Cupisnique pottery (Ulbert 1994). In these and other early and middle Initial period ceramic styles, a single-spout bottle is one of the main vessel forms; apparently such bottles were used to pour maize beer or other drink in social or ritual settings. By the late Initial period, the artisans of the Peruvian North Coast had appropriated the more elaborate and less natural stirrup-

spout bottle form from the Machalilla culture to the north, in what is now Ecuador, but the Cupisnique potters also continued to produce some single-spout bottles.

The bottle illustrated here exemplifies how the Cupisnique potters of the late Initial period transformed the single-spout bottle form, inspired by the natural shape of cut bottle gourds, and transformed it into a thoroughly unnatural, extremely beautiful, physical expression of an abstract geometric ideal. The bottle features a conical elongated spout, which tapers gradually until it turns outward into an everted open mouth, from which the liquid would have been poured. The open mouth of the vessel most closely

resembles its gourd antecedents, whereas the bottle chamber shows a fuller exploitation of the plastic potential of pottery.

Rather than imitating the rounded convex-curved sides and rounded base of a bottle gourd, the potter of this plain Cupisnique bottle in the Larco Museum Collection has produced a chamber with a flat top and a flat base. The cylindrical volume of the chamber itself, which would have held the liquid, is divided into two undecorated horizontal registers, each with concave walls. The entire vessel was polished to a high luster and then fired. A reducing atmosphere imparted the dark color to the bottle, but uneven exposure to the fire and air

2

VESSEL WITH JAGUAR IN CAVE
Cupisnique, Late Initial Period,
1200–200 B.C.
Ceramic
26.4 cm x 19.5 cm (8¾ x 5 in.)
XXC-000-059

during production left the bottle's surface with a slightly irregular dark hue. Because of its exceptional beauty and prior publication by Rafael Larco (1945: Pl. 64b), this specimen is internationally known, but judging from recent studies of Cupisnique ceramics (for example, Alva 1986) this form is extremely rare. RLB

This classic Cupisnique stirrup-spout bottle represents a low-relief feline modeled in profile beneath a hemispherical arch. The feline and arch are represented almost identically on both sides of the bottle chamber, suggesting that a mold may have been used. Cupisnique potters sometimes used molds to make ceramics, and this technological tradition continued on the North Coast up to the time of the Spanish conquest. The short spout of the bottle is connected to the chamber by a pair of cylindrical tubes curved in a form reminiscent of a horse's stirrup, from which the term *stirrup spout* derives. As in many classic Cupisnique bottles, the stirrup has a distinctive trapezoidal form. The base of the bottle is flat, giving greater stability to the vessel when it rests on a level surface. As in most fine Cupisnique ceramics, the

surface was polished to a high luster before firing and superficial reduction left it with an uneven dark coloration.

The feline is shown in profile with its hind legs flexed and its front paw raised, as if poised to attack. The paws and claws are exaggerated in size, as if to emphasize the animal's ferocity. The elongated feline tail is held upright above its rump, and the end of the tail is curved, further emphasizing the dynamism of the animal represented. The head of the feline looks backwards, with its rounded ear upright, its eyes bulging, and its open mouth exposing prominent fangs. The modeled surface enhances the animal's musculature and conveys its power. Concentric circles have been incised on the polished black surface to represent pelage markings that distinguish the jaguar from its relative, the mountain lion.

Large felines, particularly jaguars, were important symbols in the Cupisnique religious system and were frequently depicted on fine ceramic bottles, as well as on stone ritual vessels and the walls of temples. Efforts to understand the significance of this multivalent symbol have drawn upon our knowledge of the animal and its distinctive behavior, as well as its use as a symbol by historic and contemporary indigenous religious systems in the tropical forest of Amazonia and the Orinoco (for example, Reichel-Dolmatoff 1975). As the largest and most feared terrestrial carnivore in the American tropics, the jaguar serves as a natural symbol of raw power and aggression. Contemporary shamans connect its preference for nocturnal hunting and its solitary nature with their own forays into supernatural realms. Jaguars swim with facility and climb into the forest canopy to hunt, thus showing the earth, water, and sky to be their domain. It is perhaps not surprising then that indigenous religious leaders viewed, and continue to view, the jaguar as their natural alter ego and frequently claim the ability to transform themselves into jaguars when engaged in supernatural intervention on behalf of the individuals or communities they represent (cat. no 3). When religious leaders represented divinities, feline features were incorporated in their

3

BOTTLE REPRESENTING FELINE-HUMAN
DUALITY
Cupisnique, Late Initial Period, 1200–200 B.C.
Ceramic
24.8 x 13.5 cm (9¾ x 5¼ in.)
XXC-000-051

costumes to symbolize them. The central role of the jaguar in early Andean religion was recognized by such pioneering scholars as Julio C. Tello (1923) and Rafael Larco (1941), and continues to be appreciated by contemporary scholars.

The jaguar was a frequent theme on fine Cupisnique bottles, and many of these were eventually used as grave goods. Such vessels probably held *chicha* for consumption by the deceased during the journey to the next life. The illustrated vessel and most other known examples of such bottles come from looted tombs, including many Cupisnique bottles depicting jaguars that are said to have come from looted tombs in the lower or middle Jequetepeque Valley (Alva 1986: 70–71). One similar bottle was recovered by Peruvian archaeologists Jose Pinilla and Carlos Elera during the excavation of Tomb LVIII in the Cupisnique cemetery of Puemape on the shore of the Cupisnique drainage (Elera 1994: 242–243). The bottle with the modeled feline was one of two ceramic bottles placed above the bundle containing the body of an adult woman weaver. One of the bottles had a junco reed stopper sealing the top of the bottle spout, suggesting that the vessel was filled with liquid at the time of interment; gourd bowls were also included, perhaps to hold food.

The representation of the jaguar on Cupisnique pottery is limited to the chambers of bottles, but the position of the animal and the context in which it is shown varies. In some cases, the jaguar is seated or standing (Alva 1986: Figs. 180, 181, 182), but more frequently the animal is shown, as in the Larco bottle, standing in profile against a symbolic landscape. On this Larco bottle, the jaguar is framed by three concentric arcs shown in relief. The ear and front paw of the jaguar hides a portion of one arch, giving the impression that the animal is standing in front of it. On other Cupisnique bottles, the backdrop is filled with stepped or terraced volumes, perhaps representing sacred mountains (Alva 1986: Figs. 174, 186) or an environment filled with stalks of the San Pedro cactus (Alva 1986: 183, 184, 186, Burger 1992: Fig.84), the mescaline-bearing plant used by contemporary shamans to induce hallucinations during their ritual activity.

Although there appear to be a large number of Cupisnique vessels featuring modeled jaguars, no two are identical. While most are dark monochrome pieces, some are bichrome (Burger 1992: Fig.84). The modeling of the jaguar in the Larco piece has numerous parallels, as does the dynamic position of the profile body. Most Cupisnique modeled vessels show the jaguar's head frontally, rather than looking backwards in profile. Alva illustrates only one bottle, said to be looted at Chungal in the mid-Jequetepeque, with a jaguar in this distinctive position. In both poses, Cupisnique representations of jaguars differ from Chavín-style jaguars, in which the head invariably looks forward in profile (Burger 1992: Figs. 124, 141, 142, 177).

The specific meaning of the representation on the Larco piece in part depends on the significance attributed to the arch behind the jaguar. At least one other Cupisnique stirrup-spout bottle shows a similar backdrop behind the animal (Alva 1986: Fig. 18a/b), which Alva interprets as representing the mouth of a cave (Alva 1986: 71). The sense of deep space created by the concentric arches is consistent with the reading of this motif as a cave. Less compatible then, is its alternative reading as a rainbow, especially since the cave signifier is also seen as an independent motif incised on other bottles (for example, Larco 1941: 80). In the Andes, caves are often viewed as entryways or points of connection with the supernatural world, and not surprisingly, they play a special role in the mythical tales of the Andes, such as the origin of the Incas. The juxtaposition of the jaguar with a cave mouth, sacred mountain, or San Pedro cactus (or any combination thereof) would have embodied central religious concepts of the Cupisnique culture and the mythical narratives that served as its foundation. RLB

This unique bottle is perhaps the most famous example of Cupisnique ceramics in the world. Its sensitive high-relief modeling and classic polished dark monochrome surface—typical of the fine Cupisnique pottery from Moche, Chicama, and Jequetepeque—give the piece its remarkable strength. The flat base and trapezoidal stirrup likewise fit well within the orthodox conventions of classic Cupisnique pottery. No image appears on the back of the bottle. What sets this piece apart from all other known Cupisnique bottles is the sculpted split-face image that appears on the bottle's front. Part feline, part human, this image may be a representation of the dual character of the Cupisnique religious specialist and his ability to transform himself from human state to jaguar state and then back again (see discussion of cat. no. 2). Such views reflect Native American notions of the profound interconnectedness between humans and animals and this world and the supernatural realm.

The modeled chamber of the Larco stirrup-spout bottle is divided in two by an imaginary vertical axis. On the left (from the viewer's perspective), a feline visage with characteristic interlocking triangular canine teeth and round buttonlike nose is represented in a manner which works as well in profile as it does frontally. In some respects, this depiction of the chamber as a feline head can be linked to other Cupisnique pieces (Alva 1986: Fig. 169). The modeled projection above the nose may connote the furrowed brow so prominently depicted in some other Cupisnique felines (Alva 1986: Figs. 181, 182). On the viewer's right, a more naturalistic rendition of a human face is shown frontally with arched brow, almond-shaped eye, nose, and mouth. Although the two half-images join together to form a single head, they do not completely conjoin—producing a disturbing tension. On the feline side, the eye is shown as rectangular with rounded corners and an eccentric pupil—more typical of supernatural than naturalistic felines or humans (Alva 1986: Figs. 60, 91, 108). Similarly, the human face has modeled snakes projecting from its mouth and the side of the head and an extra set of nostrils positioned above the nose. Clearly, neither side represents a straightforward feline or human.

In an analysis of stone sculptures from

Chavín de Huántar, I argued that the carvings illustrate the gradual but complete transformation of human priests or their mythical antecedents from human form to jaguars or raptorial birds (Burger 1992: 157–159). This Cupisnique bottle can be interpreted as expressing the same concept, but with the process represented in a single image rather than multiple pieces. The practice of showing dual human-supernatural states on a single piece arranged around an imaginary vertical axis is rare in classic Cupisnique pottery, but it has been well documented for Cupisnique ritual vessels of steatite (Salazar-Burger and Burger 1983). In these cases, the body of the image was divided, with arachnid elements shown on the viewer's right and anthropomorphic elements on the left. A related practice in the roughly coeval Tembladera style is best known from male-female figurines, in which characteristics of both sexes appear on a single piece (Alva 1986: Fig. 463). There are also parallels in the Kuntur Wasi stone sculpture showing a frontal face with completely dissimilar eyes (for example, Burger 1992: Fig. 102). Given the centrality in Andean thought of dynamic dualism, in which contrasting but complementary characteristics join to create balance and harmony (Burger 1992, Burger and Salazar-Burger 1994), the Larco stirrup-spout bottle and other dual representations seem particularly significant. RLB

4

BOTTLE WITH FELINE-SNAKE
Cupisnique, Late Initial Period,
1200–200 B.C.
Ceramic
23.5 x 13.4 cm (9¼ x 5¼ in.)
XXC-000-067

This stirrup-spout bottle depicts two snakes with feline attributes. The head of each snake is modeled in high relief at the bottom of the vessel and its body bends upwards and doubles back so that its extreme end is immediately above the head. The two nearly identical snakes are represented facing in opposite directions on the vessel and could have been produced using molds. Each has long interlocking fangs, a flattened nose, a long eyebrow line that projects forward to the nose and far backward past a vertical band separating the head from the body. (Ophidian representations with this band have sometimes been referred to as collared-snakes [Roe 1974: 18]). Beneath the heavy brow line the round eye is depicted, and all along the body are large concentric circles representing pelage markings. When the bottle is viewed frontally, only one of the two snakes is visible.

To embolden the image, the potter has covered the bottle with red pigmented slip, incised the circles to reveal the lighter clay color in the grooves, and then painted the face, eyebrow, pupil, circular spots, and the outlines and posterior of the creature's body with a final coat of silvery-black graphite slip. The latter, made from a low-grade coal, must be applied after initial firing to prevent it from being burnt off. The contrast of red and black graphite slip, a common decorative device on finer Cupisnique vessels, particularly in the Moche drainage, was a popular alternative to the monochrome dark bottles utilized in the same area. Here, the two snakes and the stirrup-spout were highly polished, but an intermediate zone between the snakes was left unpolished; its matte finish textured by small shallow punctations. This matte-textured feature of this space strongly contrasts with the shiny smooth surfaces that flank it on both sides. The juxtaposition of contrasting colors, reflective surfaces and textures was a fundamental feature of Cupisnique pottery and that of many coeval cultures elsewhere in Peru.

The significance of the snake in Cupisnique culture is poorly understood. The distinctive pelage markings on this vessel suggest that a particular snake, such as an anaconda or boa, may be represented, but either type of snake, like

the jaguar, represents the most powerful animal of their kind. The similarity between their markings and those of the jaguar may have also added to the snakes' symbolic importance. Other examples of Cupisnique bottle chambers modeled in the form of snakes are known (Alva 1986: Figs. 172, 173, 175, 176), although none closely resembles this piece. These other snake bottles have circular markings and most have feline ears grafted onto the snake heads, but unlike the ophidian representations from Chavín de Huántar, these Cupisnique snakes generally are not rendered with the characteristic forked tongue. Rebecca

Carrion Cachot (1958) has argued that the snake had strong water and fertility associations, linking it with underground springs and other subterranean sources of water as well as rain. This interpretation worked well with later Andean notions of the *amaru* (Quechua term for snakes that were thought to rise out of springs during rain), as well as the way in which snakes appear in the Chavín style of the late Initial period and Early Horizon. The triad of raptor/jaguar/snake as symbols of air/land/water occurs so frequently that many archaeologists feel that it is a key to interpreting Andean iconography. RLB

5

PLATE WITH STYLIZED ARACHNIDS
Cupisnique, Late Initial Period,
1200–200 B.C.
Porphyry
13 cm (5 in.)
XXC-00P-347

In addition to the representations of felines, raptorial birds, and snakes that Cupisnique iconography shares with other contemporary cultures in the adjacent highlands and elsewhere on the coast, special importance was attributed to spiders in the early religious art of the North Coast. These supernatural creatures were not depicted on the bottles or bowls used for public food consumption, but they were featured on a small group of stone plates and beakers.

This plate, first illustrated by Tello in 1929, then belonged to the personal collection of Rafael Larco Herrera (1930). Subsequently five other similar stone vessels featuring supernatural arachnids have come to light on the North Coast, and similar ritual paraphernalia has been recovered in the adjacent highlands (Salazar-Burger and Burger 1983). For example, several stone vessels in this style were recovered from Limoncarro in the lower Jequetepeque drainage, including a fragmented specimen now in the collection of the Museo Nacional de Antropología, Arqueología y Historia in Lima, and one fragment has been documented from the Pacopampa area. In those cases where the stone has been analyzed, it has proved to be steatite, a soft and easily carved material with mineral impurities that give the pieces natural reddish and/or greenish hues. In some cases, cinnabar (mercuric sulfide) was rubbed into the incisions to highlight the iconography (Salazar-Burger and Burger 1996: 93).

The spider is always shown as though viewed from above with its eight legs flexed, two pairs pointing forward, two to the back. The articulations of the leg segments are usually shown, as in the Larco specimen, and the tiny nail at the end of each leg is enlarged. A pair of scissorlike jaws is shown in an accurate, albeit exaggerated, way and convey a clear sense of the spider's poisonous chelicerae. The stylizing additions of a fanged agnathic mouth and a pair of double-winged eyes relates the arachnid image to other Cupisnique supernaturals, although it is harder to identify, unless seen in conjunction with other representations. The problem of recognition is

further aggravated by an identical head added to the animal's posterior perhaps as the extension of the natural bilateral symmetry of the spider's legs. The quest for symmetry is similarly facilitated by reducing the trunk of the arachnid to a central carapacelike thorax and omitting the rear portion of the spider. This process of simplification and transformation to enhance symmetry can likewise be seen on a small cup from Dumbarton Oaks (Salazar-Burger and Burger 1986: 89–91) and a polished stone bowl or mortar from the San Pablo area of Cajamarca (Salazar-Burger and Burger 1983: Fig. 19).

The powerful arachnid image is carved stretching over the outer walls and base of the shallow ritual plate. Small representations of a bird head are shown beneath the spider's legs on either side of the plate, but their importance is clearly secondary to that of the arachnid. (On other examples, the arachnid is found portrayed with

secondary representations of felines and anthropomorphic heads.)

A better understanding of the place of the spider in Cupisnique cosmology can be drawn from a comparative study of these ritual vessels, and a fuller explication has been offered elsewhere by Lucy Salazar-Burger and the author (1983). Many pieces emphasize the arachnid's ability to catch and kill live prey in the netlike webs that it spins and weaves. In some representations, an anthropomorphized arachnid supernatural is carrying a net bag filled with decapitated heads. This iconography as well as data from Inca and modern times suggest that in the Andes, arachnids were closely linked with rainfall and fertility, and it is likely that vessels like this plate were produced as ritual paraphernalia for ceremonies designed to ensure adequate water for the irrigated crops along the North Coast (Salazar-Burger and Burger 1983: 238–243). RLB

6
SMALL BOWL WITH HEADS IN BAG
Cupisnique, Late Initial Period,
1200–200 B.C.
3 cm x 4.8 cm (1 ¼ x 3 ½ in.)
XSL-006-004

This tiny shallow vessel is an example of finely carved stone ritual paraphernalia produced by Cupisnique artisans. Its size suggests that it was made to hold a small quantity of pulverized material, such as lime for chewing coca leaf, hallucinogenic snuff, or mineral pigment. Similar Cupisnique vessels of this size and form also were made from gourds and decorated by pyroengraving (for example, Burger 1992: Pl. VIII).

The exterior of the Larco miniature bowl is decorated with a low relief carving of a net bag with interlocking fiber cords filled with a series of profile heads. The specific characteristics of these heads alternate rather than repeat: some feature a face with a downturned mouth filled with small teeth, while others show a face with an upturned mouth from which an angular fang projects. As already noted in the

discussion of cat. no. 5, the theme of bagged heads is particularly popular in Cupisnique iconography. Many stirrup-spout bottles have chambers modeled or incised as net bags with heads of different kinds filling the interstices (Alva 1986: Figs. 222–225, 248). A related motif seems to be a series of heads connected by a cord; in one such piece, two contrasting heads are linked—one with fangs, the other without (Larco 1941: 32). Are these variations in the depiction of the heads meant to contrast with human and supernatural qualities? Or were these two distinctive and recognizable characters from Cupisnique myth? It is likely that, as in the case of Moche art, images like the net bag filled with heads were part of a larger mythical scene or narrative and that their meaning will only be clarified when examined in that broader context. Although the bag-of-

heads images appear to be singular when seen on pottery bottles, they constitute part of a larger, more elaborate scene on some of the stone vessels, such as the Dumbarton Oaks Plate (Salazar-Burger and Burger 1996: 92–94). On this vessel, an anthropomorphized arachnid holds a recently decapitated head by the hair, while a net bag filled with numerous other heads hangs from the spider's head. On other stone vessels, this same scene is associated with plants, some of which bear fruit in the form of human body parts. These vessels point to a myth in which the death of a mythical or supernatural hero is linked to agricultural fertility; in this case decapitated heads say less about warfare than the mythical basis for safeguarding agricultural success (Salazar-Burger and Burger 1983). RLB

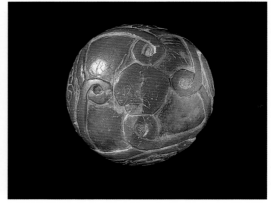

7

INCISED BOTTLE IN THE FORM OF A
SACRIFICED MAN
Cupisnique, Late Initial Period,1200–200 B.C.
Ceramic
25.3 cm x 16.5 cm (10 x 6½ in.)
005-004-002

This single-spout Cupisnique bottle is extremely unusual because the spout, rather than the bottle chamber, is modeled to convey the main theme. The uppermost portion of the spout has been formed as a human head, with the open lips of the individual serving as the bottle mouth. The chamber has a composite form with a flat bottom and straight lower sides, which are joined at an angle to its convex upper section; the latter is decorated with superficially incised Cupisnique motifs. These latter motifs suggest a religious theme, while the red-slipped bands descending from the expressionless head may signify a sacrificed individual, perhaps with his throat cut. Several Cupisnique bottles show men modeled with the their hands tied behind their back (Alva 1986: Figs.191, 252), others show recently decapitated human heads. The later iconography of the Moche suggests a possible connection between these two isolated themes. One recently published stirrup-spout bottle from Zaña shows an individual with his throat cut, exposing the vertebra in his neck. Remarkably, he holds a blade in his own hand, suggesting a case of self-sacrifice (Elera 1994: 237). In any case, its similarity to these other pieces makes it plausible to interpret this bottle as a scene of sacrifice. The Cupisnique designs incised on the chamber once again suggest that a mythical event, not a violent scene from daily life, is depicted. RLB

8

Fox (?)
Cupisnique, Late Initial Period,
1200–200 B.C.
21.7 cm x 13.2 cm (8½ x 5¼ in.)
XXC-000-061

The Cupisnique potters of the late Initial period depicted a broad range of animals on their ceramics, but these did not correspond to the animals that were important in daily subsistence. Although the population was heavily dependent on fish and mollusks for their protein, these creatures are rarely represented. On the contrary, wild animals that figured prominently in their mythology and, in some cases continue to be important in Andean folklore and traditional curing, are depicted. While the artisans were able to represent these animals naturalistically, they also recognized the potential of creating images on pottery that depart from what is observed in nature.

This stirrup-spout bottle, depicting what may be a fox seated on its haunches, appears to be an example of straightforward naturalistic representation, but it is not particularly easy to identify the animal here. When originally published, Rafael Larco (1941: 42, Fig. 56) considered it to be a feline representation, and there are

Cupisnique vessels that depict jaguars in this same pose (Alva 1986: Figs. 180, 181). But the absence of pelage markings, large clawed paws, upright rounded ears, and prominent fangs, makes this identification unlikely. A more likely, although by no means certain, reading of the image is that it represents a fox, a creature that plays a prominent role in the folklore of the Andes and the rest of the Americas. The animal in this piece has rounded eyes, tapering ears, a flattened snout, a closed mouth, and four powerful legs with no visible claws; a raised curled tail has been incised on the back of the bottle. These general features are compatible with those of a fox, albeit one that is well fed. More naturalistic and less ambiguous representations of foxes are common along the North Coast a millennium later in the art of the Moche. The dark color, naturalistic modeling, and trapezoidal stirrup spout all indicate that the piece was produced by the Cupisnique culture during the late Initial period. RLB

Woman Nursing Child
Cupisnique, Late Initial Period,
1200–200 B.C.
Ceramic
22.8 cm x 21.2 cm (9 x 8¼ in.)
XXC-000-049

Portrait of an Elderly Woman
Cupisnique, Late Initial Period,
1200–200 B.C.
Ceramic
17 cm x 18.3 cm (6¾ x 7¼ in.)
XXC-000-054

The ability to depict human forms and create portraits had been mastered by classic Cupisnique times, and although they are not common, representations of undistinguished individuals do occasionally appear on the ceramics. Nevertheless, it should be noted that the persons represented may be mythical characters who would have been easily recognizable to members of the Cupisnique culture, if not to the modern viewer. For example, how would an archaeologist be able to identify the mythical nature of a sheep or a mother-and-child figurine from a modern Christmas nativity scene?

One of the best-known Cupisnique depictions of so-called daily life is this scene of a woman and child. Modeled on a classic Cupisnique bottle chamber, the vessel shows a rather portly adult female holding a infant in her arms, apparently suckling at her right breast. The woman is seated with her legs extended. Her hairstyle—with bangs, squared short sides, and long hair down her back—is carefully represented, as is the texture of her hair, conveyed by parallel incised lines. The facial features of the woman are simplified, with almond-shaped eyes, straight thin projecting nose and straight lips created by added clay. One curious feature is that the woman is apparently not wearing any jewelry or clothing; this is in sharp contrast with some other representations of females from the art of the North Coast during the Initial period (Alva 1986: Figs. 463, 464). Clinging to the woman with both arms, the child has long hair, suggesting that this is also a female. Judging from the figure's size, it is a young girl rather than an infant. These somewhat anomalous details (the absence of clothing and the surprising size of the child) may be signals that the vessel represents a mythical, rather than generic family, scene.

A vessel in the Larco Museum Collection showing the head of an elderly individual illustrates the sculptural skill of Cupisnique artists. This careful treatment is of a different order than that applied to the faces of the mother and child on the bottle described above. Unlike most of the finely crafted Cupisnique vessels in this exhibit, this piece is a jar rather than a bottle. Its straight-sided neck emerges directly from the modeled chamber. Like most of the bottles, the jar has been highly polished and superficially reduced to produce the distinctive dark and lustrous monochrome appearance. To enhance its impact, the face of the individual has been smoothed but not highly polished, and consequently it remains more textured and less reflective than the rest of the vessel. The face of the individual is heavily lined with wrinkles that extend over the forehead, cheeks, and chin. The rounded contours of the face are skillfully modeled, suggesting an underlying bone structure and musculature. The eyes are narrowed, and the thin-lipped mouth is shown clamped shut and downturned, producing a serene but severe expression. The lustrous zone surrounding the face suggests that the individual might be wearing a shawl or head piece, but this seems inconsistent with the small ears that project from the sides of the head. The lower lobes of the ears are traversed by holes to indicate piercing. It is likely that ear ornaments once hung from the face on the jar.

What individual is being represented and why? Some existing Cupisnique bottles show modeled figures with wrinkled faces. One such piece (Alva 1986: Fig. 252) shows an elderly hunchbacked male with a puckered mouth. He is on his knees with a rope around his neck and his hands tied behind his back. Another Cupisnique bottle (Burger 1992: 90) has a very different representation of an elderly male seated with crossed legs and wearing a loincloth and headband. The man's face has a serious but unperturbed expression and large earspools adorn his lower ears. Significantly, the entire back of the individual's body is covered with elaborate incised religious motifs, suggesting that the individual represented is a priest or mythological figure. This portrait jar may represent this same figure, although there is not enough evidence to be certain. RLB

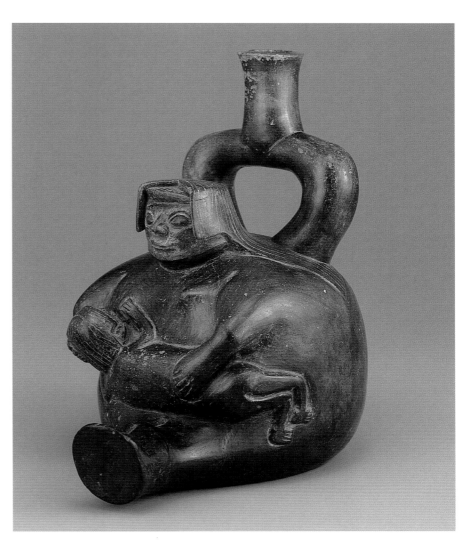

11

BOTTLE WITH TWO OWL HEADS
Cupisnique, Late Initial Period, 1200–200 B.C.
Ceramic
22.2 cm x 13 cm (8¾ x 5 in.)
XXC-000-089

This modeled and painted Cupisnique bottle features two owl heads at the juncture of the stirrup spout and chamber. The bottle has been covered with red slip, but through modeling, incision, and the addition of silvery-black graphite slip the potters produced an elaborate vessel for holding corn beer or some other liquid. The use of contrasting red and silvery black slips was popular on the North Coast during the late Initial period and excavations at Caballo Muerto in the Moche Valley have produced many fragmented vessels decorated in this manner, which were discarded around the temple buildings (Luis Watanabe 1976). Imported vessels with red and graphite decoration were recovered in the Ofrendas Gallery at Chavín de Huántar. The stirrup on this vessel has a rounded rather than trapezoidal form, a contemporary variant of the classic Cupisnique bottle.

The two owl heads are dominated by large, projecting circular eyes, the pupil and exterior of which are silvery-black while the iris is polished red. A small pincerlike beak projects outward and, like the eyes, is carefully shaped and polished. The heads of the owls have been left matte for contrast, and, curiously, they have neither a feathered nor plain surface, but rather are covered with small, unevenly spaced protuberances. This texture is reminiscent of some Andean fruits, especially the cherimoya. The treatment of the heads may be used to indicate that these are not typical owls.

The red bottle chamber is decorated with two incised geometric motifs painted with zoned graphite slip. The twice-repeated motif on the upper surface of the chamber has an inverted V-form ending in a more complex design, which may be a conventionalized two-headed cat-snake in profile. On the side of the chamber, twice repeated, is an inverted stepped motif ending in a volute. Popular in Cupisnique and later Moche art, this motif has frequently been interpreted as representing a sacred mountain with water associations. The owl, like the geometric design just referred to, has a long history in the art of the North Coast and appears frequently on Cupisnique bottles, bowls, and jars during the Initial

and Early Horizon periods (Alva 1986: Figs. 351, 361, 413, 419, Larco 1941: Figs. 42,125). This nocturnal animal is often linked to shamanic activity. While characteristic of Cupisnique iconography, the owl, like the spider, is absent from the contemporaneous religious art of Chavín de Huántar. RLB

12

BOTTLE WITH MODELED MANIOC TUBERS
Cupisnique, Late Initial Period,
1200–200 B.C.
Ceramic
23.2 cm x 16.5 cm (9¼ x 6½ in.)
XXC-000-52

While the animals commonly represented in Cupisnique art are wild, the plants shown are usually domesticated or at least cultivated. Nonetheless, it is likely that the selection of items has a mythological rather than a dietary rationale. In this blackware bottle, the entire chamber has been sculpted as a cluster of manioc tubers. Other Cupisnique bottles with similar representations of manioc have

been published (Alva 1996: Figs. 190, 192, 198, 219). Although manioc is generally considered to have been introduced onto the Peruvian coast from moister and more tropical regions of northeastern South America, this high-carbohydrate crop flourished in the coastal environment and was eaten during the Initial period. According to Carlos Elera (1986), the small twisted manioc roots that are

represented here resemble a local noncommercial variety of the plant still found in some of the more isolated sections of the North Coast.

Profile heads, with eccentric eyes and fanged mouths, which have been incised on this bottle, indicate its probable function in an agricultural ritual. Other Cupisnique bottles showing manioc have analogous fineline motifs on the modeled tubers. RLB

13
BOTTLE DECORATED WITH APPLIQUÉ NUBBINS
Cupisnique (?), Late Initial Period,
1200–200 B.C.
Ceramic
23.5 x 15.5 cm (9¼ x 6¼ in.)
XXC-000-044

14
BOTTLE WITH RAPTORIAL BIRD
Chavín or Late Cupisnique, Early Horizon,
500–200 B.C.
Ceramic
20.3 cm x 14.2 cm (8 x 5½ in.)
XXC-000-058

Just as Cupisnique potters mastered the finishing of ceramics and were able to achieve lustrous surfaces without the use of glazes, they also learned to shape and texture pottery surfaces to produce a roughened organic appearance. The chamber of this bottle has been thoroughly transformed by attaching small pieces of clay, which were then incised with vertical lines. This technique, known as appliqué nubbins, creates a surface reminiscent of organic materials like tree bark or the surface of a mollusk.

The potters may have been interested

simply in the aesthetic effect of the texturing. If so, bottles like this would be the equivalent of cat. no. 1. The rough matte surface covered with appliqué nubbins on this bottle contrasts with the polished shiny surface of the undecorated stirrup spout. The doughnutlike shape of the stirrup and the thickened rim of the spout is not typical of the North Coast, at least in the late Initial period. Fragments of similar vessels have been recovered in the late Initial period contexts from Chavín de Huántar (Burger 1984), but it is not yet known where such bottles were produced. RLB

By the middle of the first millennium B.C., many of the large coastal centers had gone into decline, but highland centers enjoyed a period of unusual prosperity and growth. Chavín de Huántar, in particular, grew in prestige and influence as a center of cult practice and pilgrimage. Many coastal and highland groups were drawn into its socioeconomic network, and some adopted elements of the Chavín cult and imitated the style best known from the stone sculpture at Chavín de Huántar.

This stirrup-spout bottle depicts a raptorial bird, probably a harpy eagle, with its wings and tail feather extended and its beaked head turned upwards toward the sky. Diagonal lines are used to indicate the wings' feathers. Thickened appliqué bands mark the wing structure and the bird's body. The powerful legs and taloned feet of the raptor are carefully shown. Birds, in general, were associated with the celestial journeys of shamans and priests, and some Chavín

sculpture suggests that its priests claimed the ability to transform themselves into eagles. The attention given to the harpy eagle is explained by its unusual size and strength, a position of importance in the animal world shared by the jaguar and anaconda. On this and other examples of Chavín art, however, the creatures represented were supernaturals with avian traits rather than naturalistic animals, which explains the presence of the crossed fangs of the feline and other ferocious carnivores placed within the mouth on this bottle and in many other similar images.

When birds were represented on Cupisnique pottery, they were usually owls, parrots (Alva 1986: Fig. 246), or some other relatively small coastal bird. Those few Cupisnique pieces that show some type of raptor (for example, Larco 1941: Figs. 109, 110) depict the creature in profile with much of the body abbreviated. In contrast, the position of the eagle on this bottle is based on the long-standing conventional representation of eagles with fully spread wings on the stone sculpture at Chavín de Huántar; depictions of harpy eagles in this pose are present from the earliest-known phase at the site (Rowe 1967: Fig. 11) and continue until the final phase at the temple (Burger 1992: Fig. 6b). The Larco Collection bottle (cat. no. 14) can be considered as an expression of Chavín influence on the North Coast, if not a direct import from the highlands. Similar bottles showing crested eagles and jaguars are known from many parts of Peru, and they may have been widely exchanged (Burger 1992: Figs. 235, 236).

The thick rounded stirrup form and conical spout with a sharply flanged lip are formal characteristics shared with the Janbarriu phase assemblage at Chavín de Huántar (Burger 1984), and so a dating for the Larco bottle of between 500 and 200 B.C. is probable. Vessels like this one, as well as other ceremonial paraphernalia (such as gold object #179), have been used as evidence of the involvement of cultures of the North Coast in the Chavín cult (Burger 1993). At the same time, the Cupisnique cultural tradition is transformed rather than abandoned during the Early Horizon, hence the preference of some to refer to this cultural pattern as a late phase of the Cupisnique culture (Elera 1993). RLB

15

MORTAR
Pacopampa Chavín, Early Horizon,
700 B.C.–A.D. 1
Stone
7.1 cm x 10.9 cm (3¾ x 4½ in.)
XSL-010-005

PESTLE
Pacopampa Chavín, Early Horizon,
700 B.C.–A.D. 1
Stone
5 cm x 10 cm (2 x 4 in.)
XSL-010-005

During the Early Horizon period, numerous public centers flourished in the highlands. After Chavín de Huántar, perhaps the largest of these was the center of Pacopampa in the Chotano drainage of northern Peru. Pacopampa was integrated into Chavín's economic and social sphere, and during the Early Horizon it appears to have added the Chavín cult to its own local religious system (Burger 1992). Pacopampa ritual objects are material expressions of this relationship.

This mortar and pestle was one of a pair collected in the Pacopampa area by Rafael Larco. The mortar is carved into a composite animal form with the body of a four-legged jaguar; circle dots represent the feline's pelage markings. The jaguar-like upright ears and fanged mouth are consistent with the feline portrayal, but the head also features a massive beak, suggesting the most conspicuous attribute of a crested bird. As in other examples of Chavín art, collared snakes emerge from the creature's eyes. A guilloche band with profile faces in the interstices is incised on the rim of the mortar, represented as the back of the creature; the squared eyes and L-shaped fangs are typical of late Chavín iconography. On the upper lip of the mortar is the image of a braided cord.

The grinding end of the mortar's pestle is enlarged and left undecorated for functional reasons. The side that was held, however, has been carved into the form of a serpent with prominent fangs. The concentric circles with central dots suggests its character as an anaconda or boa. It was probably of special religious significance for the serpent pestle to grind material in the composite crested eagle-jaguar mortar, symbolically unifying the great spheres of the universe (water, land, sky).

The small size of the mortar would make it impractical for grinding bulky staples like maize. It would have been appropriate for preparing mineral pigments or hallucinogenic snuff. The latter interpretation is supported by the frequency of snuffing equipment at Pacopampa and other coeval sites and the importance of psychoactive substances in the Chavín cult (Burger 1992: 107, 153–159, 200–203). Small ceremonial mortars similar to those at Pacopampa have been found at Chavín de Huántar and elsewhere in the Mosna drainage (Tello 1960; compare Burger 1992: Fig.145, 146). RLB

MACE HEAD
Salinar, Late Early Horizon,
200 B.C.–A.D. 100
Stone
10.9 cm x 8.7 cm (4¼ x 3½ in.)
XSL-006-018

On the North Coast, the collapse of the Chavín sphere of influence and the demise of the late Cupisnique culture marked the end of culture patterns which were rooted, in many cases, two thousand years earlier in the late Preceramic period. It also saw the emergence of more stratified and warlike cultures. For cultures like the Salinar, the surviving material culture shows that religious concerns are less prominent than they had been, and the monumental architecture at their centers is far smaller in scale. During this period, burials from along the coast document a sharp increase in the interment of headless bodies or solitary heads and skeletal analysis reveals that head wounds were more common during this period (John Verano personal communication). These statistics, combined with a proliferation of fortresses and other defensive architecture (Willey 1953), suggest that the final two centuries B.C. were times of trouble.

Finely crafted mace heads, like this one, are artifacts among the most

characteristic of the Salinar culture of the North Coast. Exquisite mace heads were carved from hard stone material, like diorite, and six of these were illustrated by Larco in his volume *Los Cupisniques* (Larco 1941: 92, 95). Given the absence of metal tools during this early period, these artifacts would have been produced by painstaking pecking, abrading, and polishing. Although Larco believed these objects to be Cupisnique, subsequent work by the Virú Valley Project and more recent research on the North Coast has shown them to come from Salinar sites (Burger 1996). Other maces, like the Larco specimen, have a circular socket drilled up their central core to facilitate hafting on a wooden shaft or staff. The vertical ribs and circular spikes could have had functional as well as decorative purposes, and there can little doubt that a mace head of this kind could be lethal. Because the care and skill devoted to carving such mace heads far exceeds what would be necessary to produce an effective club head, it seems likely that these objects may have also served as the emblematic staffs of people in authority. The use of the mace head both ceremonially and as a weapon would not be exceptional: in many unrelated cultures macelike objects serve both purposes (Burger 1996: 84–86).

The Larco mace head has long vertical ribs alternating with circular projections or spikes. This arrangement may have been inspired by the natural form of the San Pedro cactus (a mescaline-bearing cactus whose stalks were boiled to prepare a hallucinatory brew), and it is interesting in this regard that a San Pedro-like staff is held by priest or mythical figure in one of the sculptures from Chavín de Huántar (Burger 1992: Fig. 125). The combination of ribs and spikes (or nubbins) characterizes most of the published Salinar mace heads, although some have only ribs (Larco 1941: 125). The Larco specimen appears to be unusual in that the ribs extend down to the bottom of the mace head. RLB

MONKEY ON ALL FOURS
Salinar, Late Early Horizon,
200 B.C.–A.D. 100
Ceramic
24 cm x 14.5 cm (9½ x 5¾ in.)
Xsc-000-167

In vessel form, decorative theme, and production method, Salinar ceramics show many continuities with Cupisnique, the religious intensity and artistic refinement that characterizes the finest of the Cupisnique vessels is generally lacking in Salinar pottery, but it is frequently replaced by a refreshingly straightforward depiction of humans and animals. Most Salinar pottery was fired in an oxidizing atmosphere and orange to beige wares replace the dark monochrome pottery typical of the Initial period and Chavín-related styles of the Early Horizon. As in the earlier styles, the finest Salinar pottery tends to be the bottles that were used to serve maize beer in public contexts.

This bottle naturalistically depicting a monkey on all fours is an excellent example of Salinar pottery. The primate is shown without human features, standing on a squat bottle chamber. The stirrup with its short tapering spout emerges out of the monkey's head and back, so that the liquid from the chamber would have had to pass through the body of the hollow modeled animal before emerging from the spout. The primate's stance, five-digit hands and feet, prominent ears, and sunken eyes suggest firsthand familiarity with monkeys. Salinar contact with primates is likely, given that monkeys were frequently kept as a pets on the pre-Hispanic North Coast and can survive in the tropical forests of far northern Peru and southern Ecuador. Like the use of the stirrup-spout bottle, the depiction of monkeys in Salinar pottery continues in the tradition of the preceding Early Horizon style, sometimes known as late Cupisnique. Primates, sometimes on all fours, were shown on late Cupisnique pottery in a manner not unlike the Salinar piece, although some of the late Cupisnique primates appear to be much more than simple portraits because of the addition of jaguar spots or religious motifs (Alva 1986: Fig. 273, 280, 281). The possibility that the late Cupisnique primates may represent known characters from specific myths or folktales is raised not only by the unusual body adornment on some of them but also because in some cases they are shown eating or touching their genitals (Alva 1986: Figs. 194, 196, 205, 359).

Discovering the Salinar style in 1933, Rafael Larco subsequently excavated Salinar material from more than two hundred tombs, some of which were found stratigraphically beneath graves from the Moche culture (Larco 1948: 20). In many of these tombs, one to three pieces of Salinar pottery had been placed alongside the extended body of the deceased, along with gourd bowls filled with meat, squash, maize, and shellfish. Many of the bodies were covered with a dark red colorant and then with stones. Pieces of gold sheet metal were sometimes found in their mouths (Larco 1944: 16–20). RLB

18

BOTTLE WITH GEOMETRIC DECORATION
Salinar, Late Early Horizon,
200 B.C.–A.D. 100
Ceramic
22.5 cm x 15 cm (8¾ x 6 in.)
XSc-009-001

19

ARCHITECTONIC BOTTLE
Salinar Style, Late Early Horizon,
200 B.C.–A.D. 100
Ceramic
16.7 cm x 13 cm (6½ x 5 in.)
XXC-000-815

Some of the finest Salinar vessels are bottles with a single conical spout and strap handles, rather than stirrup-spout bottles. This bottle form had existed during late Cupisnique times, but its popularity increased dramatically as Salinar potters attempted to forge a distinctive artistic style that could express newly emerging cultural patterns.

In some cases, as in the bottle with geometric decoration, the Salinar potters drew upon the tradition of nonfigurative designs that were used to decorate the sides of Cupisnique bowls and bottles. On this bottle, a repeating stepped block is shown in a dark reddish-purple hue against a naturally orange field; a vertical column precedes and is connected to each of the stepped-block motifs. A red band encircles the bottle chamber above the geometric designs, which are defined by incisions and highlighted by slip painting before firing. Repeating geometric motifs, including step motifs, were typical of Cupisnique bowls along the North Coast during the Early Horizon (compare Alva 1985: Fig. 458). These vessels were often bichrome or polychrome, although the painting technique employed usually involved post-fire pigments, which were adhered with organic resins. The continuation of this mode of decoration, but with a shift to slip painting is reminiscent of a parallel shift that occurred along the South Coast at roughly the same time, when the Paracas ceramic style transmuted into the early Nasca style. It is difficult to know whether geometric designs like the one on this bottle are symbolically charged symbols or simple decorations. The use of the step-block design throughout the Formative and into the Early Intermediate Period and its association with altars at Cardal (Burger and Salazar-Burger 1991) and sacred mountains in Moche iconography, suggest that more than tasteful design may have been involved in its use as decoration for this exquisite drinking vessel.

The bottle depicting a building offers an unusual opportunity to imagine what structures built of largely perishable materials may have looked like during this time. The squat flat-topped chamber of the bottle may represent a low adobe platform. The building is a three-sided structure, trapezoidal in ground plan, with a flat sloping roof. The adobe walls had step-block patterns cut into them, serving to both ornament the building and allow light and air to enter. Geometric openings in walls, including some produced by a stepped-block motif like those seen on this bottle, have been documented by archaeologists working on the North Coast. Lintels crowning the step designs on both lateral walls supported a crossbeam, which was also sustained by a central housepost. The flat roof, perhaps made of a flexible material such as reed mats, was supported by three pairs of circular beams, which in turn rested on the crossbeam near the front of the building; the roof then sloped down

to where it was supported by the back wall of the building. If the depiction on this bottle is accurate, red paint was used to decorate the building. The desert environment of the coast makes constructions like this one both practical and attractive. The flat roof is sufficient protection from the mist and infrequent light precipitation. The windowlike openings in the sides and the completely open front of the building would have guaranteed ample light and badly needed air circulation during the hot midday sun. These features would have allowed a building like this to be used effectively during the daytime. On the other hand, this design would have offered little in the way of privacy or security, consequently it seems likely that some special type of public building is being represented on the bottle, rather than a common house. Other Salinar bottles depicting of buildings are known, including one showing a circular construction (Larco 1944: 9). RLB

20
FELINE WITH RESIST PAINTING
Gallinazo (or Virú), Early Intermediate
Period, A.D. 1–100
Ceramic
17.2 cm x 17.5 cm (6¾ x 7 in.)
XSc-008-004

The Gallinazo culture—which developed in the Virú Valley, where it followed the local variant of the Salinar culture (Puerto Moorin) and preceded the Moche occupation of the valley—produced ceramics of considerable charm through an uncluttered forthright style that emphasized modeling and resist or negative painting. This bottle in feline form typifies the Gallinazo style not only in the use of these two techniques but also in its strap handle and single conical spout. The idea of modeling a feline body to serve as a bottle chamber dates back to Cupisnique

pottery of the late Initial Period and continues through the late Cupisnique and Salinar styles. Yet the Gallinazo feline with its stylized face featuring pancake eyes, rounded teeth, gumdrop nose, and giant ears, as well as its skin heavily decorated with stripes, circles, and solid dots, seems fundamentally different from the awesome jaguar of the Cupisnique culture. This transformation can be seen in many examples of Gallinazo pottery, which draw upon distant Cupisnique roots but seem far more secular in their intent.

The best-known Gallinazo site is in

the middle Virú Valley covering over 5 square kilometers, a massive site that appears to have been one the Central Andes first urban centers and possibly the capital of its first multivalley state. The Gallinazo style, with its distinctive modeling and negative decorations made through the application and charring of an organic wash after initial firing, apparently was closely associated with this Virú-based polity and its expansion into the neighboring valleys of Santa and Moche. RLB

21

WARRIOR IN REED BOAT
Gallinazo (or Virú), Early Intermediate
Period, A.D. 1–100
Ceramic
19.9 cm x 9.6 cm (8¾ x 3¾ in.)
XXC-000-144

This typical Gallinazo piece with its single conical spout and strap handle shows a human figure holding a square shield in one hand and a club with a pointed-disk mace head in the other. These elements suggest that a warrior is being represented; the large circular earspools and distinctive headdress suggest that the warrior is an elite individual. The V-shaped facial markings, perhaps corresponding to facial paint or tattoos, and the designs on the headdress and shield may have helped the Gallinazo viewer identify the person being represented. The body of this important individual is shaped as a reed boat, such as those used by the traditional fisherman on the North Coast today. The wavy designs, shown in resist paint, reinforce the maritime theme. Yet the conflation of the boat and body point to a mythical scene, and the way in which the arms and the legs of the figure cling to the boat could not be more unnatural. Moreover, reed boats like the one represented are quickly waterlogged during the day's fishing, and there is no evidence that the Gallinazo or later Moche conducted warfare using boats. They did use boats, however, to travel to offshore islands in order to engage in ritual sea-lion hunts and make religious offerings. Later Moche bottles represent trips by supernaturals or priest impersonators in reed boats carrying ceremonial equipment and sacrificial victims. RLB

22

MONKEY WITH FISH AND SHRIMP
Gallinazo, Early Intermediate Period,
A.D. 1–100
Ceramic
15.8 cm x 8.2 cm (6¼ x 3¼ in.)
XXC-000-127

23

MAN PLAYING DRUM
Gallinazo, Early Intermediate Period,
A.D. 1–100
Ceramic
20 cm x 9.8 cm (8 x 3⅝ in.)
XXC-000-142

If Gallinazo ceramics relate to myths or folktales that have been lost or forgotten, we can still appreciate some of the humor implicit in these representations. It is hard not to smile at the sight of the small monkey sitting perilously on the back of a grinning fish whose eyes seem to look at its passenger. The expressiveness of the fish acts as a foil for the impassive monkey. At the opposite base of the vessel's arced handle is another creature, possibly a shrimp judging from the legs and face. If so, this animal is shown on a colossal scale, at least twice the size of the monkey. On this bottle, a rectangular boxlike chamber has been covered with geometric designs possibly suggesting a watery environment.

Another bottle, depicting a cross-legged man playing a drum could, be a scene taken from daily life or a well-known moment from a popular Gallinazo myth or folktale. While drums are often recovered archaeologically, scenes like this are the only evidence of how they were used. Also of interest are the resist technique details of the facial and body paint: the darkened zone around the eyes, cheek marks, and elaborate decoration of the torso are all elements that are rarely preserved on corpses despite the desert conditions on the North Coast. Finally, the turbanlike headgear and the absence of earspools present an interesting contrast with some other Gallinazo individuals, such as the one portrayed in cat. no. 21. RLB

24
LARGE HEAD OF MOON ANIMAL
Recuay, Early Intermediate Period,
A.D. 1–650
Stone
25.5 cm x 41 cm (10 x 16 in.)
XSL-009-001

During the Early Intermediate period, public expressions of political power and religious devotion often took the form of platform mounds or pyramids built on a truly monumental scale. On the coast, sun-baked adobes were the preferred material to build edifices that were then decorated with colorful polychrome friezes. Coeval cultures in the highlands created public constructions from local quarries, and the remarkable masonry edifices were then ornamented with stone sculptures. The Recuay culture, a highland contemporary of the Moche, was centered in the Callejon de Huaylas and extended in the east to the valleys that constitute the Callejon de Conchucos and on the west onto the upper slopes of Nepena and Santa valleys. Apparently organized into small, independent militaristic polities, the Recuay territory is dotted with poorly known platform mounds and fortresses. Recuay is best known for the ceramics and stone sculpture that have been looted from its sites. Although much of the iconography involves symbols of power and leadership, there are depictions of creatures that seem to be supernatural in character and related to Recuay religious cosmology. Perhaps the

best known of these is the so-called moon animal, a feline or foxlike creature with a triangular form projecting from its face, which plays a principal role in Recuay art and is common on fine Recuay pottery. On these kaolin pieces, a feline creature with a curled tail, large clawed paws, a round eye, and an open heavily toothed mouth is often depicted. On top of the animal's snout is a triangle and extending back from the head is an anomalous bent or curved appendage (see, for example, Lumbreras 1974: Figs. 127a, b). This figure is one of many supernaturals found among the Moche, and it has widely been seen as deriving from their Recuay neighbors.

The stone sculpture in the Larco Museum Collection is a tenon head from the Pashash area in the northern Callejon de Huaylas. The style of the sculpture indicates that it was produced by the Recuay culture. The circular eye, open mouth filled with teeth, and angular band extending from the front of the snout towards the back of the head identify this creature as the feline supernatural, which is often referred to as the moon animal because of its association with crescents and other celestial imagery in the coeval

Moche style. As is typical in most Recuay sculpture, there is an emphasis on stylistic simplicity, sharp angular or circular lines, and flat surfaces. While the best-known pieces are monoliths that were free-standing or incorporated into masonry walls, this piece was carved so that its undecorated shaftlike back could be inserted into a wall socket while the carved supernatural visage projected out of the wall in tenonlike fashion. Pashash, the area from which the sculpture is said to come, features one of the largest known masonry platforms of the Recuay culture, and it is conceivable that its origin is this complex or a nearby site (Grieder 1978). The utilization of sculptured tenon heads can be traced back to the earliest constructions at Chavín de Huántar, thus this Recuay piece can be seen as a continuation of the North Coast tradition of architectural ornamentation. However, until post-Chavín highland sculpture is more thoroughly understood, it will be impossible to determine whether this tradition is continuous or the result of deliberate reintroduction of the technique. RLB

25
HOUSE WITH FIGURES
Moche III, A.D. 200–450
Ceramic
32.3 cm x 20.5 cm (12¾ x 8 in.)
072-003-005

26
HOUSE ON PLATFORMS
Moche III, A.D. 200–450
Ceramic
19.8 cm x 15 cm (7¾ x 5⅞ in.)
XXC-000-166

In the desert climate of the North Coast of Peru, shelter from the elements is rarely needed. Houses are positioned to protect from wind. Rain only comes about once every ten years. Structures are often very simple. Open-sided, shedlike buildings are depicted in many Moche fineline scenes (cat. no. 99). The houses in these two vessels appear to be made of adobe bricks, the common material for more permanent, high-status structures. The house as a cosmic model and a temple is a widespread concept. These seemingly sacred houses may represent tombs, houses of the dead. It is also possible that they are places for sacrifice; one unpublished example of a house with an attendant figure has a warrior and a nude captive painted at its base. Both examples here are tended by people, possibly priests guarding the dead. In cat. no. 25, the house stands on a globular pot with two figures seated in front of it and a broad spout rising from it. At either side of the roof top, a step-triangle motif, a symbol of status and/or sacredness— which may be a diagram for mountains— indicates the importance of the house. A courtyard may be indicated by a low wall that projects from the house; each of the figures is seated on a painted area that resembles a fringed carpet but could suggest a platform, because it extends beyond the house and courtyard. The figure on the left has a headband and wears a vertically striped garment usually seen on certain priestly figures who appear to engage in funerary rites. He holds a staff or stick diagonally across a painted door at the center front of the house. The door and his hand are incised; the staff is in relief. This might be the staff or cane of a footless or otherwise deformed person (cat. no. 73); it might be a staff of office. There are wooden examples of such staffs, sometimes

intricately carved (cat. no. 100). The other figure has a headdress tied under the chin. A whiplike object, possibly a sling, rests between them; it is an object that appears occasionally in scenes with priestly figures, sometimes with men with a missing foot (Arsenault 1993; Kutscher 1983: Abb. 295).

Elevating the house in cat. no. 26 on two round platforms, one on top of the other, with a steep ramp leading up them, further indicates its importance. At the top of the ramp stands a figure in relief, who, like a figure at the other house, wears a vertically striped garment and holds a staff or walking stick. He stands beside an open door. The serrated design on the roof, which appears often on Moche structures, garments, and the outlines of mythical animals has not been satisfactorily explained. The wave motifs on three sides undoubtedly refer to the sea. There is an opening at either side of the roof, where the two sections meet; this is unusual, as is the crescent shape cut into the dark band painted around the structure. This vessel has a stirrup spout, the characteristic Moche form, which was not very practical but was ancient and was probably thought of as ancestral and sacred. Significant subject matter appears most often on stirrup-spout bottles. EPB

27
LOADED LLAMA
Moche II, A.D. 100–200
Ceramic
20.2 cm x 13.2 cm (8½ x 5¼ in.)
XXC-000-191

28
LLAMAS
Moche II, A.D. 100–200
Ceramic
21.7 cm x 21 cm (8½ x 8¼ in.)
XXC-013-004

Llamas, originally and essentially highland animals, were bred on the North Coast (Donnan 1978: 112–115; Shimada 1994: 47, 187–189). Their remains have been found there, and some Moche vessels represent a mother llama with her young. Unlike most other animals in Moche art, which are frequently anthropomorphized and sometimes mixed with other animal traits, llamas are depicted quite realistically, as these two examples are. The flowerlike motif on the head of the animals shown here is surely a stylization of the hair growing on the brow.

The llamas in cat. no. 28 are playing or rutting; the one in cat. no. 27 is a working llama. Llamas were not only among the few domesticated animals in the Americas but also the only pack animal. When loaded, like this bright and alert llama (cat. no. 27) with bundles projecting on either side, they can carry about 100 pounds. The amount they carry depends on the length of the trip. Llamas are said to spit with great skill and strength when they are displeased, but apparently this reputation is exaggerated. When overloaded, they will simply sit and not get up until the burden is lightened. Because llamas have no difficulty adjusting to changes in altitude, they were used in trade between highlands and coast, and in travel across the mountains toward the Amazon Basin. The checkerboard design on this pack suggests that it might contain coca leaves, for garments with this motif are sometimes worn by participants in the ritual chewing of coca leaves (cat. nos. 76, 79; Kutscher 1983: Abb. 125). Coca (*Erythroxylum novogranatense*), the plant from which cocaine is derived, was grown in some Moche valleys, but it surely originated on the other side of the mountains.

A cord with a dark pattern runs through the llama's right ear and hangs down along the right leg, a kind of marking still used to identify the owner of an animal, often on sheep and goats as well as llamas.

The llama and the finer-wooled alpaca, which thrives only in higher altitudes and is not sturdy enough for load-carrying, are the two domesticated New World relatives of the camel. Moche woven garments often contain soft alpaca fiber, along with cotton that the Moche grew (Uceda, Mujica, and Morales 1996: 15). Alpaca fiber would have been a trade item from the highlands. It is possible that the very fine hair of the wild vicuña was sometimes imported from the highlands; the vicuña is also a high-altitude animal, which was hunted by early man and is still hunted today, illegally. The guanaco, the fourth New World camelid, is also wild and hunted; it was known on the coast relatively recently. All of these animals contributed to the development of civilization in the Andes from very early times, providing not only wool but meat, fat, hide, and sinew; camelid dung fertilized the potato and other crops.

Llamas were important sacrificial animals for the Inca in later times, as many of the early Spanish chroniclers noted; llamas of different colors were offered on different occasions. The Moche people frequently placed llamas and llama parts in the burials of important people, as offerings or provisions for the afterlife (Alva and Donnan 1993: 120, 161, 215; Donnan 1995: 146–147; Donnan and Mackey 1978; Shimada 1994: 101, 151–154). EPB

RESTING STAG
Moche IV, A.D. 450–550
Ceramic
25.5 cm x 25.5 cm (10 x 10 in.)
091-005-005

IGUANA OR LIZARD
Moche III, A.D. 200–450
Ceramic
27.2 cm x 29 cm (10¾ x 11½ in.)
XXC-013-005

The white-tailed deer (*Odocoileus virginianus*), distributed from Canada well into South America, is a favorite in the myth and iconography of many peoples. Although there are other deer species, this one is usually depicted, perhaps because of the male's showy antlers, as well as the species' wide range. Deer were an important food source for the early hunting ancestors, for they were plentiful animals, as the white-tailed deer is today in many parts of its range. Among the many variations of roles that deer play in the origin myths all over the Americas are the aboriginal grandfather, the culture hero who turns into a deer, and the supernatural first couple who had many children, some of whom were human, some of whom were deer. Deer are depicted in many materials by various pre-Hispanic civilizations in the Andes. One is featured, for example, on a pair of gold ear ornaments with turquoise and shell mosaic, found recently in a rich tomb at the Moche site of Sipán (Alva and Donnan 1993: 77–81).

Deer, among the most important animals for the Moche, are shown realistically or as anthropomorphs (cat. nos. 104, 105, 106). This stag is depicted with the head rendered in detail and the body more roughly defined, except for the carefully delineated tail. The patterning on the body, which resembles the marking on a fawn, may be a way of indicating the texture of the fur. EPB

Naturalistic iguana depictions are rare in Moche art. An anthropomorphic iguana, wearing a condor headdress and priestly human garments, is a frequent companion of the major Moche god (Kutscher 1983:Abbn. 275, 276, 278, 305). That iguana, who faces the god and appears to applaud him, must have been a well-known, named character in Moche myth.

Rafael Larco Hoyle (1938: Fig. 102) identified the animal in this sculpture as *Iguana tuberculata,* an earlier name for *I. iguana,* the common iguana, and surely the source for the anthropomorph. This image does not depict the common iguana's distinctive serrated tail and frilly crest along the spine; it may instead represent a lizard, a close relative of the iguana. The straight, fat legs on this example are not realistic for either family, nor are the odd patterings—the spots on the legs, a netlike design on the head, and a dentate pattern with stripes across the back and the tail—although some lizards have dentate designs rather like these on their backs. A gold-and-

31

Dog
Moche I, A.D. 50–100
Ceramic
18 cm x 9 cm (7 x 7½ in.)
091-003-005

turquoise bead or clasp showing a lizard with similar markings was found at the site of Moche (Alva and Donnan 1993: Fig. 14). A lizard or iguana motif is the primary decoration for an elaborate pair of gold and turquoise ear ornaments (cat. no. 149). These were creatures worthy of depiction in precious materials, perhaps because both iguanas and lizards slough their skins, a trait that makes them symbolic of regeneration. EPB

This engaging spotted dog has elegantly drawn nostrils and nicely matched facial markings. In most Moche depictions of effigy dogs, the forelegs are pressed against the body. This one, with separated forelegs, projects a sense of imminent movement; the open mouth with tongue showing also gives it liveliness. This bottle was published by Rafael Larco Hoyle (1948: 48) as an example of Moche I style, in the ceramic seriation he established.

The dog, one of the few domesticated animals in the New World, was valued because it assisted hunters; a dog appears in a number of Moche deer-hunt scenes (cat. no. 106). Dog remains or dog effigies have been found in burials in the Moche region and many other areas (Alva and

Donnan 1993: 123, 159–161; Donnan and Mackey 1978: 144). These may have been the hunting dogs of the men with whom they were buried.

In folk literature throughout much of the Americas, dogs escort the dead on the journey to the underworld (Benson 1991), which may be another reason that canines are buried with humans. In many Moche fineline scenes—including the Presentation Theme—a dog accompanies a god in depictions that probably have astronomical meaning (cat. nos. 84, 107; Donnan 1978: figs. 239, 240, 270); the dog may escort a sky deity to the dark underworld. In the real world, dogs bury and dig up bones; they walk with noses to the ground; they eat carrion; they have many associations with the underworld. EPB

This puma (*Felis concolor*) rests like a well-behaved house cat with head alert, forepaws together, and tail neatly draped over the left rear leg. Nevertheless, the puma (known also as mountain lion, cougar, panther, or, sometimes, catamount) can be as fearsome a power symbol as its relative the jaguar. It is almost as large, and it is an excellent hunter. Pumas have the greatest natural distribution of any mammal in the Western Hemisphere—except for human beings. It is the world's most adaptable cat. Pumas were more important to mountain than to coastal people—it does better in high, dry mountains than its spotted relatives—but pumas were clearly known in the coastal valleys of northern Peru, although depictions of them are relatively rare. Pumas are solitary and wary of people, but they hunt the same food that men do.

The dark and light areas of the body are more prominently marked here than on a real puma, but the distinction is aesthetically appealing. A similar vessel was found in the Moche Valley (Donnan and Mackey 1983: 150–152, Pl. 9). The stylistic similarities between these bottles suggest that both may have been made there. EPB

33
JAGUAR
Moche II, A.D. 100–200
Ceramic
18 cm x 18.3 cm (7 x7¼ in.)
089-004-001

Although some Moche depictions of jaguars are realistic, few Moche artists would have seen these animals because jaguars are not indigenous to the coast. Jaguars prefer moist forests—and so are often widely associated iconographically with water and rain—but they can survive in a variety of environments when necessary. Some cubs may have been brought over the mountains for Moche ritual occasions, and it is possible that a few jaguars wandered down to the coast.

This early Moche pot suggests that the potter had never actually seen either a jaguar or a smaller feline—a margay or an ocelot. The ears are large and round, the markings are polka dots; the stripes on the legs are overemphasized and misplaced (in nature, there are stripes on the chest); the large, clawless paws resemble human hands. There is a diagonal line on either side of the brow.

However it might be represented in art, the jaguar was an important power symbol throughout the pre-Hispanic world, with whom rulers, warriors, hunters, and shamans identified. Moche captives cower in the grasp of a jaguar (cat. no. 78). The major Moche god wears a headdress adorned with a jaguar head and paws (cat. nos. 82, 84), and some important mortals wear the same headgear. The animal epitomizes physical power. It is the largest cat in the New World, and, for its size, the most powerful cat in the world. It leaps at the neck of its prey, a method of attack appropriate to the symbolism of a people who were in the habit of beheading sacrificial victims. The jaguar is also an avatar for shamans and

priests. Mostly nocturnal, it sleeps in caves and dark places; it moves silently through the forest, evoking a world of mystery. It climbs trees and swims in streams; it moves between one world and another. EPB

34
CRESTED ANIMAL
Moche I, A.D. 50–100
Ceramic and mother-of-pearl
20.3 cm x 14.2 cm (8 x 5½ in.)
XXC-007-006

A mythical animal, with a disproportionately large, fanged mouth, is seated with paws raised. A creature of this type is common in Moche—and some other Andean—art (Kutscher 1983: Abbn. 309-313; Shimada 1994: 92-93). Sometimes it seems to derive from a fox, sometimes from a feline. Often scrolls in the upper and lower registers frame the motif, with the lower scroll like a stylized tail and the upper one like a crest. In this example, three inlaid triangles framed in a step motif, a symbol of importance or sacredness, have been added to the upper crest. The step motif appears on many examples of the animal.

This creature, which is unlike most Moche mythical beings, may have been introduced into Moche iconography from the contemporary Recuay culture in the mountains to the east, with whom the Moche had some exchange (Anton 1972: Pls. 87, 88, 91). The Moche version has been called a dragon but is more often referred to as a moon animal, moon eater, or moon monster, because, when painted on the surface of a vessel, it sometimes stands in a crescent and/or has star shapes around it. The moon association was not usually present in the first depictions of this creature, but in later Moche art the figure may have referred to a constellation that is sometimes near the moon. It surely does not represent the moon itself (Benson 1985). The motif, which endured for centuries and appeared in several cultures, probably had different meanings in different times and places.

Rich inlay is a trait that appears only in early Moche ceramics. The thickened, tapering rim of this spout also indicates its early place in the sequence established by Rafael Larco Hoyle (1948: 28–29), as does its taut, compact form. EPB

35
Owl with Shell
Moche IV, A.D. 450–550
Ceramic
26.5 cm x 12.7 cm (10½ x 5 in.)
082-005-009

36
Standing Owl
Moche III, A.D. 200–450
Ceramic
39 cm x 26.5 cm (15½ x 10½ in.)
XXC-013-006

Owls are widely associated with death because of their predation, nocturnal nature, mournful voices, and frequent habitation of grave sites. On many Moche effigy vessels, a small, nude human figure with the tufted hair of a captive (see cat. nos. 78, 96, 97) is tied to the back of a giant owl, who is probably carrying the figure to the other world. Here, at the back of a realistic great horned owl (*Bubo virginianus*), a gastropod shell is tied onto the owl's body with a snake, which the owl holds in place with its claws. This subject may relate to the depictions of owls with human captives on their backs.

The great horned owl is found all over the Western Hemisphere in a variety of environments, apparently including the Peruvian guano islands (cat. no. 48). Owls appear in coastal or island scenes on Moche pottery, often in fantastic combinations of godly figures, sea lions, seabirds, fish, and shells (Kutscher 1983: Abb. 277). Many wooden objects, considered offerings, were found under the guano, and a considerable number of these have owl attributes (Kubler 1948). If the sun's evening path across the sea was seen as the way to the watery underworld, the owl's part in this iconography would be to carry the dead to the afterlife. Aside from this sea association, it is not clear why this owl is bearing a shell on its back.

Trumpets were made from gastropod shells. They are a prominent element in the rite centered on the chewing of coca leaves (cat. nos. 76, 79), but trumpets apparently also marked moments in other rituals, as they do in some places today. EPB

In Moche art owls are represented realistically and anthropomorphically in many roles. An important role was that of supernatural warrior or war god; associated with this role was the owl as sacrificer of war captives. Such owls hold a knife in the right hand, a decapitated head in the other. Some apparent owl sacrificers hold only the cutoff head, not the knife. These owl-humans are shown clearly as a man with an owl mask over his face (Anton 1972: Pl. 141; Benson 1972: Figs. 3–9). He may have a winglike cape, but he is otherwise human. These are the only instances in Moche art of a clear portrayal of a ritual impersonator. The actual sacrificer is always a supernatural being. The example in cat. no. 36 is an unusual portrayal and somewhat ambiguous, but it appears to be a supernatural being, not a human in owl costume. It might show an eye mask of a horned owl over a human face; but the arms are not human, and the feet have three short claws or toes. The owl wears a kilt with a slit design and a shirt or short tunic with a double swirl motif, which suggests a sea connotation.

This vessel is exceptional in its large size and its high-relief forms. The basic shape outlines a curving double-headed serpent like that framing the participants in coca-rite scenes (cat. no. 79). Seen frontally, it has a design of alternating dark and light squares, which make a checkerboard pattern with the sides of its arched body. In South American myths, rainbows and the Milky Way are often thought of as serpents; here, the nocturnal owl suggests the Milky Way. Certainly, there is an astronomical connotation in this composition. The framing serpent might confirm that the enclosed figure is supernatural, but this is not true in the coca-rite scene—although that occasion was so sacred that it might be considered a supernatural experience. A wave motif painted around the rim of the open spout of this vessel adds a sea association, which is seen also with the owl in cat. no. 35. EPB

37
DUCK
Moche III, A.D. 200–450
Ceramic
12.8 cm x 17.7 cm (5 x 7 in.)
XXC-000-154

This very elegant vessel, with its gracefully flared Moche III spout, portrays a duck with variegated colors and textures on the wings. It is perhaps a cinnamon teal (*Anas cyanoptera*), a surface-feeding, or river, duck, indigenous to both North and South America (Phillips 1986, II: 390–401). On the North Coast of Peru, it inhabits swamps with tule reeds, from which the Moche people made rafts. The marshes and the rivers that run through the desert also provided important food resources, and many Moche vessels show scenes with reeds, fish, and birds (cat. no. 40; Kutscher 1983: Abbn. 58, 59, 66, 67).

This bird does not seem to be the Muscovy duck (*Cairina moschata*), which is frequently pictured on Moche ceramics, often as an anthropomorphic warrior or runner (Kutscher 1983:Abbn. 179, 287, 289, 290). The Muscovy, a large, strong, aggressive duck with a crest, was one of the few domesticated animals in the pre-Hispanic Americas. One reason for its successful domestication may have been that it likes maize, the staple food of most pre-Hispanic cultures. Like the cinnamon teal, the Muscovy duck often inhabits swamps along the banks of streams and rivers (Phillips 1986, I: 57–67). EPB

38
PELICAN
Moche III, A.D. 200–450
Ceramic
20.5 cm x 12.5 cm (8 x 5 in.)
XXC-000-161

The Peruvian pelican may be a subspecies of the widely distributed brown pelican (*Pelecanus occidentalis*) or a separate species (Harrison 1985: 104, 287); they are very closely related. The white chest plumage of cat. no. 38 indicates that it is a juvenile. The dark beak and feathers are outlined in white dots, seemingly a decoration rather than an attempt at naturalism. Pelicans generally have a broad wingspan, which allows strong and graceful flight. They forage in flocks, flying low above the water, diving for fish they have spotted, scooping up a great deal of fish in their large beaks, and then draining the water in the bill that serves as a sieve. Moche fishermen must have admired the skills of these birds, but they were probably particularly interested in pelicans as inhabitants of the offshore guano islands.

The pelican is one of the primary producers of guano, which was surely collected by the Moche from the offshore islands for use as fertilizer, as it was by the later Incas (see Rostworowski essay this volume). Even today, flocks of hundreds of pelicans can be seen nesting together on these islands. It is a sight that must have greatly impressed the Moche people.

Pelican life was, and is, affected by the current that comes from the north into the Humboldt Current, usually around Christmas—hence its name, El Niño, the Spanish appellation for the Christ Child. This warm current drives marine life out of the cold Humboldt stream, and the birds suffer from the scarcity of food; they either leave the area or die. Fishing becomes difficult for people as well, and guano production is diminished. What affected the pelican also affected the Moche. EPB

39
CRAB
Moche III, A.D. 200–450
Ceramic
21.4 cm x 18.2 cm (8½ x 7¼ in.)
XSC-013-003

40
CRAYFISH
Moche IV, A.D. 450–550
Ceramic
26.2 cm x 27 cm (10⅜ x 10⅝ in.)
105-005-005

This crab, resting on a globular platform, is presented in elegant and complex detail, with realistic legs and claws meeting center front and with color variation and incised scaly patterning on the casing. This swimming crab, a member of the family Portunidae, is shown naturalistically; the long arcs may indicate excreting activity rather than supernatural attributes. Crabs go through various metamorphoses in their life cycle, which probably gave them significance in addition to their connotations of food and the sea. Shellfish were a vital food resource for many early peoples, who clustered on shores and stream banks, where food was easily available. Crabs figure in Moche iconography in various depictions, frequently as supernatural personages with a face on the shell (cat. no. 92). They may be shown with the fish monster (cat. no. 85) on a line or about to be sacrificed by the major Moche god (Bourget 1994a: 433–436; Kutscher 1983: Abbn. 260, 262A, 266).

This kind of full-round figure, placed atop a globular or boxlike support, is called a "deck figure" in Moche studies. It is a common form of design for stirrup-spout vessels. EPB

A crayfish is posed above a waterscape rich with fish, reeds, and other aquatic life. Rafael Larco Hoyle (1938: Fig. 113) identified this crustacean as a member of the family Astacidae, crayfish, freshwater versions of the lobster. It has projecting eyes, a pointed snout, and a long body; its claws frame a painted waterlily blossom (*Nymphaea*). Many Moche vessels depict life at sea, on shore, or on the rivers. Not only were the Moche a seagoing people, they were inhabitants of an arid desert, to whom water, water creatures, and water plants had deep and vivid significance. A crayfish sometimes appears with a deity

41
Bivalve Shell
Moche IV, A.D. 450–550
Ceramic
24.8 cm x 17 cm (9¾ x 6¾ in.)
106-004-009

42
Fish
Moche IV, A.D. 450–550
Ceramic
30 cm x 16 cm (11¾ x 6¼ in.)
083-003-008

head, in the water with fish, or about to decapitate a water bird (Kutscher 1983: Abbn. 243-246). It is not clear whether this being is a crayfish demon or the major god metamorphosed to accomplish a certain task.

Like the crab (see cat. no. 39), this is a deck figure, placed here above an elaborate fineline scene. EPB

Shells were symbols of the sea and of the waters of the earth, and they were imitated in many materials. This scallop (family Pectinadae, perhaps *Cryptopecten*) is not commonly represented in Moche art. There are many depictions of gastropod shells, but bivalves are rare. *Spondylus*, the spiny oyster (*Spondylus princeps*), which was traded into Peru from Ecuador at least from Cupisnique/Chavín times (1200–200 B.C.) and was highly valued by Andean peoples, makes virtually no appearance in Moche art until the last Moche phase. It has been found in Moche graves, however, as have other bivalves (Alva and Donnan 1993: 154, 215; Shimada 1994). Bivalves may have had male-female symbolism, which would have added to the fertility connotations of their association with water. EPB

Fish life is more plentiful in cold water than in warm. The frigid waters of the Humboldt Current, flowing up from the Antarctic along the coasts of Chile and Peru, normally provide one of the world's richest fishing grounds. An important food source for local consumption and for inland trade, fish were also a frequent motif in Moche art, as realistic representations, as mythic monsters (cat. nos. 84, 85, 89), or as scene-setting elements (cat. no. 40). The Moche were fishermen, and they never forgot it. This delicately detailed fish is probably a member of the large family of pompanos and jacks (Carangidae). EPB

43
TOAD
Moche II, A.D. 100–200
Ceramic
18.2 cm x 17.5 cm (7¼ x 7 in.)
104-004-009

This toad has highly stylized markings similar to those on the jaguar in cat. no. 33. (Jaguar and toad/frog traits are sometimes combined in Moche depictions of fantastic animals.)

Frogs and toads are associated with water and vegetation, and some Moche frog vessels have plants painted on their backs. In addition to their fertility connotations, all anurans are at least somewhat toxic, which gives them special significance. Cat. no. 150 is a necklace of gold frogs with turquoise eyes; some of the more toxic frogs are gold-colored. Some frogs—notably

Dendrobates, the poison dart frog—produce a toxin used by some peoples in hunting and fishing. Some toads, such as the widely distributed marine or giant toad (*Bufo marinus*), emit a fairly powerful toxin from glands at the side of the head; this toxin may have been converted by certain pre-Hispanic groups into a psychoactive drug for ritual use. Rafael Larco Hoyle (1938: Fig. 100) identified this toad, whose toxin glands are visible behind its eyes, as a *Bufo*. EPB

44
TUMBO PLANT
Moche IV, A.D. 450–550
Ceramic
22 cm x 16.6 cm (8¾ x 8½ in.)
109-005-014

Tumbo (*Passiflora mollissima*) is a member of the passionflower family, with tendril-bearing vines, which usually have showy flowers. Margaret Towle (1961: 68, 113) tells us that seventy species of *Passiflora* are known for Peru. *P. mollissima* has an edible fruit, granadilla, which was well known in pre-Hispanic times. Its remains have been found in archaeological excavations.

The spout-with-handle vessel seen here is a typical Moche form but much less common than the stirrup-spout bottle. This beautifully composed bottle, although almost in the shape of the fruit itself, shows the whole form of the plant in a remarkably complex, compact design. A small, spotted frog rests under the vine. The frog may be *Dendrobates*, the poison dart frog, a highly toxic genus, used by some people in hunting. Poisonous or otherwise, dangerous animals seem to have been particularly significant to pre-Hispanic peoples. EPB

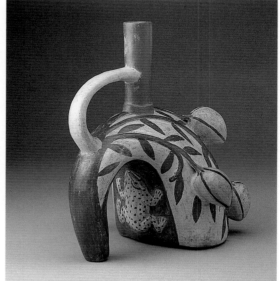

45
HEAD OF A SEA LION
Moche IV, A.D. 450–550
Ceramic
23 cm x 17.8 cm (9 x 7 in.)
094-003-003

46
SEA LION
Moche II, A.D. 100–200
Ceramic
16.5 cm x 12.8 cm (6½ x 5 in.)
094-002-008

47
SEA-LION HUNT
Moche IV, A.D. 450–550
Ceramic
24.2 cm x 15.3 cm (9½ x 6 in.)
XXC-000-189

Sea lions appear in Moche art as effigy vessels, as portrait heads, and in sea-lion hunts and scenes of life and ritual on the guano islands (cat. no. 48). At the time of the Spanish conquest, the South American sea lion (*Otaria flavescens*) was hunted for food, hide, and fat; it was probably hunted for the same resources in Moche times.

Sea-lion hunts are sometimes shown in fineline painting with the priestly figures, small houses, and pottery jugs that mark a scene as ritual (Kutscher 1983: Abbn. 88, 89). In an unusual low-relief rendering (cat. no. 47), a striding, central figure has two narrow prongs in his headdress. (This type of headdress is usually found on Moche men who go to sea.) He holds a big club and hits the head of a large sea lion. Around him are sea lions of various sizes and a seabird. Another man is bashing the head of a very large sea lion under the handle of the bottle, and a third figure attacks the rump of another sea lion. Two sea lions on one side are in high relief. The form of the bottle is uneven, as if the potter had attempted to imitate the shape of a mound of guano. Such scenes may have taken place on the mainland but are more likely to have occurred on the off-shore islands, where sea lions are plentiful and where ritualists are out of sight of land, on an island white with guano, surrounded by a vast sea (Benson 1995).

Both the effigy sea lion lying on its side (cat. no. 46) and the portrait head (cat. no. 45) are depicted with a round stone in the mouth. Sea lions have the habit of engorging beach pebbles up to the size of a tennis ball; according to Judith King (1991: 172), more than twenty pounds of stones have been found in a sea-lion stomach. It is not known whether the ingestion of stones helps in the digestive process, acts as ballast, or performs some other function. Christopher Donnan (1978: 136) reports that stones from the stomachs of slain sea lions are used today by folk healers. The sea lion's digestive juices are thought to give the stones medicinal properties.

In the colonial period on the coast of Peru, it was believed, according to Father Pablo José de Arriaga (1968: 64), that the dead were carried across the sea to an island by sea lions. This may well have been a very ancient belief, a variation on the widespread theme of a dog's escorting the dead across a body of water to the underworld or other world. EPB

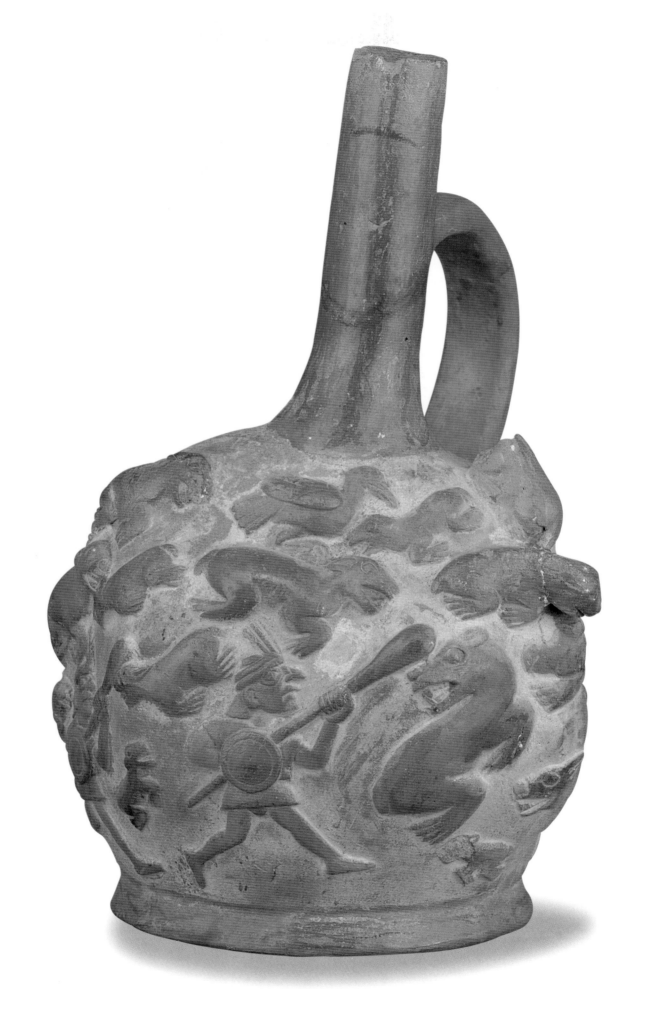

48

GUANO ISLAND
Moche I, A.D. 50–100
Ceramic
12.8 cm x 13.5 cm (5 x 5¼ in.)
XXC-000-167

Islands off the coasts of Peru and Chile are gathering places for seabirds who deposit large amounts of guano, which in recent times was one of Peru's biggest exports. In the nineteenth century, Peru supplied most of the world's fertilizer from the guano on these islands. That the islands were frequented by Moche people is attested by quantities of Moche objects left on them as offerings (Kubler 1948; Benson 1995) and by depictions like the one on this bottle, which is very similar to a drawing published by Adolf Baessler (1902–03: Fig. 62) at the beginning of this century. Ritual and practical life are merged in presentations like these.

In this complex scene, a pile of guano or guano-covered rock rises at one end of

the bottle spout. A figure climbs up it, and, above him, there is a bird; both are rendered in relief. The bird is presumably a depositer of guano. The other high area in the scene is a structure with two figures, in full round, at the side near the guano pile. One figure, in the clasped-hands pose usually associated with ritual, may be a woman. The other is a man holding a vessel; depictions of pottery also usually indicate ritual. A capped figure holding an unidentified object sits outside the structure. Two sea lions formed of unslipped clay rest on the outer edge of the vessel. On the side opposite the structure, there are two large enclosures, one with a bridge over it, each containing two sea lions; a small structure houses another

sea lion. All these animals are made of unslipped clay, as are two rafts outside of this area and another on the end. Birds are indicated at the sides.

An enclosure near the large structure is decorated with two painted motifs that are probably war clubs. Many of the objects, mostly wooden, that were left on the islands by the Moche have war iconography, representing weapons, warriors, and captives, so it is not surprising that weapons are shown here. War was a rite related to the control of land and water for agriculture, and war may have been fought for control of the guano islands; Moche objects have been found on islands outside the mainland Moche region. EPB

49
SEABIRD
Moche IV, A.D. 450–550
Ceramic
34.5 cm x 35.8 cm (13½ x 14 in.)
XXC-008-001

This white bird with a dark area around the eye has been called a cormorant and a gull, but it is difficult to identify it. It looks like a cormorant, one of the major guano-producing birds, but there is no white cormorant species. Seabirds would have had had many associations for the Moche, particularly the cormorant, because of its deep dives below the surface of the water. Water was surely the entrance to the Moche underworld; such a belief about water, and especially the sea, exists in many places in the Americas.

The curve of the bird's neck on this unusually large vessel is an elegant form, showing great skill on the part of the potter. Although the bird seems generally to be realistically rendered, its asymmetrical shape is reminiscent of that of a guano island. The spout, with a chevron band around the bottom, comes from the bird's right shoulder, which is higher and wider than the left. The white color also might be a reference to guano. There is a dark spot on the rump. For all its seeming realism, this may be a visual bird/guano-island pun. EPB

50
DRUM
Moche IV, A.D. 450–550
Ceramic
18.5 cm x 8.5 cm (7¼ x 3⅜ in.)
XXC-000-158

A vessel in the form of a drum is unusual, although three-dimensional and fineline figurative vessels show such drums. The drum is usually held upright, resting in the lap of the player (Anton 1972: Pls. 113, 163; Kutscher 1983: Abbn. 160, 161), but in some examples the figure is standing (Castillo Butters 1994: Fig. 41). A human or supernatural figure holding a drum hovers over the top of some complex guano-island compositions. The figure is sometimes a priest, sometimes a skeleton, and often an anthropomophic animal, most often a sea lion or cormorant.

This drum stands upright in the position in which it would have been held. Drums seem to be used in activities related to the sea and often appear with other musical instruments in scenes with the dead and in what are likely funerary rites, passages to the other world. EPB

51
RELIEF FANTASY SCENE
Moche IV, A.D. 450–550
Ceramic
26.5 cm x 13.8 cm (10½ x 5½ in.)
086-005-003

The shapes of this vessel suggest potatoes with faces, which are depicted in Moche art. The faces are usually deformed or diseased, perhaps because the potato develops underground, metaphorically in the underworld. In recent times, in certain Peruvian valleys where the best potatoes are grown and certain disfiguring tropical diseases are endemic, the guardian of a potato field was required to be a victim of one of these diseases (Benson 1975: 114, n.6; see also cat. no. 69).

On this vessel, the rough potato shapes form a confused conglomeration of motifs. At the top of the pile are two faces: one has a disfigured nose; a larger one is a little lopsided. There are hands and arms, not obviously attached. A curled-up sea lion rests on top of what appears to be a monkey, with a skull behind them. At the bottom, there is a human couple with a larger head shown

face up, a small head on top. Each head has a tied headdress. In the middle tier, a vague body with a head face up rests on a big asymmetrical face, next to a sea lion and above a bird. Other faces have light hoods and/or garments. There is also a ceramic jug, usually a symbol in a ritual of death or sacrifice.

A number of Moche vessels have distorted shapes depicting creatures—sometimes supernatural—and forms united in strange, unnatural ways (Kutscher 1983: Abb. 277). They often portray sea lions, seabirds, fish, and shells, sometimes gods, captives, and owls; they apparently show guano islands. This scene seems to be related to these depictions as well as to the potatoes with distorted faces. Whether such images are induced by ritual consumption of the San Pedro cactus or some other psychoactive drug, whether they are underwater distortions or images read in rocks, or whether there is some mythical, religious, or philosophical justification for them is not clear. This vessel seems to relate potato agriculture to guano. The Museo Nacional de Antropología y Arqueología, Lima, calls a similar vessel a "mythical potato." EPB

52
MOUNTAIN
Moche IV, A.D. 450–550
Ceramic
21 cm x 15.6 cm (8¼ x 6¼ in.)
111-003-009

53
MOUNTAIN WITH PLANTS
Moche III, A.D. 200–450
Ceramic
18.7 cm x 12.2 cm (7½ x 4¾ in.)
111-004-009

The Andes, rising close to the coast and continuing toward the Amazon Basin, were a constant presence for the Moche people. The sun came from the mountains; precious water for food cultivation flowed in rivers from the mountains; trade of elite and ritual goods came from the mountains; and sometimes enemies came from the mountains.

Mountains were sacred, as they were and are in many places in the world. *Apu*, the term the Inca used for mountain, indicates that they considered the Andean peaks to be gods. Modern ethnographic accounts indicate that this is still true. Mountains were surely sacred also in Moche times. They were earth's contact with the sky, and they housed caves, which were probably thought of as entrances to the underworld, as they are in many cultures.

Moche vessels show mountains depicted in various ways. Often, there are five peaks, and the mountain resembles a hand. A relationship between landscape and body parts is a common theme in the Andes. Many bottles show, in relief, a scene of sacrifice in the mountains, usually before a seated deity (Bourget 1994b: Fig. 5). Some unpeopled mountain vessels take the form of geometrically rendered peaks on a square box. Cat. no. 52 seems to be a cosmic model based on the four world directions and the sky, both of which were basic to Andean thought. Cat. no. 53 has three peaks with a plant at the front of each and also peaks with plants below. A somewhat similar mountain bottle with plants was found in a grave at Moche (Donnan and Mackey 1978: Pl. 7). EPB

54

SNAILS ON MOUNTAIN OR CACTUS
Moche III, A.D. 200–450
Ceramic
20.2 cm x 20.5 cm (8 x 8 in.)
107-005-001

Snail hunts in the hills are depicted in Moche art. John Gillin (1945: 26) described snail hunts at the town of Moche during the moist winter season, when occasional expeditions are made into the upper valleys to gather the large snails that appear at that time. Snails are often found near or on cacti, which usually appear in the hunt scenes. This bottle, although it resembles mountain images, also looks like a cactus, which it may represent. It may deliberately imply both meanings.

The land snail may have had special meaning for the Moche because it resembles a creature from the all-important sea. Sea shells were rich symbols for most pre-Hispanic peoples, perhaps especially for the coastal Moche. That the snail hunt was a rite is suggested by the number of fineline snail-hunt scenes on stirrup-spout vessels showing hunters wearing the white, tied-cloth garments of priest-shamans and carrying long sticks to pick up the snails and small net or woven bags in which to put them (Lavalle 1989: Pl. 1). One bottle illustrates a mountain sacrifice scene with nine skeletal figures; among the live figures there are snails and cacti (Hocquenghem 1987: Fig. 186). Another bottle portrays snails, cacti, and other plants in a battle or ritual scene with warriors clothed to represent two groups of people (Hocquenghem 1987: Fig. 178). These scenes may all depict related rites. EPB

55
YACON
Moche III, A.D. 200–450
Ceramic
22.4 cm x 25 cm (8 ¾ x 9 ⅞ in.)
109-004-002

Yacon (llakhum; [*Polymnia sonchifolia*]) grows to three or four feet in temperate valleys and at fairly high altitudes in the Andes (Coe 1994: 185; Towle 1961: 96). A relative of the dahlia, the plant has yellow flowers and edible spindle-shaped roots that contain sugar and starch. The roots are best eaten raw, like a fruit. One of the early Spanish chroniclers, Bernabé Cobo, described it as sweet, watery, and rather like a turnip (cited in Coe 1994: 185). He noted that it was even better when dried in the sun and that it lasted remarkably well when taken to sea for some weeks. In colonial times its consumption was identified with a Catholic religious celebration held at the time of an earlier Inca feast. In the Moche era also, it may have been food for a special occasion. Effigies of edible food may have been placed in Moche burials for the nourishment of the dead, as offerings to lords of the other world, or in commemoration of a certain occasion. EPB

56
YUCA
Moche II, A.D. 100–200
Ceramic
14.6 cm x 19 cm (5 ¾ x 7 ½ in.)
110-003-005

In many places in the Americas, yuca (manioc, cassava [*Manihot esculenta*]), not maize, was the staple food. The plant has clustered roots ending in elongated tubers. It is easy to grow; it does well in environments not suitable for maize cultivation; and it can be used in many ways. Eaten frequently in various forms in the Neotropics today, the plant is best known in the United States in the form of tapioca. *M. esculenta* has been found in many excavations on the coast, including Cupisnique sites; it grows also in the mountains, up to 7000 feet (Towle 1961: 61). It was once thought that there were two species of yuca, one sweet, one bitter. It has now been demonstrated, however, that when yuca is grown in poor soil, in which there is hydrogen cyanide, the plant becomes not only bitter but also poisonous (Coe 1994: 16–18). Sweet manioc is easily prepared as a vegetable. Bitter manioc must be grated and squeezed to remove the poisonous juice, which is sometimes boiled down to make a sauce. The starchy matter remaining after the removal of the poison can be made into bread, which is cooked on a clay griddle over the fire, or it can be fermented to produce beer.

The shapes of yuca make a handsome bottle, and there are several depictions of it similar to this one. Like maize, it is also portrayed with a god head emerging from it (Donnan 1978: Fig. 234). EPB

57
SQUASH
Moche IV, A.D. 450–550
Ceramic
24.8 cm x 12.8 cm (10 x 5 in.)
109-005-010

Maize, beans, yuca, and squash were staples in much of the pre-Hispanic world, with the potato an important addition in the Andes. There were a number of New World squashes, and they were prepared in a variety of ways. The warty, or crookneck, squash (*Cucurbita moschata*) has a wide distribution, from North America down. A vine with yellow or yellow-orange flowers, the warty squash develops fruits of various shapes,

usually oblong or crook-necked. Its seeds have been found in Preceramic levels at Huaca Prieta (2500 B.C.), in the Chicama Valley near the Moche site that comprises Huaca del Brujo and Huaca Cao Viejo, and in early levels at other sites on the North Coast (Towle 1961: 91). It was domesticated earlier than maize on the Peruvian coast (Coe 1994: 39). Farming on the coast began in pre-Moche times with the development of desert irrigation.

The water that flowed from the mountains was utilized by Moche farmers in fairly complex canal systems. Short-term cultivation plots were developed during heavy El Niño rains, as they are today, and flooding at such times deposited soil-enriching silt (Shimada 1994: 52).

The rough texture of this warty squash is remarkably well rendered; it makes a pleasing contrast to the polished smoothness of other Moche vessels. EPB

58
POTATOES
Moche IV, A.D. 450–550
Ceramic
24.2 cm x 21.5 cm (6½ x 5¼ in.)
109-004-011

59
PEPINOS
Moche III, A.D. 200–450
Ceramic
18.2 cm x 17 cm (7¼ x 6¾ in.)
110-004-009

The importance of the potato (*Solanum tuberosum*) in northern European diets today indicates how its introduction from the New World in the mid-sixteenth century revolutionized staple foods used there. The potato is important also in the Andes, especially at high altitudes, where only underground crops, tubers and rhyzomes, can be reliably cultivated; potatoes were also a notable crop in the coastal valleys.

The pepino (kachun [*Solanum muricatum*]), a relative of the potato, bears the Spanish name for cucumber, but the Andean vegetable is not related to the cucumber and does not resemble it. The ovoid fruit of the pepino, five to six inches long, with longitudinal stripes, grows on a bushy shrub that is native to Peru (Towle 1961: 84). Pepinos are not often found archaeologically—they are soft and pulpy, not easy to preserve—but they were described by early Spanish chroniclers as being cultivated on the coast; the Moche Valley was particularly famous for them (Coe 1994: 189–190). They are seen fairly often in Moche art. Still a common food in the Andes, they appear sometimes in U.S. markets.

One of these vessels depicts four potatoes, the other four pepinos. The cosmology of the ancient Americas was based on the four world directions or the four corners of the world, a theme that seems to be implicit in the form of these bottles. EPB

60

BOWLS OF FOOD
Moche IV, A.D. 450–550
Ceramic
24.5 cm x 15 cm (9½ x 6 in.)
108-003-008

These bowls probably represent gourds, which were halved and used for containers in the era before pottery was made. The upper bowl contains peanuts (*Arachis hypogaea*), a plant indigenous to the Andes; remains of peanut pods are commonly found in North Coast archaeological excavations (Towle 1961: 42). The lower gourd probably contains red peppers. Representations of filled gourd bowls like these may have been made especially for burial and placed in a grave. In many depictions, such containers are tied together and/or placed one on top of another (cat. no. 74).

A finely made necklace of gold beads and silver beads in the shape of peanuts was found by Walter Alva in one of the splendid burials at Sipán (Alva and Donnan 1993: Fig. 96). The fact that a ruler wore and was buried with such a necklace demonstrates the high status of the peanut and probably also indicates that the ruler was responsible for a successful peanut crop.

Red peppers (*Capsicum*) belong to the same family as potatoes and tomatoes (Solanaceae, the nightshade family); they are mentioned in early Spanish accounts as one of the few spices the Incas had, and apparently a very appreciated one (Coe 1994: 60–62, 193). There are several species in Peru (Towle 1961: 80–82), one of which was found at the Preceramic site of Huaca Prieta. EPB

61
PEANUT-MAN PLAYING FLUTE
Moche IV, A.D. 450–550
Ceramic
22.5 cm x 21 cm (8⅞ x 8¼ in.)
063-004-005

A peanut playing a flute was a serious Moche subject, reflecting a belief in animism. Here, a peanut shell seems to be worn like a suit by a plump human figure with a carrying cloth tied around the neck. This kind of cloth, thick in back as if bulging with its contents, is often worn by priestly figures in Moche ceramic scenes. The peanut figure is playing a *quena*, the native flute that is still an important Andean instrument.

Music was an important part of ancient culture; various figures are shown playing *quenas*, panpipes, trumpets, and drums in mythic and ritual scenes, probably primarily funerary rites (cat. nos. 84, 109). The instruments had fairly specific status (Benson 1975: 116–117), with panpipes holding the highest rank: they are usually played by supernatural beings or by the largest, best-dressed figures in a scene (cat. no. 84; Donnan 1992: Fig. 95), and sometimes they float over an important figure. Occasionally, an anthropomorphic peanut plays panpipes, but more often it holds a *quena*, an instrument that is generally middle-ranking, played by priestly shamanic figures. The drum held a lower status, often played by figures with deformed faces or by anthropomorphic animals. Various kinds of rattles are depicted. Trumpets are rarely shown in use, but the ceramic trumpets that exist are richly decorated, often with high-status figures or feline heads (Anton 1972: Pl. 109, 110; Tello 1939: Pl. 38).

Vegetables, frequently depicted with faces, were also ranked in importance. Maize was at the top—its face is that of a god (cat. no. 63)— and potato tubers, which ranked much lower, have deformed faces (cat. no. 51). The peanut, perhaps holding a middle status, has a plain human face. EPB

62
MAIZE WITH BIRD
Moche IV, A.D. 450–550
Ceramic
21.8 cm x 15.7 cm (8½ x 6¼ in.)
109-003-013

63
MAIZE WITH GOD HEAD
Moche IV, A.D. 450–550
Ceramic
25.8 cm x 17 cm (10¼ x 6¾ in.)
110-001-011

Out of a cluster of maize (*Zea mays*), with four peaks of maize ears, emerges the head of a deity with fanged mouth (cat. no. 63). In most of the highly developed cultures of the New World, maize was the most important plant, as a status symbol, if not always as the primary staple. Other faces appear with other vegetables, but the major deity appears commonly with maize and rarely with any other vegetable. This is surely not a maize god as such, but a demonstration of the sacred nature of the plant.

A single ear of maize is clearly represented on the front of cat. no. 62. An upside-down bird, probably a vulture, pecks at it. Many New World accounts of the origin of maize tell that a bird discovered the precious grain. Here, the bird-head form echoes the upper, curving, striated shape, which may depict flowing water. The top part of this vessel resembles scenes of mountain or wave sacrifice, where the long hair of victims flows like water over the mountain peak (Hocquenghem 1987: Figs. 182–186, 189). Because Moche sacrifice is usually related to agriculture, there may well be a link between all these vessel themes. EPB

64

PORTRAIT HEAD
Moche IV, A.D. 450–550
Ceramic
31.7 cm x 22.5 cm (12½ x 8¾ in.)
XXC-000-012

This man wears a headdress with bird heads facing forward. The two lines by the eye are a Moche artistic convention in drawing a number of birds and animals, which makes it unclear exactly what creature is being portrayed. These birds are probably aplomado falcons (*Falco femoralis*), although they may be ospreys (*Pandion haliaetus*). Both birds have wide distributions; both are of the order Falconiformes, raptors related to eagles and hawks. A dark bird appears on either side of the headdress. A dark band crosses the top with a bird painted on either side, and a dark bird with light wings and a light pleated design appears below. The chevron on the front of the headdress is a relatively common headdress motif, particularly with birds. The man wears ear ornaments that were probably closed tubes of sheet gold, a type of ornament that does not appear to be specific to an occasion, as some ear ornament types are.

An almost-identical portrait of this man, in the Museo Nacional de Antropología y Arqueología, Lima, has a knife blade painted above the chevron (Tello 1938: Pl. 1). A similar portrait, excavated in the 1940s from a rich burial in the Virú Valley (Strong and Evans 1952: Pl. XIIA–C), has a somewhat different face. These may all represent the same Virú Valley personage, but the nature of their relationship is not immediately obvious. EPB

65
PORTRAIT HEAD
Moche IV, A.D. 450–550
Ceramic
32.8 cm x 20 cm (13 x 8 in.)
XXC-013-002

This portrait-head bottle has backward-looking sea(?) birds on the headdress and pendant-blade ear ornaments, which do not normally appear with a bird head-dress. The chevron between the birds, a motif seen on many bird headdresses, may refer to wings or flight. The backward-looking birds are depicted on other head-dresses, but their significance is unknown.

The man has a large nose and high cheekbones; a bit of hair shows under the headdress, and there is a rectangle of dark face paint on the outer side of each cheek, a pattern normally seen on impor-tant people and even on the major god. Some patterns of face paint are associated with specific rituals, but this one seems to be generally used. The "paint" may well have been a vegetable or mineral dye, applied for official occasions. Sometimes there is depiction of tattooing—or linear painting—on the chin or throat of por-trait heads or figures (cat. no. 74).

The Moche portraits are the most specific ever made in the pre-Hispanic Americas, where portraiture is very rare. We can, so far, only guess who these men were, but they were important enough to have multiple portraits made in the un-usual stirrup-spout vessel which was the typical form of Moche portraiture. As far as one knows, most portrait heads and finely made and decorated vessels were found in burials; possibly they were made strictly for burial, although they may have had some special use prior to burial.   EPB

66
PORTRAIT OF AN OLDER MAN
Moche IV, A.D. 450–550
Ceramic
28 cm x 19 cm (11 x 7½ in.)
052-004-003

One can sometimes find Moche portraits of the same man at various ages. This bottle portrays an older man wearing a headdress painted with a fish monster, which probably derived from a shark (cat. no. 85). The fish monster, who often holds a sacrificial knife in its human hand, is a common motif of Moche art, but it is rarely seen on a headdress. This man may have had a successful sea-going past; he may have earned the right to wear this motif by having battled the fish monster successfully, possibly in shamanic initiation. Headdresses do not appear to be straightforward emblems of family or clan. The same man may wear headdresses of various shapes, and the use of motifs does not seem to fall into any consistent pattern. The designs seem to symbolize attributes or activities rather than lineage or office. Designs most often painted on portrait headdresses are the step motif or a snake or a geometrized snake or ray. Birds are the most common motif in relief.

Moche portrait headdresses usually have a basic cotton cloth body with a valance that descends in back and around the sides. Hair is normally hidden. Cloth elements are tied over the basic garment in various ways. Often there are ties under the chin, and there is usually a design on the cloth over the brow. EPB

67

PORTRAIT HEAD
Moche IV, A.D. 450–550
Ceramic
29 cm x 17.6 cm (11½ x 7 in.)
084-004-005

68

FULL-FIGURE PORTRAIT
Moche IV, A.D. 450–550
Ceramic
23.5 cm x 17.7 cm (9¼ x 7 in.)
035-003-007

Moche portrait-head vessels are common. Full-figure portraits are rarer; those that exist are usually seated cross-legged in the hands-on-the-knees pose seen in less-individualized depictions of prominent people, or they are holding a bag or a flute or some other ritual object.

The same man, with swollen lids, puffy face, and a half-smile, is portrayed twice here, and in a number of other portrait-head vessels. Rafael Larco Hoyle (1939: Fig. 135) noted that portrayals of this personage were repeatedly found in the Santa Valley, where the man was probably a high-ranking leader. He has the scar of a cut on the right side of his lower lip, which also appears on other depictions of him. Scars, on different parts of the face, are among the traits used to identify subjects of other portraits also. An interesting question for Moche scholars is whether these are scars from battle wounds or scars from ritual activities.

Many Moche headdresses have a strap under the chin, but this cloth headdress that fits the face closely, wrapping under the chin, is unusual. It is as if the tight cloth were containing his over-full face or giving him some comforting support. This man wears the same basic headdress in each portrait, but the designs on the undercloth of these two examples are different, although both derive from the head of a snake or a ray, a motif that appears on some—but not all—of his depic-

tions, as well as on some other individuals. A number of portrait heads might be made in the same mold but usually had different decoration painted on the surface. On the full-length portrait (cat. no. 68), the headdress design is repeated on the cuffs and the squarish badgelike design near the neckline. This design is not a separate badge, but probably a supplemental-wool-weft weaving on the cotton plain weave of the garment; its meaning

is obscure, but its shape resembles banners found in burials at Sipán or banners and bags carried in fineline ceramics (Alva and Donnan 1993: 60–67; Kutscher 1983: Abbn. 114, 115). This figure wears a tie at the waist and a long skirt or overgarment. The combination of the light top and the dark bottom is uncommon. Dark circles are placed in a row, like a bracelet, on each forearm. EPB

130

69
PORTRAIT HEAD WITH DISFIGURED FACE
Moche IV, A.D. 450–550
Ceramic
28.3 cm x 18.8 cm (11⅛ x 7⅜ in.)
XXC-000-201

This portrait vessel was published by Rafael Larco Hoyle (1939: Fig. 214) as representing a man who had been mutilated in castigation. Some faces, indeed, appear to have been cut and deformed, but the disfigurement here—with the skin drawn taut over the bones—is more likely the result of a tropical disease such as leishmaniasis or verruga, diseases with similar symptoms; both produce faces that look almost mummified. The headdress here is of a type worn by important men, but the monkey ornament is unusual. It is possible that the monkey and the disease that this man suffers are endemic to the same region.

A portrait of another man with a similarly disfigured face wears elaborate circular ear ornaments and a distinctive headdress with two backward-looking, long-beaked birds (Wasserman-San Blas 1938: Pl. 162). Other portraits show the same accessories and the same facial proportions, with skin rather tightly stretched over the cheekbones and nose but not yet noticeably diseased; this is apparently the same man portrayed before the full effect of the disease can be seen (Ubbelohde-Doering 1952: Pl. 213). This series of portraits depicts an obviously prominent person, who retained status even with disfigurement, as the one in cat. no. 69 presumably did also. Special status and sacredness may have been accorded to those who suffered these diseases and other physical handicaps. EPB

70
MAN SEATED ON PLATFORM
Moche IV, A.D. 450–550
Ceramic
22 cm x 21 cm (8¾ x 8¼ in.)
XXC-000-190

71
SEATED MAN
Moche III, A.D. 200–450
Ceramic
16.4 cm x 13.5 cm (6½ x 5¼ in.)
XXC-000-149

Both vessels depict an elaborately dressed man seated cross-legged with hands on knees, a common pose for prominent Moche men. The garments are slightly different, but each has a broad collar or pectoral, and both wear a headdress with a feather ornament in the shape of a fan at the back and two ornamented disks at the brow (Benson 1982). Both men have bracelets, which would have been made of copper or gold. There are short appendages and incising on the back of the headdress of cat. no. 71. The man in cat. no. 70 has elaborate ties depending from his

headdress strap, with a drawing of a long-beaked bird on the back of the headdress fan. A long streamer from the headdress ends in a fringe that rests on the platform at either side. He also has the knife (called *tumi* by the later Incas) that appears in the head-dresses of many important Moche people. This probably refers to sacrifice and, hence, to warfare; it is often worn by men in warrior garments, although it was not a weapon of war. Both of these men wear the short garments of warriors. The ear ornaments of the two figures are different. Circular ornaments, attached to a tube that went through the ear lobe, were nonspecific, non-status ornaments (cat. no. 70). Plain tubular ear ornaments, without the round frontal, were also fairly generally worn (cat. no. 71). The holes in all these ornaments were probably inlaid with

turquoise; the eyes were likely also inlaid. Earlier Moche bottles often had inlay (cat. no. 34).

In cat. no. 70, the man sits on a platform or throne. Only important people sat on platforms. Cat. no. 71 may have been placed on some sort of stand. These men seem to be rulers or chieftains seated in official posture. The pose and dress endured through a considerable length of time. Cat. no. 71 is earlier than cat. no. 70, and so the two vessels cannot depict the same man, although these men may have ruled the same territory. These were probably portraits. Full-figure portraits are usually less individualized than the portrait-head bottles, for attention is focused on the accessories that exhibit official status rather than on the person. EPB

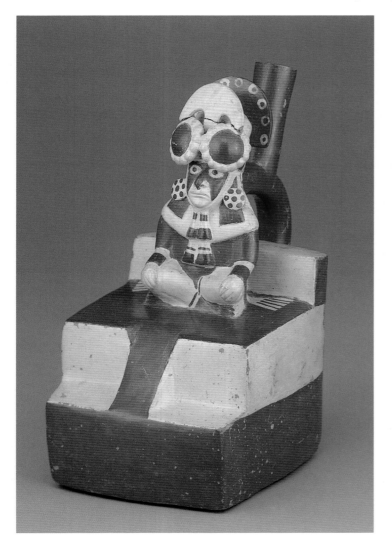

72
RULER WITH FELINE
Moche IV, A.D. 450–550
Ceramic
20 cm x 10.5 cm (7⅞ x 4⅛ in.)
032-005-003

The box form of this vessel serves as a throne or platform for a man in a turbanlike headdress with what is probably a feather cluster at the back and a chin strap that has two pendants with widening dark elements below. He also wears round ear ornaments and a necklace or collar. Like many prominent Moche people, he has face paint, which, in this case, forms a kind of moustache and goatee. In front of him is an object, probably a bag for ritual materials.

The right hand of this man rests on the head of a small feline with a long tail draped over the side of the supporting box. (This was certainly a power object.) There are stripes on the feline's legs and peanut- or beanpod-shaped markings on the body which are typical Moche renderings of feline pelage. In nature, the pelage markings of the margay are closest to these, but this animal may be intended to represent an ocelot or even a jaguar cub that had been brought from the tropical forests on the other side of the Andes. EPB

73
MAN WITH MISSING FOOT
Moche IV, A.D. 450–550
Ceramic
26.3 x 21 cm (10½ x 8½ in.)
069-004-005

This remarkable figure holds a thick stick diagonally in both hands. It is presumably algarrobo (*Prosopis chilensis*), one of the few trees that grow in parts of the desert, and so was generally used as a source of wood (Larco Hoyle 1938: Fig. 41; Shimada 1994: 49). His right foot is shown; his left foot is missing, replaced by a prosthetic device. In a tomb found by Walter Alva at Sipán, a woman and a man, buried near the ruler, lacked left feet; a young man, interred near the entrance to the tomb, had both feet missing (Alva and Donnan 1993: 51, 122, 123, 143). There are other depictions of men with a single foot and a prosthetic device; they are dressed usually in fairly high-status garments (Arsenault 1993). Some are surrounded by objects that probably indicate funerary offerings or possibly feast preparations or elements of a shamanic table. They appear also in "dance-of-death" scenes, accompanying a deceased lord. Daniel Arsenault (1993) has called such figures "stewards"; one might think of them as priests with stewardly duties who accompany a lord to the other world. The figures in cat. nos. 25, 26 may represent such a person.

This man wears a tied headdress (similar to but less elaborate than those on portrait-head vessels; hair shows at top and sides), tubular ear ornaments on prominent ears, and a white tunic with lines or fringe at the bottom and a badgelike woven design on the chest. His face is a distinctive portrait of an older man, as are some of the other one-footed depictions. A lizard is incised from the outer corner of each eye, and an arching animal over the upper lip at either side; facial marking is found also on other examples of this kind of figure. EPB

PRIEST/SHAMAN WITH RITUAL OBJECTS
Moche III, A.D. 200–450
Ceramic
23.7 cm x 21.8 cm (9¼ x 8½ in.)
108-005-001

This man has a distinctive face—strong features with thick lips and perhaps blind eyes. Rather crude incising on the chin, a repeated sideways chevron motif, may represent tattooing. The sideways chevron, a motif of unknown meaning, appears also on the spout of a seabird vessel (cat. no. 49). Bodies with tattooing have been found in archaeological excavations (Donnan 1978: 28). This man wears a cloth headdress with a diagonal fold line, a strap that fits tightly under the chin, and two little knots on top like clasps. His plain dark upper garment has long sleeves; a light garment is seen below. He sits as a deck figure on a dark circle, looking slightly upward, his hands folded right over left. Below him, on one side, is a drawing of a stirrup-spout bottle with swirl motif and, on the other side, a *florero* with a widely flaring bowl and a small base; S's and waves decorate it, suggesting a message having to do with the sea and perhaps the other world. Pottery depictions can be used as symbolic language on ceramics. Here, the vessels seem to refer to food preparation—perhaps for a feast, more likely for a funerary offering—because two containers are centered between them, probably gourds tied together loosely (cat. no. 60). Dots between the gourds might indicate either contents (beans, for example) or something that is hot, effervescent, or perhaps full of some supernatural spirit. Above these are what look like two spits with food on them.

This is one of a number of stirrup-spout bottles on which well-dressed, priestly deck figures sit atop a painted scene with ceramics and other evidence of food preparation (Benson 1975: Figs. 27, 28). Like some of the other examples, he may be missing a foot. EPB

75

CURER WITH PATIENT
Moche IV, A.D. 450–550
Ceramic
23 cm x 20.2 cm (9 x 8 in.)
069-004-005

76

MAN WITH LIME GOURD
Moche III, A.D. 200–450
Ceramic with inlay
17.5 cm x 14.7 cm (7 x 5 in.)
XSC-007-004

This curer is a seated man, wearing a tied-cloth headdress with the side-flap extensions seen on some portrait-vessel headdresses; he has tubular ear ornaments, a necklace, a stepped tunic, and a belt. The patient may be a woman, although the hair does not appear to be braided, as women's hair usually was. The curer's left hand is on the patient's stomach, his right hand on the chest. The patient wears something like a hospital gown along the outside of the body and over a raised knee. There are more obvious depictions of female patients, and some curers were women. Anthropomorphic owls are also portrayed as curers.

On this curer's right is a gourd. On his left is a rectangular box with six small round objects in it. These may be stones, which still have various uses on shaman's tables on the North Coast (Joralemon and Sharer 1993). They may even be stones from the stomachs of sea lions (cat. nos. 45, 46). This man has a coca bag on a cord around his neck, as participants in the coca rite do (cat. no. 76). Leaves of the coca plant were undoubtedly used medicinally in the past, as they are today. Other depictions of curers also sometimes have coca bags. EPB

Coca leaves, of the plant from which cocaine is made, have long been sacred in the Andes. The chewing of the leaves has been a significant ritual, one that was particularly important to the Moche. This handsome early Moche pot has numerous associations with the rite. A man, seated with feet together, holds in a very lifelike way a gourd, which contained powdered lime, probably made from shell, and the stick that was used to place a bit of lime in his mouth with a few coca leaves, which were carried in a woven bag at his back. This bag was suspended around the neck by a cord. Many effigies are shown wearing the coca bag, but depictions of figures holding a gourd are relatively rare.

The eyes and the designs on the face of this figure are inlaid with turquoise or chrysacolla. The Maltese cross and circles represent the face paint frequently seen

on those engaged in the coca rite. The hairlike cap or caplike hair appears on many early depictions of coca-chewers; on later bottles, it is seen only on men wearing a coca bag around the neck and holding a tunic (cat. no. 77). The ears are pierced in three places to receive pendant-disk ear ornaments (cat. nos. 96, 97); the hole on the lobe is larger than the upper ones. Miniature metal ear ornaments, probably of copper, would likely have been placed in these holes. The layered garments have borders of step and bird motifs. The basic garment is sleeved. The Moche may have invented the sleeved tunic.

The outer, scarflike garment is tied on the right shoulder of the figure. The tying of garments is obviously significant in Moche art: garments were indicative of status and ritual, and the way they were worn encoded a symbolic language. EPB

77
MAN WITH TUNIC
Moche IV, A.D. 450–550
Ceramic
26 cm x 16.5 cm (10¼ x 6½ in.)
XST-004-001

A man who is either capped or bare-
headed (it is difficult to tell which) holds
a tunic in front of him. If it is dark hair, it
may be shaved on top; other vessels
showing this subject suggest this possibility (Lavalle 1989: Pls. 159, 160). The
man has the Maltese-cross-and-circle face
paint seen on participants in the coca-
chewing rite (cat. nos. 76, 79). A coca
bag, suspended on a cord around his
neck, hangs down his back at his left
shoulder. Many examples of these figures
holding a tunic seem to illustrate a moment in the coca rite. Often the upheld
tunic bears designs worn by participants
in the ritual. Most designs appear to represent woven patterns; this one looks as if
a pectoral or collar, perhaps of metal,
with flower- or star-shaped pendants suspended from the jagged edge, were hanging over a fairly plain tunic. Circles and
angular S's decorate its border.

Cloth was of great value in the
Andes. Offerings of cloth were made, and
later Inca rulers gave gifts of tunics and
other fine woven garments. Garments
were significant for the wearer in life, and
they were placed in graves at death. They
denoted status, occupation, and ritual
association. This is one of many pieces
that show the role of a woven garment in
the context of Moche ritual, although it
is not clear what that role was. The garment must have been held up for some
sort of display before being donned for
the rite or perhaps offered along with the
coca. EPB

78
MAN WITH FELINE
Moche IV, A.D. 450–550
Ceramic
23.8 cm x 14.5 cm (9¼ x 5¾ in.)
071-002-003

A nude man, blind in one eye, wearing neither headdress nor ear ornaments, and seated with a feline standing at his right shoulder, is a composition that is fairly common in Moche art (Benson 1974). The man is usually grimacing, and his hands are clasped in front of him in a gesture of respect or pleading. Both man and jaguar look as if they were facing a higher being or were engaged in a ritual scene. Some modeled examples, including this one, have the Maltese-cross face paint seen on participants in the coca-chewing rite (cat. nos. 76, 77). This man may have been captured in a battle—real or ritual or both—enacted at some stage of the coca rite. He may have been either beheaded or fed to the jaguar shortly after this moment. A man and a jaguar, in a somewhat similar arrangement, also appear in fineline depictions of the Presentation Theme (Donnan 1978: Fig. 240), but there the human figure is tied with rope and lacks face paint, and the feline holds a sacrificial knife. That scene is part of a different ritual, involving captive sacrifice and ritual presentation of the victim's blood.

In Moche thought, the jaguar was surely both attacker and protector, and, in depictions like this, it is not easy to tell which role it is playing. Jaguars usually attack the neck or head of the victim, and this one is in position for attack. On the other hand, the jaguar, looking out over the man's shoulder and holding him with both paws, seems to claim and protect the man. It is possible to entertain both views. This scene may depict part of a shamanic initiation, given a widespread belief that surviving an encounter with a jaguar qualifies the survivor as a shaman.

The man's outstanding ears indicate that he had been an important person who had worn large ear ornaments that declared his high status—and extended his ears with their size and weight. EPB

79
FINELINE COCA RITE
Moche IV, A.D. 450–550
Ceramic
27.3 cm x 15.5 cm (10¾ x 6 in.)
084-004-005

This vessel design is divided into two scenes. On one side, an arching double-headed serpent, probably representing the Milky Way (the dark spots likely indicate a night scene), forms a cavelike enclosure over two men. Each holds a lime gourd in one hand and the stick to remove the lime in the other. Between them is a weapons bundle, consisting of a round shield and two clubs. Both men wear pendant-disk ear ornaments. The man at the left has a fairly simple headdress, with two upward projections in front, and a longish white garment with lines at the bottom and three rectangular panels at the top (such panels are associated with coca-cult garments). The figure at the right has two *ulluchu* fruits at the front of his headdress; his garment has a large snake-head as a pectoral. Both head-dresses have long, dark hangings at the back. The shapes below this scene suggest mountains or rough terrain as a setting.

On the other side of the vessel, a standing figure with a god's mouth, *ulluchu* headdress with fan, and pendant-disk ear ornament, stands alone in the night, his hands together in a Moche gesture that seems to denote respect or reverence. A bag, probably for coca leaves, hangs from his arm; it is larger than the bags worn by the humans, but it may be that this is a god carrying coca leaves for all the Moche people. At his back, a plate-metal object depicting a stylized bat or jaguar is attached by a cord to his neck. This may be an object similar to the metal-platelet banners found at Sipán by Walter Alva (Alva and Donnan 1993: 60–67). The god wears a loincloth and a shirt of metal platelets. In front of him is another weapons bundle and, be-yond that, another metal animal, two lime gourds, a jaguar headdress resting on a rectangular bundle, and three round bundles, possibly containing coca leaves. Below all these objects are outlines of plants, probably cacti. It is not clear whether this is a coca god or whether it is the major Moche god with coca-associated accessories. If the latter is true, the jaguar headdress may be his regular head-dress, which has been set aside for the occasion; it perhaps confers some special attribute to the bundle under it.

The coca rite was associated with battle. It is not clear whether the warriors engaged in the ritual before battle, whether a mock battle was part of the rite, or whether this was a post-battle celebration and offering of a sacrificed captive. The weapons bundles suggest that this might have been a pre-battle ritual, in which the coca was offered to the weapons to give them life or strength.

A bottle with a related scene in the Linden-Museum, Stuttgart, shows the double-headed serpent above the god figure, and three coca-chewers in the open night sky (Kutscher 1983: Abb. 125). Details of dress and accoutrements are different, but the bottles may form a pair. EPB

FINELINE RUNNERS WITH FOX FIGURE
Moche IV, A.D. 450–550
Ceramic
25.3 cm x 17.2 cm (10 x 6¾ in.)
006-004-003

Runners carrying bags is a common Moche theme. On some pots, the runners are human; on others, they are anthropomorphs with human bodies and animal heads and attributes. Clothing normally comprises a loincloth and belt and a headdress with a round or blade-shaped upward projection. The figures have been nicknamed "bean runners," because beans sometimes float in the air around the runners, but other vegetation also appears in the scenes. The bags may have contained beans and other seeds, perhaps for a planting rite, perhaps for divination; there might have been other shamanic equipment as well. Rafael Larco Hoyle (1939: 121–123) published photographs of actual bags that had been found containing white powder and a piece of quartz, a shamanic substance. In a burial at the Huaca del Sol at the site of Moche, Christopher Donnan and Carol Mackey found a bag containing quartz crystals, stones, beads, an animal-bone fragment, and plant remains (Donnan and Mackey 1978: 66–68).

On this bottle the runners are a falcon with a circular headdress, a hummingbird with a shovel-shaped headdress, and a bifid-tongued centipede, also with a shovel-shaped headdress. Floating among them are birds, beans, cacti, *Tillandsia* (a species related to the pineapple; both are Bromeliaceae), and *ulluchu*, a fruit that contains an anticoagulent and is related to papaya. The figures run through a landscape indicated by patches of sand. There were probably roads, like Inca roads, but of less extent than the vast Inca network. Later Inca runners carried messages all over the empire. The activity of Moche runners appears to have been more ritualistic, at least the runs that were immortalized in the ceramic depictions.

Seated cross-legged on top of the vessel is an anthropomorphic fox, wearing a loincloth and belt, and tying his runner headdress, which has a monkey face on its circular projection. Foxes appear frequently as runners, and probably most human runners have a fox head on the front of the headdress. (Here, they

are probably monkey heads.) Copper or gilded-copper fox-head headdress ornaments still exist (Alva and Donnan 1993: Fig.199; Benson 1972: 5–31; Shimada 1994: Fig. 2.8). The fox's swift running speed (around 45 mph) may explain, at least in part, the association with this

rite. Foxes play a wide range of prominent roles in Moche art, from full-length anthropomorphic figures dressed in the finery of human chieftains to fox-head ornaments at the ends of litters or reed rafts. The fox head is one of the most common Moche motifs. EPB

81

FINELINE PAINTED BEANS
Moche IV, A.D. 450–550
Ceramic
28.6 cm x 17 cm (11¼ x 6¾ in.)
073-004-005

The beans (*Phaseolus lunatus*) placed in horizontal rows on this bottle all have the same design, a dark top and a dotted lower half. In the presentations on some bottles, bean markings are varied (cat. nos. 82, 83), one of the reasons that led Rafael Larco Hoyle (1939: 85–124) to propose that the patterning was a form of writing. Beans with pecked markings were found in the Santa Valley. One might also wonder if the placement of the beans on this bottle composed a counting device. Larco Hoyle (1943) published a number of other bottles with beans in this kind of linear arrangement but in varying numbers. Whatever their significance, beans were a design element of considerable iconographic importance,

and they were a basic food crop in much of the pre-Hispanic world—as they are in many parts of Latin America today. Some Moche vessels show beans fitted out as warriors with helmeted heads; beans came to life to join and support (and nourish) Moche warriors (Kutscher 1983: Abbn. 203–212).

At the spout juncture of this vessel, a step motif ending in a snake head seems to indicate the importance of the subject, whatever it may be. Some spouts are undecorated or only minimally so; some have subject matter that is directly related to the iconography of the body of the vessel; some, like this one, seem to comment on or add to the iconography. EPB

82

FINELINE SCENE, GODS WITH BEANS AND STICKS
Moche IV/V, A.D. 450–800
Ceramic
26.7 cm x 17.7 cm (10½ x 6¾ in.)
066-004-007

83

FINELINE SCENE, GODS WITH BEANS AND STICKS
Moche IV, A.D. 450–550
Ceramic
28.8 cm x 15.3 cm (110¼ x 6 in.)
XXC-000-123

These two vessels show a rare theme, which is rooted in mythology and may be related to divination or astronomical calculation. The more complex design, cat. no. 83, is presented in three tiers. Two godly figures sit at the top, one on either side, with desert sand between them. Each holds a bundle of sticks. Their headdresses almost meet, so that the fruit depicted at the top of the pot is above both heads. On one side is a richly dressed figure: he wears a large, semicircular headdress with two rosettelike ornaments and a chin strap; round ear ornaments; a collar or pectoral, probably

81

83

beaded (cat. no. 143); and a tunic with sleeves with a step motif. His fanged mouth ends in an arrow shape. Facing him is a bird-headed anthropomorph wearing a two-pronged headdress with owl-head ornament and a short tunic and scarves of metal platelets. These figures are known from other mythic, ritual, and astronomical contexts, notably the Presentation Theme and related scenes (cat. no. 107; Donnan 1978: 158–173; Benson 1982, 1984). Here, each figure holds a bundle of sticks; the bird points to one of the variegated beans that rest between them, and the larger figure balances a bean in his right hand.

On the middle tier is a litter surrounded by curving radiances, with carrying poles that end in snake heads; this must belong to the larger figure above, for a litter awaits him in other scenes, and one scene shows him riding in it (Hocquenghem 1987: Fig. 176). Next to

82

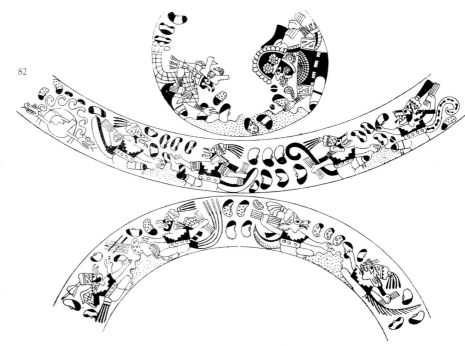

82

82

84

FLORERO WITH PAINTED SCENE
Moche IV, A.D. 450–550
Ceramic
26.5 cm x 45 cm (10½ x 17¾ in.)
XXC-000-210

the litter on this bottle, a seated anthropomorphic fox faces his twin. Both are dressed in cloth headdresses with feathers and step-motif shirts or tunics with decorated sleeves. Next are two other animals, both with fox faces; one has a monkey tail and one a jaguar tail. On the lowest tier are two other pairs: perhaps a falcon and a macaw, and two mammals, a deer with its tongue out and an animal with whiskers and a long, bushy tail, perhaps a tayra (*Eira barbara*), a relative of the weasel. The last three pairs wear a costume like that of the foxes, but it lacks sleeves.

The gods at the top surely have astronomical identities. The prominent figure has likely ridden the litter to the sky. The flying bird needs no litter. All the figures may represent sky beings.

Each figure holds a bundle of sticks. Variously marked large beans, usually grouped, float between the paired figures, who often seem to be juggling them. It looks like a game, but serious matters are surely implied. Rafael Larco Hoyle (1939: 85–124; 1943) and others, following him, have argued that beans had a form of writing incised on them. The designs on the beans in a single context are often different. Divination may be under way here. The numbers of beans may relate to crop prediction or to astronomical calculation. The motif on the spout, a common way of depicting feline pelage, also resembles a bean pod and may have that meaning here.

Anne Maria Hocquenghem (1987:144–147) suggests that this is a summer-solstice ritual related to agriculture fertility. The fruit that appears at the top of the vessel and in front of the major figure is the *ulluchu*. Henry Wassén (1986) has observed that, because *ulluchu* contains an anticoagulant, its depiction signifies sacrifice.

A similar scene is painted on both sides of cat. no. 82: two different gods sit facing each other. The figure on the right has accoutrements of the major Moche god: stepped shirt, belt with two snake extensions, snake-head ear ornaments, and an elaborate, almost-full-bodied jaguar headdress with a fan. He has the wrinkled face that this god often has and a round nose ornament with a beaded bor

der. The facing figure has the same shirt and ear ornaments but only one snake extension at his belt, with different markings. His head is bare, and his long hair flows down his back. Moche gods are rarely bare-headed, for bare-headedness is usually a sign of defeat. Long hair is also unusual; it is seen on face-down figures presumably falling from mountain peaks or wave crests but rarely in other circumstances (Hocquenghem 1987: Figs. 182–186, 189).

On both sides of the pot, a few beans rest on the sand between the figures, and the long-haired figure points a bean in his left hand toward the other god. In his right hand, he holds a bunch of sticks; the linear drawing of sticks and hair is similar. The more elaborate god opposite him holds a bean in his raised right hand in both scenes. On one side, the bean is bracketed by two X's, formed by sticks; one X floats or falls between the chin and left hand of the bare-headed figure. On the other side, two X's have fallen toward the outstretched arm of the bare-headed figure, so that there are three X's in front of him and none before the god with the headdress. There has been a transference, but the meaning is not obvious. Both gods have white hands on one side of the bottle, black hands on the other. Black hands are a late Moche trait of unknown meaning. The more prominent figure here gestures with his left hand: on the white-hand side, the hand is lifted and facing out; on the black-hand side, it is probably turned up, and he is pointing. There seems to be a time sequence from one side to the other, in which X sticks are dropped, and hands change color and gesture.

The bare-headed figure might be a human captive sacralized by the ritual and/or the presence of the god; it might be the god himself in another manifestation, or his twin in some mythic tale of defeat. It is unlikely to be an unrelated deity, for he has no other traits. Whoever they are, these are not the deities on the other bottle. EPB

The *florero*, or flaring bowl, is a less common shape for elaborately painted pottery than the stirrup-spout bottle, but significant scenes are sometimes presented on its broad rim.

This *florero* presents a series of mythic encounters concerning the major Moche god, who is probably a culture hero as well as a deity with mountain, sky, and sun assocations. Of the five scenes, four show the major god engaged with a mythic creature. The fifth portrays three musicians who form a group: two playing panpipes, with a drummer between/behind them. All lack headdresses but have long, dark, flowing hair. Not ordinary musicians, they all have the snake-belt appendage and the snake-head ear ornaments that are attributes of the major god. All have the god's arrow-shaped mouth, which is drawn most clearly on the larger piper. These attributes might imply that the god could be a musician and three beings at once or that musicians could have godly traits; these pipers are likely to be supernatural musicians in a mythic context, not deities but sacred beings.

The four additional scenes may simply show various exploits of the god, but they appear to be sequential. Luis Jaime Castillo (1989: 175) has argued, in a book on the iconography of this vessel, that the order of the scenes does not read around the rim but back and forth across it. This is quite possible. In this description, however, they are presented in sequential order.

To the viewer's right of the musicians, the god confronts a fish monster (cat. no. 85). The god, presumably the culture hero of the Moche people, with sky and solar attributes, holds a knife in his raised right hand; the fish has a knife in his raised left hand. Both knives are tied to ropes that end in snake heads. The movements of the antagonists mirror each other. The god's left hand is raised before the fish's face; the fish's right arm is extended. The fish tilts slightly back as the god advances; the god appears to be winning. (On other vessels, the god is beheading the monster.) The god wears a shirt with step motif; the fish monster has a striped shirt. The god has a wrinkled, half-black face; round ear ornaments; snake belt extensions; and the semicircular headdress with two extensions usually worn by the supernatural owl warrior.

In the next scene, the god, in the same garments, is held between two anthropomorphic vultures dressed as women in capes and sashed tunics. On the viewer's left is a condor or turkey vulture in a striped tunic. The bird on the right, in a white tunic, is probably a black vulture. The left bird seems to be holding the god's right arm with her right hand, as if she were taking his pulse. The bird's left fist is between the god's shoulder and his tilted-back headdress, from which one projection is falling. She may be pulling the god's head back or supporting him. The right bird holds in her left hand what is probably a bag. Her right fist is at the god's other shoulder, near the snake-head ear ornament, which seems to dart a forked tongue at the bird. In sacrifice scenes, women and vultures assist those about to be sacrificed. The sun dies in the sea every evening off the coast of Peru. In much indigenous belief, the sun goes to the underworld at night. This god may be dying in the underworld sea, escorted by vultures, who clean the bones of the dead.

A black-and-white dog, standing directly behind the god and facing away from him, makes the transition to the next scene. Dogs are widely believed to escort the dead across a body of water to the underworld. In this scene, the god wears his customary jaguar headdress with fan; the pattern of his stepped shirt shows light above and dark below, rather than the reverse, as in the previous encounters. His raised right hand holds a knife (its cord is likely eroded). His left hand reaches toward the bag clutched at the chest of the round creature facing him. This being, long puzzling to iconographers, was identified by Steve Bourget as a fish (Bourget 1994a: 441–442). It is probably a porcupine fish (*Diodon hystrix*), which can inflate itself to a round body. All over its body are sharp spines that contain venom. Here, this anthropomorphized fish wears a plain semicircular headdress with one extension (the other eroded?). He has a god's mouth, a round ear ornament, and black hands. Holding the bag in his right hand, he grasps a knife with snake-head rope in his left.

If this sequence of scenes describes a voyage through the sea, the two kinds of fish may be encountered at different depths

85
FINELINE FISH MONSTER
Moche V, A.D. 550–800
Ceramic
31 cm x 15.7 cm (15½ x 10½ in.)
XXC-013-006

or may have a different latitude range. The location of the fish may be a telling part of the narrative.

In the last scene, in this order of reading, the major god, dressed in the same fashion, faces a figure with projections like radiances emanating from his body. He wears the metal-platelet shirt and headdress with flared projections that are associated with the owl-warrior deity (Kutscher 1983: Abbn. 190, 191, 267). The headdress is essentially the one the major god started out in. The major god again holds a knife in his right hand and, in his left, a light-colored bag, which he likely acquired from the round fish. The opposing figure holds in his left hand a knife on a cord that ends in a very large snake head. In his right hand, he holds a dark bag.

Bags like these appear in other ceramic scenes, and actual bags published by Rafael Larco Hoyle (1939: Fig. 187) are of very similar form. They are usually held not by supernatural beings but by priests in rites apparently related to sacrifice (cat. no. 98). They probably contained shamanic material. Gods were shamans. Here, supernaturals have shaman's bags, which may hold "day" and "night" or the power to create them.

The major god, having gone through a sequence of events, now faces a being with a dark bag and garments associated with an owl; the radiances may be those of a celestial body visible at night. The major god has also arrived back at the musicians. Constance Classen (1993: 18–19) and others have noted that, in Inca times, music/noise, being liminal, marked a transition from day to night, night to day. Musical instruments are usually depicted with seemingly dead figures and with probable funerary rites that may induce new life.

Many Moche scenes must have astronomical significance. The figure with platelet armor appears in the Presentation Theme (cat. no. 107) and scenes related to it; sometimes he has radiances. Other scenes also suggest sky connotations. Does this vessel present iconography of a day-and-night cycle? Is it a specific astronomical event? There are many unanswered questions about this remarkable piece. EPB

A fish with a human arm and leg was a common Moche motif. The design seen once on either side of this bottle has a particularly well-developed human arm and leg, with a small bracket motif repeated on the limbs and the fish body. There is a large fanlike tail and a big fin. Pointed, tapering projections emerge from the body and the head. Usually the fish holds a sacrificial knife, as this one does. Sometimes the fish also holds a decapitated human head, but in this example, shells, fish, and perhaps sea anemones surround it. Various bits of sea life float between the two bodies, which virtually meet at the top. On the stirrup are snakes and circles that look as if they might be bubbles from underwater.

The fish monster has been variously identified as a bonito (Donnan 1978: 38) and as a fish whose toxin can be used as a hallucinogen (Bourget 1994a: 426–432);

it might be a shark or some other fish with symbolic behavior or attributes. The various depictions of the demon do not always seem to derive from the same fish. The fish monster may have personified the sea and its dangers for Moche fishermen going out in reed rafts. It may simply have represented the dangers of the fish, its teeth and toxin. It is also possible that the monster depicts the conquered god of another group. It is sometimes shown being caught or decapitated by the major Moche god, who may thus be demonstrating the power of the Moche people or acting as the Moche culture hero winning out over danger. Cat. no. 84 suggests that the encounter with the fish monster occurs among other encounters on the major god's passage through the sea; but, because the scene was often shown in isolation, it must have been a particularly important one. EPB

86

FINELINE FALCON WARRIOR
Moche IV, A.D. 450–550
Ceramic
30 cm x 16 cm (11¾ x 6¼ in.)
083-003-008

87

BAT SACRIFICER
Moche IV, A.D. 450–550
Ceramic
22.8 cm x 21 cm (9 x 8¼ in.)
078-005-003

Warriors, like runners, are often portrayed with human bodies and animal or bird heads and attributes. Beyond the real world, there was an equivalent other world, in which the traits of special creatures were taken on to give extra power—the power of the falcon as a swift predator who can fly and attack, for example. Human-falcon warriors are also depicted running through desert sands, and runners also can be half-falcon. This creature—with falcon head, crest, feathered breast, wings, and tail, and one hand that is a cross between a hand and a claw—has a warrior's kilt and human legs and holds a weapons bundle as he flies over an undulating landscape.

The dark and light markings around the eye are reversed, but this could be the aplomado falcon (*Falco femoralis*) or the American kestrel or sparrow hawk (*F. sparverius*). It is also conceivable that it is an osprey (*Pandion haliaetus*), an adept predator that nests near water; although found over most of the world, it is rarer in the Southern Hemisphere. A prominent theme on Moche ceramics, these raptor-warrior creatures appear also on elaborate ear ornaments of gold, stone, and shell (cat. no. 148). EPB

The bat was a potent symbol in Moche art, as it was in many other pre-Hispanic cultures (Benson 1987). Bats that feed on fruit and nectar are important plant pollinators and seed distributors. The Moche may have had an inkling of this, for they sometimes depicted bats with fruit or vegetables. Bats that insert their heads into flowers to feed have sacrificial connotations, and vampire bats are even more strongly suggestive of sacrifice. The common vampire bat (*Desmodus rotundus*), whose range includes the North Coast, probably fed on human blood more frequently in pre-Hispanic times than it has after the Spanish introduction of horses and other large domesticated animals in the sixteenth century. The vampire bat delicately punctures the skin and, with an anticoagulant in its saliva, keeps the blood flowing. This behavior is appropriate symbolism for warriors and sacrificers with whom the bat is sometimes identified in Moche iconography. Owls, who were more prominent as warriors, also appear as sacrificers.

This humanized bat, standing with mouth open and wings outspread, wears a headdress common on important (usually divine) warriors, with a symbolic knife in the center and a step motif on either side. The headdress, which is tied under the chin, has attached ear ornaments or protectors. The bat wears a round-bead or disk collar or pectoral and a kilt with a border that probably consists of pendant metal disks. In his right hand, the bat holds a war club, and his left hand grasps a small, nude, human captive, whom the bat is undoubtedly presenting for sacrifice. The bat is not holding a knife and about to decapitate a human being, as he is in some depictions, but the implications here are clear. The supernatural nature of the bat is emphasized by his immense size compared to that of the human captive. EPB

88
BAT WARRIOR
Moche IV, A.D. 450–550
Ceramic
23 cm x 20 cm (9 x 8 in.)
078-005-001

89
GOD POLING A FISH/RAFT
Moche III, A.D. 200–450
Ceramic
21.7 cm x 29 cm (8½ x 11½ in.)
075-004-005

In this complex image, an anthropomorphic bat, holding with a large human hand and arm a huge upright war club, dominates the strange composition. The bat wears a semicircular headdress with a jaguar-head ornament and circular ear protectors or ornaments. He has a wing at the back, and, in front, a human leg with a large thigh, wearing a kilt with pendant danglers. Swirl motifs adorn the tunic and the border of the kilt. The bat's other large human hand holds a sacrificial knife near the head of a small, seated human warrior holding a club, who seems to be pressed against the bat.

The fact that the human warrior is holding a club makes it unlikely that he is a captive. Weapons and garments were usually confiscated on capture (cat. no. 87; Kutscher 1983: Abbn. 102, 105, 106). This warrior is dressed; he has a step motif on his belt and, like the bat, a swirl motif on his tunic. He appears to be a Moche warrior, ready for battle, in the embrace of a paradigm of the war-and-sacrifice beliefs of the Moche people. The bat image appears to conflate the ideas of the bat sacrificer and the animated weapons bundle (cat. no. 95). The scene may be part of a pre-battle ritual in which the warrior, possibly under the influence of a drug, puts himself under the aegis and inspiration of the supernatural bat.

Bats, the only mammals that truly fly, are anomalous creatures that play a shamanic role in Moche iconography. Sometimes they are depicted in priestly dress, and they often hold the pottery that is associated with funerary rites (Benson 1987; Kutscher 1983: 157–159). EPB

The Moche used bundles of reeds to make rafts of a kind still made today on the North Coast (Benson 1972: Fig. 4–1). In the complex design of this bottle, a god poles, with a broad, snake-headed paddle, not a raft but a very large fish. In other supernatural Moche sea scenes, a raft made of reeds may have, as a finial, the head of a fish, a snake, or a fox (Kutscher 1983: Abbn. 314–319). The god's headdress, with a projection rising at center front, is worn by fishermen; this projection ends in an animal head. The deity wears a stepped shirt and a loincloth with circles on it; he has snake-belt appendages. This may be a sea deity, but it is likely the major Moche god who has gone to sea. At the side of the cabin, or hold, hang what are probably floats for a fishing net and an object—perhaps a garment—of metal platelets.

The god faces a woman in the stern. She is tied at neck and loins; the lower ties go around the fish's tail. The woman looks skyward, her hair flowing behind her. Another, smaller woman leans against the god's back; he wears her almost like a trophy at the center of his belt. Some Moche bottles show the god attacking a woman who has a child. Others show the god making love to a woman in a house, which seems to be on a shore or an island; two women watch them (Benson 1972: Fig. 6–7; Hocquenghem 1987: Fig. 125). These may all be segments of a story, perhaps a creation myth. EPB

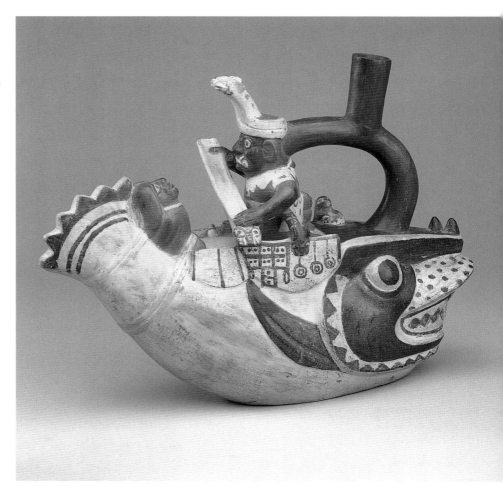

90

HEAD OF A GOD
Moche IV, A.D. 450–550
Ceramic
28.6 cm x 17 cm (11¼ x 6¾ in.)
073-004-005

91

GOD WITH ARTHROPOD LEGS
Moche IV, A.D. 450–550
Ceramic
20.5 cm x 23 cm (8 x 9 in.)
074-004-004

This deity depiction is reminiscent of portrayals of a god or gods in the older Cupisnique/Chavín culture (1200–200 B.C.). Moche potters, who sometimes imitated or adapted the earlier pottery designs, have merged some Cupisnique/Chavín elements with Moche ones in this piece. The ears or ear ornaments, comprising one swirl above another, the oddly fanged mouth, and the dilated eye are motifs seen on tenoned heads at the site of Chavín de Huántar, as well as on Cupisnique pottery from the coast (Larco Hoyle 1941). But the sea-lion heads that emerge from the brow and cheek—replacing the usual snake head on the ear ornaments—are motifs unknown to the earlier culture.

There are small abstract motifs on nostrils, under the nose, and on the mouth outline, as well as on the brow of the sea lions. Eyebrows drawn in vertical lines, as these are, are rarely seen except on depictions of captives. A connected circle design like a necklace continues around the neck, and dark hair comes down plainly in the back. From the outside corner of each eye, a horizontal line projects, and a slightly longer line goes out from the side of the mouth. The mouth line is crossed by a prominent dark X, a most unusual Moche motif. The X suggests a pre-Hispanic method of mending ceramics, by making one or two holes on each side of a break and tying or sewing them to hold the break together.

What myth might have inspired such a depiction? Was there a story about a god with a mended face? Was there a sea-lion deity, and how might he have related to the Chavín culture? EPB

The deity portrayed here has the attributes of the major Moche god: a wrinkled face, snake-head ear ornaments, a semicircular headdress with an animal head and peanut/bean-pod pelage on the band, a necklace, and a shirt with a step motif. He holds a knife in his right hand and, in his left, a small human head with long hair, which he has presumably just cut from a human body. On his rear half are four arthropod legs and two snake-belt extensions that come from the stirrup spout and curve up at either side; the latter are also attributes of the major god. This may be an example of the god's taking on attributes of a creature in nature in order to accomplish a purpose—in this case, a sacrifice/offering. It is not clear whether he is a crab, a scorpion, a spider, or another such creature, all of which can be found as sacrificers in Moche art.

GOD WITH CRAB GOD
Moche IV, A.D. 450–550
Ceramic
25.7 cm x 24 cm (10 x 9½ in.)
XSC-013-009

This curious traveling-on-the-belly pose has similarities to certain poses in other depictions. An example is an anthropomorphic fox warrior holding a club in both hands, as he appears to inch forward, legs at the side (Lavalle 1989: Pl. 55). Whether this refers to a lack of human feet or a method of sneak attack is not obvious. EPB

Supernatural crabs appear in various roles in Moche art. Here, a crab, standing erect on human legs, has a deity face depicted on its body, as do a number of other Moche supernatural crab portrayals. There are crabs in waters off Japan with markings that resemble a face; a similar species may exist off the coast of Peru, which would have suggested this motif.

The crab appears to be a member of the family Grapsidae. It stands on one side of a rock(?), while the major god stands facing it on the other side, wearing snake-head ear ornaments and a headdress with jaguar head surmounted by a knife. (This head has been restored.) The god's belt extensions may have sea-lion heads instead of the conventional snake heads.

The major god does not appear to be battling or sacrificing a crab demon, as sometimes happens in fineline depictions (Kutscher 1983: Abbn. 259A, 260, 262A, 264–266). Instead, this crab seems to be supporting the god, a theme that appears also on other full-round vessels and may be similar to the depiction of vultures supporting the god in the sea sequence of cat. no. 84. Here, the crab claws reach upward toward the head of the god. The god's right hand rests on a crab claw; his left hand is grasped in the crab's other claw. In many examples, the crab faces the god; here, the crab is belly out.

Supernatural crab portrayals are confusing. A crab with human head is sometimes portrayed with the fish monster on the end of a line (Kutscher 1983: Abbn. 249–252, 255). It is not clear whether this is a crab supernatural or the major god transformed into a crab in order to deal effectively with the fish monster. Sometimes the major god is about to behead a very elegantly accoutered crab (with a face on its body), who seems to be the equal of the god (Kutscher 1983: Abbn. 259A, 265, 266). The crab clearly had an important role of its own. In this instance, it is apparently helping the major god. EPB

93
SKELETAL FIGURE WITH VULTURE
Moche IV, A.D. 450–550
Ceramic
24.6 cm x 15.5 cm (9⅞ x 6⅛ in.)
042-003-004

94
KNEELING WARRIOR
Moche III, A.D. 200–450
Ceramic
22.5 cm x 17.7 cm (8¾ x 7 in.)
XXC-000-197

The Moche usually depicted the dead with a skull and a skeletal ribcage and a live body for the rest. The dead seem not to have been thought of as truly dead, for they dance, play musical instruments, sit on thrones, or fondle women. Here, the ribcage is not skeletal and the face grimaces in pain; the man was probably tied alive to a tree with three ropes across the chest and three across the hips just above the phallus; his hands are tied behind him. Human sacrifice was usually related to agriculture and probably petitions for good crops. This man stands on a vegetable, perhaps a pile of potatoes but more likely lucuma, the fruit of a relatively tall tree (*Lucuma bifera* or *L. obovata*), which has been found archaeologically on the North Coast and is used as a food today. A turkey vulture (*Cathartes aura*) pecks at an eye socket of the man's skull.

Vultures pecking at a human figure are a fairly common theme in Andean art. Significant because they are transformers of death and filth, vultures were sacred at a number of places in Peru and elsewhere. The Andean condor (*Vultur gryphus*), the most splendid vulture and one of the world's most impressive birds, is commonly shown in Moche art, along with turkey and black vultures. Vulture headdresses are worn occasionally by prominent human figures on Moche vessels and regularly by an anthropomorphic iguana who is often seen with the major god. EPB

Kneeling on the right knee may have been a movement in pre-battle ritual for warriors; it is a common pose for effigy figures in warrior's dress. The wrinkled-face man of this stirrup-spout vessel wears a wrapped-cloth headdress with a chin tie. The headdress has a fan-shaped ornament, probably of feathers, at the back. There are round ear ornaments or ear protectors. The two rounded ornaments at the front, likely formed of small bundles of feathers, are associated with certain prominent figures in Moche art (Benson 1982). The warrior has a square shield tied to his left wrist. Both fists are

hollow, and the figure probably held a club of wood or copper, fitted through one or both hands (Uceda, Mujica, and Morales 1996: 10). A blade-shaped rattle, imitating one of copper or gold, is suspended at his side.

Warriors had very special status in Moche society, for warfare was an important ritual activity, which also achieved the practical goals of gaining or defending land. The sacrifices that were thought to nourish and honor the gods or spirits of nature were those of captives in some sort of warfare. A very high percentage of Moche art depicts warriors and military activity. EPB

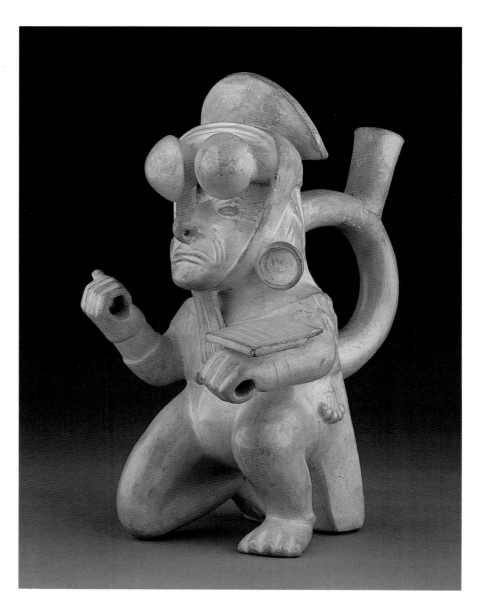

95
FINELINE WEAPONS BUNDLES
Moche IV, A.D. 450–550
Ceramic
27.2 cm x 21.6 cm (10¾ x 8½ in.)
046-003-006

96
CAPTIVE
Moche III, A.D. 200–450
Ceramic
23 cm x 22 cm (9 x 8⅝ in.)
061-004-005

97
HEAD OF A CAPTIVE
Moche IV, A.D. 450–550
Ceramic
42.6 cm x 17.6 cm (16¾ x 11¾ in.)
XSC-017-001

Two humanized weapons bundles are depicted here as warriors: the heads are war-club heads, the bodies are round shields; gracefully running human legs and arms with hands that carry spear-throwers and spears are added. Typical of warrior's gear are the helmet—the end of the club—with a knife element on top and fan ornaments on the broad part of the club, a streamer down the back, and a blade-shaped ornament at the waist. The weapons bundle is a common motif on Moche ceramics, and individual weapons can be pictured anthropomorphized and taking captives (Kutscher 1983: Abbn. 268–271). In murals on the adobe walls at the Huaca de la Luna (Pyramid of the Moon) at the important site of Moche, various elements of warrior's gear are animated and attack warriors in unchar-acteristic dress (Bonavia 1985: 73–85). Murals at Huaca la Mayanga, Lambayeque, published by Duccio Bonavia (1985: 99–104), show a series of

them, each holding a goblet, presumably for sacrificial blood. A *huaca* was a sacred place or object, and what was depicted in these buildings was integral to Moche cosmology and the means of expressing it.

These two figures not only convey liveliness and movement, they express also the concept that weapons could come alive to help the Moche cause. A similar idea is expressed later, in Inca times, when it was said that the stones around Cuzco turned into warriors to defend the city. There is in the Andes a strong sense of animism, of the life in things, a life that was inherent in sacred places and objects and was instilled, through sacralizing ritual, in weapons and other kinds of objects important to Moche survival. The tie painted around the neck and down the front appears on otherwise undecorated jars. It seems to represent a cord like that at the necks of captives (cat. nos. 96, 104). EPB

Although Moche captives were stripped of garments and war paraphernalia, these men still wear the pendant-disk ear orna-ments seen on participants in the coca-chewing rite (cat. no. 79). The use of double ear ornaments is uncommon but exists on other figures; cat. no. 76 has three holes in the ear for attachment of disks. In some instances, separate ele-ments were added, but the ear ornaments and hanging wires on cat. no. 97 are part of the ceramic production. Both of these heads have a hank of hair over the brow. Conquest was signaled by grasping the hair of the defeated. Both of these men were surely due for the sacrifice that was related to the coca-rite. Captives associ-ated with the coca-rite usually have

hands tied behind them. Captives in the Presentation Theme scenes usually have hands tied in front (cat. no. 107).

Cat. no. 97, although probably a generic depiction, has qualities of an individual portrait: low brow, staring eyes, and distinctive lines by the nose. The slight asymmetry of the face adds liveliness.

The man in cat. no. 96 sits with great dignity, despite the rope that goes around his neck and ties his wrists behind him. His moustache and goatee are unusual; Amerindians have relatively little facial hair, and little is depicted in Moche art. The eyebrows here are prominently drawn, a trait seen on other faces but

rarely (cat. no. 90). These unusual characteristics and a skin color that is paler than that of other figures are found on a few other vessels. He may have been a character in legend. EPB

98

Scene with Captive
Moche IV, A.D. 450–550
Ceramic
19.7 cm x 23 cm (7¾ x 9 in.)
061-004-009

A captive with a stout rope around his neck is being led by a group of men who are not in military dress but in the tied-cloth garments worn by priests and sometimes by kingly figures. Often military and religious actions appear to merge; there was a moment when the captive was handed over to the priests or perhaps when the military leader put on priestly dress for the sacrifice that followed conquest. The roped figure here is very likely to be both a prisoner of war and a sacrificial victim, probably a particularly significant one, for he is surrounded by six important men. The two largest and most elaborate of these figures stand one in front of and one behind the captive. The man at the rear bears a human-headed club (cat. no. 95). The rope securing the captive is held in both hands of the man at the front. These three figures are flanked by two men on either side (a pattern perhaps related to the four world directions). The frontal flanking figures hold a tied bag, which appears in other ritual scenes; it probably contains shamanic materials (cat. no. 84). The other flanking figures have both hands on the arms of the captive. The priestly figures all wear essentially the same garments and headdress seen on portrait vessels. The two large figures, which are slightly more elaborately dressed, may have been intended as portraits; their faces have more strength and realism.

The two dark lines around the top of the boxlike base may not be simply decoration but may mark off the space above as sacred or liminal. EPB

99

Fineline Scene with Captives
Moche IV, A.D. 450–550
Ceramic
30.5 cm x 15 cm (12 x 6 in.)
XXC-000-119

Two dark, sandy peaks with a steep chasm between them dominate one side of the vessel. A naked man falls upside-down into the chasm, arms and legs flung out. Three naked men, climbing uphill, are approaching the same fate; the first one is poised to leap into the chasm. A cut-off human arm and leg, both tied with cord, float near them. (Offered body parts often appear in Moche scenes, and extra bones have been found in burial and sacrifice sites.)

Above the falling man, and facing the three climbers, floats a helmeted, anthropomorphic fox with an exaggeratedly long tail and a weapons bundle. He seems to be in charge, directing the sacrifice and epitomizing the spirit of the military triumph that led to it. Just above him, at the top of the vessel, two vultures with skirts and human legs stand in the air, each holding a cloth and two sticks(?).

High on the other side of the bottle is an open-sided house, with one snake above and another at the side. In the house a man sits, wearing the cloth garments seen on full-figure portraits. He holds a goblet toward a man in a short tunic and loincloth, who has a disk or bowl in his hands and wears a cloth headdress with a diagonal line. These two figures seem to refer to the vessel exchange in the Presentation Theme (cat. no. 107); they may be ritually re-enacting that mythic scene.

Four naked men run by them toward the sacrificial hill; the middle two bear a litter in which a fifth man sits. Only the weaving (or twining) of the litter is visible where the lower part of his body would be, but he is bare-headed and apparently also naked. The litter, however, indicates that he is someone of importance. The running figures come down a hill (on one side of the chasm), and run past a simple house in which two figures, surely women, sit with a stirrup-spout vessel in the air between them. A vulture (with female human lower half) guards the door; a tied, cutoff arm floats above it. Two curving lines lead around this house to the hill where the three men climb to their fate.

This composition shows several Moche artistic conventions. The double curving lines are a device to indicate a path and the direction of the movement. Thus, the hill from which men jump into a chasm seems not to be the hill that the litter-bearers descend to run by the houses. But, for economy's sake, and to keep the captive/sacrifice action on one side of the vessel and the ruler/priest presence on the other, the space has been conflated; two separate hills are implied. Steve Bourget (1994b: 93–97), however, believes that this scene depicts a rite held at Cerro Blanco, an isolated hill just behind the Huaca de la Luna, an important ritual structure at Moche, where he has found sacrificial remains (Uceda, Mujica, and Morales 1966: 35–36). If the ceramic scene represents Cerro Blanco sacrifice, then the artistic conventions must be somewhat reinterpreted, but the basic sequence of the scene remains the same. EPB

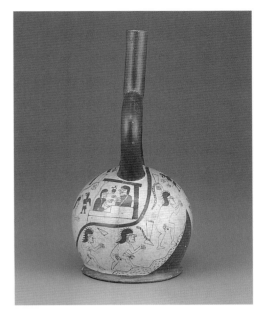

100
CAPTIVE FIGURE
Moche IV, A.D. 450–550
Wood
10.5 cm x 8.5 cm (4¼ x 3¼ in.)
XXC-00M-202

This wooden piece, probably a staff head, is hollowed out vertically; inside, it is circular at the top and square at the bottom. The seated male figure wears headgear that resembles a pillbox hat, small round ear ornaments, and a plain, short garment. His hands are tied in back with what appears to be a two-headed serpent. Cords depicted in Moche art often end in serpent heads, another manifestation of the concept that objects have life, the animation of the live things they resemble.

Moche wooden staffs with elaborately carved heads are known (Lavalle 1989: Pls. 244–246). Quantities of wooden objects, including staffs and staff heads, have been found, preserved in guano, on islands off the coast of Peru, where they must have been placed as offerings in fairly elaborate rites. Many of the objects show captive figures. Those published by George Kubler (1948) and by others are somewhat different in detail from this one, but this piece may well have come from such a source, which has produced the greatest quantities of Moche wooden objects. Wooden staffs are still used in curing and other ceremonies on the North Coast (Donnan 1978: 124–127; Joralemon and Sharon 1993). EPB

101a
SPEAR-THROWER FINIAL
Moche IV, A.D. 450–550
Bone with inlay and pigment
3.8 cm (1½ in.)
XSC-049-017

101b
SPEAR-THROWER FINIAL
Moche IV, A.D. 450–550
Bone with inlay and pigment
6.4 cm x 9 cm (2½ x 3½ in.)
XSC-049-016

A fierce-looking feline head, with nose, snout, ears, and whiskers painted black, forms a finial on this spear-thrower (cat. no. 101a). The eye is inlaid with shell and possibly pyrite. On cat. no. 101b, an entire anthropomorphic feline sits with its elbows on its knees, holding something to its mouth; a feline tail, attached to the human body, curls at its left side. The eyes are inlaid with shell and a black substance; there is red pigment around the tail, mouth, fingers, and ears.

The spear-thrower, the most common weapon among the high cultures of what is now Latin America, was essentially an artificial extension of the arm. Moche spear-throwers usually had a decorated end that must have had some identifying or talismanic function that lent power to it. A feline portrayal would have added a particularly strong symbol to the weapon that was impelling a spear toward the enemy. In a different context, a bird head—probably that of a vulture—forms the spear-thrower finial in a deer-hunting scene (cat. no. 106). Spear-throwers, as powerful symbolic objects probably limited to use by the elite, were sometimes sheathed in gold (cat. no. 147).

Bone—especially that of llamas and deer—was used to make lapidary and practical objects (Shimada 1994:210–213). Llama bones were frequently employed for tools; deer bone was rarer and was probably reserved for objects of ritual significance. EPB

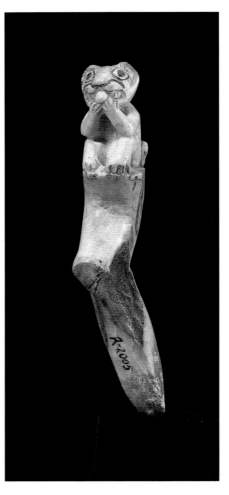

102
SPEAR-THROWER FINIAL
Moche IV, A.D. 450-550
Bone with red and black pigment
5.6 cm x 10.4 cm (2¼ x 4 in.)
XSC-049-014

103
SPATULA-SCEPTER
Moche IV, A.D. 450–550
Bone with inlay
3.8 cm x 3.5 cm (1½ x 1⅜ in.)
XSC-049-022

This remarkably complex design is centered around a bare-headed frontal man with a hank of hair that identifies him as a captive. He stands with knees bent and wears a short, striped tunic. This kind of garment is seen on certain priestly figures, but it is uncommon on captives. The figure is otherwise unclad. Three birds (vultures?) peck at a snake that he holds; the snake is enclosing and biting another figure, which is upside-down and splayed, not unlike the falling figure in the sacrifice scene on cat. no. 99. The snake passes under the falling figure's chin, like a rope. Another serpent head on the other side may also belong to this snake. Two-headed serpents are common in Moche iconography. The principal and largest figure rests its left hand on the head of a small, seated, bare-headed man who also wears a striped garment. A feline with its mouth at the head of the upside-down figure tops the composition.

The iconography of this weapon finial is convoluted and somewhat obscure, but it includes powerful symbols—snakes and felines—as well as the captives who were the spoils of war. Snakes have many kinds of meaning. Since some are fatally toxic and others strong enough to crush their prey, snakes constitute a serious threat. They also have regeneration connotations, because they shed a dry skin and acquire a fresh, new one. Hence, snakes can refer to agriculture, with which Moche battle seems to have been closely connected. This weapon seems designed to aid a warrior by invoking the powerful feline, the multifaceted serpent, and the sacrifice of captives that will be the ritual finale of the battle quest. EPB

Implements like this one come in various materials—among them, gold, silver, and copper—and in many shapes; they have been called scepters, spatulas, chisels, and knives (Benson 1984). Their use or uses are known, but they were also clearly ritual objects, based on functional tools. Some are simply made, but many are worked with complex designs, often showing scenes of capture and sacrifice. They have been found throughout the Moche region. At Sipán, Walter Alva found, in one tomb, an implementlike scepter in either hand of the buried lord, and, in another tomb, two of them, placed away from the body. All of these were of gold and/or silver, superb works of metallurgy, royal possessions to be taken to the other world.

Three figures are carved on this bone implement, one on each of its sides. A striding warrior, wearing platelet armor and a helmet with a knife, holds a club in his left hand and raises a round shield in his right. Opposite him is a warrior wearing a stepped shirt and a semicircular headdress, and holding a club and a square

shield. A bird hovers over his head. Eagles, falcons, or hummingbirds, so placed, apparently encouraged or symbolized military prowess. Both human figures have a curving line on the cheek under the eye from nose to cheek edge. The two figures face another warrior on the third surface. The shield of the figure in the platelet shirt touches the brow of this middle figure, who holds an unusual club and a round shield. His headdress has two raised hands and a face; these and his tunic with rectangular panels are elements of a costume seen in the coca rite (cat. no. 79). His head is bent backwards; his leg is also bent. He is a conquered warrior. Some inlay is left in the ear ornaments and in the hands or forearms, perhaps in a bracelet. The two main figures here appear on other spatula-scepters; the coca iconography is unusual on this kind of object. The scene, however, is reminiscent of fineline scenes on ceramics, in which warriors in Moche dress are winning over warriors in dress essentially like that of coca-chewers (Kutscher 1983: Abb. 115). These are presumably either ritual battles or depictions of historical battles, probably involving access to coca regions. EPB

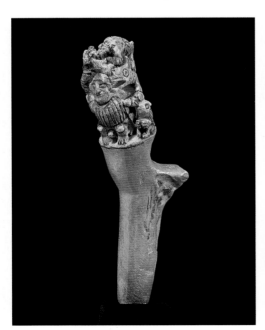

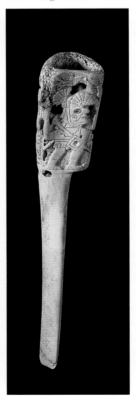

104

SEATED ANTHROPOMORPHIC STAG
CAPTIVE
Moche IV, A.D. 450–550
Ceramic
24.5 cm x 20 cm (9¾ x 8 in.)
XSC-000-194

105

SEATED ANTHROPOMORPHIC STAG
Moche IV, A.D. 450–550
Ceramic
25.8 cm x 14.5 cm (10¼ x 5¾ in.)
XSC-007-002

Many creatures in Moche art are part animal, part human. They seem to depict not disguised humans but creatures from the other world that is parallel to the human world. Most of them, including the fish monster (cat. no. 85), have human hands, as do these deer, whose humanoid bodies sit cross-legged. In cat. no. 104, human hands seem to emerge from a deer suit; however, the head, feet, and small, leafy, curled tail are those of a deer. (The ears of cat. no. 104 have been restored.) This stag appears as a captive and/or sacrificial victim, with a cord around its neck, its eyes wide open, and its hands in a gesture of respect or obeisance. Genitalia are prominently depicted, as is usually true of Moche human captive figures (cat. no. 96). Dying deer are usually shown with the tongue lolling out of the mouth, as this one is. In nature, the velvet on young antlers bleeds easily and may have reinforced the concept of the deer as a sacrificial creature.

In contrast, the seated deer in cat. no. 105 is elegantly dressed, wearing a pectoral over a tunic with sleeves and a belt. Elaborately garbed deer hunters sometimes wear such pectorals. This stag also has a bracelet on each wrist. The left hand is an upturned, hollow fist; the right hand faces down and is cupped over the knee, as the hands of important seated human figures often are (cat. no. 68). The antlers form an impressive headdress. Like no. 104, this creature has deer ears, feet, and tail. The monochrome light-colored slips on this pottery lend the mixed creature a uniform identity; the

difference between deer and man is smoothed over, not emphasized.

Seated stags can also be portrayed as warriors (Anton 1972: pl. 147). In nature, stags fight each other, and their running speed and jumping power lend them symbolism for human warriors.

Deer traits that are emphazised in these anthropomorphic renderings are: hoofs that can cause severe damage, antlers that resemble weapons, ears with extremely acute hearing, eyes with excellent vision, and a tail that rises like a white flag to warn of danger. EPB

106
FINELINE DEER-HUNT SCENE
Moche IV, A.D. 450–550
Ceramic
30.2 cm x 10 cm (12 x 4 in.)
XXC-000-111

The deer hunt (discussed by Donnan, this volume), one of the most common themes depicted on Moche IV pottery, was surely a ritual sacrifice of great significance (Kutscher 1983: Abbn. 69–87). Deer were driven into enclosures made of netting and then speared by important people in ritual dress like that worn by the two figures on this bottle: a garment with a broad pectoral or collar and dark-and-light rectangles at the waist, a pendant projecting at the rear, and a kilt with a decorated border. These costume elements are not only characteristic of most deer-hunter depictions, they are seen only in circumstances that relate to the deer hunt. The elaborate cloth-and-feather headdress and the round ear ornaments, probably of gold with shell and turquoise inlay (cat.

nos. 148, 149), are not specific to the hunt ritual but are general prestige accoutrements. Deer hunters were men of very high status, often assisted by small figures in priestly garments.

Most deer-hunt scenes show vegetation; three kinds of plants are depicted here. In many regions, the stag's woodlike antlers—the fastest-growing animal tissue—develop in synchronization with the growth of plants. This connects them to agriculture, as do their leafy-looking ears and tail; this leafiness is often emphasized in the drawing on bottles. Sometimes leaves, vines, or branches become entangled in stag antlers, and, of course, deer eat the farmer's crops. Here, a stag is shown on one side. It seems to have only one antler, and the pedicel, from which the other antler must have

recently fallen, may be indicated on top of the head in front of the ear. If this is so, this hunting rite would have taken place at the time of antler-shedding. The antlerless, speared deer on the other side of the vessel could be a doe or a stag that has shed both antlers. Genitalia are not shown here, as they are in some deer-hunt scenes.

A black-and-white dog was a member of this hunt, as is true in a number of deer-hunt scenes, for the dog helped track the deer. A similar dog accompanies the major god in the Presentation Theme (cat. no. 107). In other scenes related to death and sacrifice (cat. no. 84; Kutscher 1983: Abb. 267), the dog escorts gods, humans, and perhaps also deer to the other world. EPB

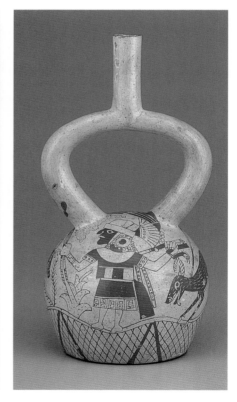

107
FINELINE PRESENTATION THEME
Moche IV, A.D. 450–550
Ceramic
24.3 cm x 15 cm (9½ x 6 in.)
XXC-000-133

Christopher Donnan (1978: 158–173) identified a scene that has been pictured on a number of Moche vessels, especially in the latter part of the seriation, as the Presentation Theme because it "involves the presentation of a goblet to a major figure." He has now adopted the term Sacrifice Ceremony, which relates to the contents of the goblet, presumably human blood taken from captives who are normally shown in the same scene. Because there are other sacrifice ceremonies, the original name is retained here.

Figures appear on two levels in this example. The upper space is marked as supernatural, sacred, or celestial space by the two-headed-serpent skyband (cat. nos. 36, 79), of a general type found throughout pre-Hispanic art. An arm (or foreleg) at either end of the snake holds a heart to its mouth, referring to the sacrifices on the lower level. On the upper level, the major figure at the left is a warrior, accompanied by a spotted dog (cat. no. 31). He is wearing a helmet with a knife-shaped ornament, a short tunic or shirt, a kilt, and a back flap. Snake-head radiances emerging from his head or helmet suggest that he is a solar deity. This figure was introduced rather late into Moche iconography, perhaps for political reasons, so a ruler could identify with him as the all-important sun. In his left hand, the warrior holds a goblet of what is likely sacrificial blood. An *ulluchu*, a fruit with natural anticoagulant, floats above the cup, reinforcing the notion of sacrifice. (Wassén 1986). These fruits appear at various critical places in the scene.

The details of this section of the design are almost identical to those on a vessel in the Museum für Völkerkunde, Munich. On that vase, which has often been published (Donnan 1978: Fig. 239), the goblet is being taken by the next figure, an anthropomorphic bird warrior. In most examples of the Presentation Theme, this latter figure derives from an owl; here, he is a more generic bird, perhaps hawk, falcon, or osprey. (These birds sometimes have interchangeable roles.) The bird warrior's right hand is raised; he holds a disk or plate in his left hand. Behind him is a woman, who appears in other late Moche contexts and may be a moon goddess (Benson 1985, 1988). Her long braids end in snake heads; two more snakes emerge from the back of her neck. She wears a distinctive

headdress and holds what is apparently a cup and its cover. Her garment is divided vertically in different patterns. Behind the woman stands a warrior figure with a god mouth; his hands are clasped in a gesture of veneration. He is dressed as the owl warrior is in related scenes, with a garment of metal platelets and a half-round headdress with two projections. It is unusual to have both this figure and a bird warrior in this scene. The right-hand figure may be the human ruler in a sacred or supernatural

state, joining the godly figures and emulating the bird-warrior, who surely has an astronomical identity that has not yet been discovered.

Peripheral figures on this level comprise an anthropomorphic jaguar warrior with a spotted tail, carrying a a folded cloth or bag over his shoulder, who walks away from the radiant god; an iguana or fish warrior (there is a serrated tail or fin), also with a cloth, who floats upward in front of the right-hand warrior; and an eroded small figure with an

animal mouth and a priestly headdress, sitting before a weapons bundle. The bags or cloths carried by these figures probably held shamanic materials, for this scene depicts interaction between the mythic world and human ritual.

On the lower level, three anthropomorphs—two birds and a fox—sit next to a radiant litter, placed below the rayed warrior; it is undoubtedly the vehicle in which he has traveled or will travel through the sky. A jaguar—jaguars are often associated with the sun—sits in the litter, which has a step form and a snake head at either pole end; it is supported by two decapitated heads. Two figures, a bird-headed warrior and another apparently human figure in a priestly headdress, sit in front of the litter. A jaguar-tailed, claw-footed warrior looks back toward the litter, holding a captive with his left hand and grasping a knife in his right. The seated captive/sacrificial victim has hands tied in front; blood drips from his nose. A weapons bundle with a jaguar head separates this group from one in which the woman from the upper scene (or her agent—the headdress is variant) holds a knife in one hand and touches the neck of another tied captive with her other hand. The scene ends with a weapons bundle, a motif that also decorates the spout. The Presentation Theme most likely treats an astronomical event, personified by gods and accompanied by ritual warfare and sacrifice. This pattern is common in pre-Hispanic cultures. EPB

108
FINELINE SACRIFICE SCENE
Moche IV, A.D. 450–550
Ceramic
26 cm x 14.3 cm (10¼ x 5¾ in.)
XXC-000-112

This sacrifice scene has many elements of the Presentation Theme, described in cat. no. 107, but with some variations. On one side stands a warrior with radiances, a fanged mouth, a helmet with knife, face paint, a beaky nose with an ornament, and a big knife-shaped rattle at his rear. Feather ornaments are attached to his garments, and metal disks hang at the edge of his kilt. He carries a club and points toward an *ulluchu* fruit above two jugs, which have vegetation at the neck. Below these, another *ulluchu* floats over a captive with tied hands, who is facing a warrior with animal head and clawed feet; this figure holds a cup. Such figures are often shown as sacrificers. A bowl hangs in the air above him, over a goblet held by the major figure on the other side of the bottle, who has a semicircular headdress with four curving rays and an indistinguishable animal head. He wears a nose ornament; square, framed ear ornaments with pendant snakehead; a snake trailing down the back from the headdress; and a long, metallic pendant from the headdress. Various weapons bundles float in the scene, and between the two major figures is a human-headed club with hands holding an object. What may be a litter rests below it. EPB

109
FINELINE RIBBON DANCE
Moche IV, A.D. 450–550
Ceramic
31.3 cm x 16.2 cm (12¼ x 6⅜ in.)
XXC-000-120

Dancers on Moche vessels appear as a line of men, warriors and/or priests, or gods and anthropomorphs (Kutscher 1983: Abbn. 151, 152, 300, 301). In some scenes, they hold hands as they move forward; in others, they hold a long ribbon, like that seen here, probably of woven cotton. Some examples show the warriors grasping the ribbon to hold a loop of cloth in hand. Here, ribbon dancers are featured on the upper register; hand-holders are relegated to the lower level. A large figure with a god mouth and a helmet dominates one face of the bottle. On either side of him is a figure in a kilt; two similar figures approach on the other side of the bottle. On the lower level, musicians, who appear in several other dance scenes, play flutes and drums, and, occasionally, panpipes or rattles. Loose warrior clothing floats in some other examples, as it does here; this spout is covered with warrior's tunics and, on either side, a head-dress with ear protectors and a collar.

Early Spanish chroniclers reported that, at the January calendrical rite of the Incas, participants in a ritual battle danced with a gold cord or chain through the city of Cuzco, visiting the major temples. Christopher Donnan (1983: 100), surmises that Moche dances were also urban rites. Ribbon dances took place in the Moche settlements or centers like those in Cuzco, whereas the coca ceremony and the ritual deer hunt were rites held outside the city.   EPB

110

TEXTILE WITH PROFILE FIGURES (detail)
Moche-Huari, Middle Horizon,
A.D. 650–1000
Cotton or wool
115 cm x 82 cm (45¼ x 32¼ in.)
XST-036-001

Among ancient Andean societies, as among other cultures that produce textiles by hand, clothmaking was a central economic activity and textiles held enormous social, political, religious, and aesthetic value (A. Rowe 1996: 330). From Spanish sources on the Inca and from the archaeological record, we know that textiles served myriad functions in antiquity. Some of these are still familiar today: garments encoded distinctions of social status, occupation, and ethnicity. Some are now more foreign: cloth was sacrificed by burning at Inca religious rituals; it was given to celebrate important stages of the life cycle, such as adoles-

cent initiation or marriage; and it was exchanged during diplomatic negotiations (Gayton 1961, Murra 1962). To judge from ceramic representations, it is likely that cloth also was a well-developed and important medium among the Moche. Unfortunately, very few Moche textiles have survived, probably in part because their homelands in the north are subject to periodic flooding more severe than that which occurs in southerly areas of the desert coast.

This textile was created during a period known as the Middle Horizon, either after the Moche collapse or very late in Moche times, when the Huari culture

came to power in the central highlands of Peru. There is no agreement about the nature of Huari interaction with or impact on late Moche civilization (see Schreiber 1992: 271–75). A distinctive synthesis of the two styles is known in a group of little-studied textiles, many of them from the Huarmey Valley, an apparently vigorous center just within the Moche southern frontier (Prümers 1990, Conklin 1979). Because so few Moche textiles have survived, it is difficult to know whether the style of these later textiles—which is much more geometric than that depicted on Moche ceramics— was common earlier or perhaps the result of interaction with Huari.

The apparently human figures placed within a lattice of stepped red diamonds are reminiscent of Huari figures who hold staffs, a traditional implement of authority, to each side of their bodies. Repeated across the bottom of this field is a geometric, three-pronged motif flanked by disks, often found in the headdresses of Huari figures. The series of smaller-scale stepped red elements can be traced through the art of both cultures. SEB

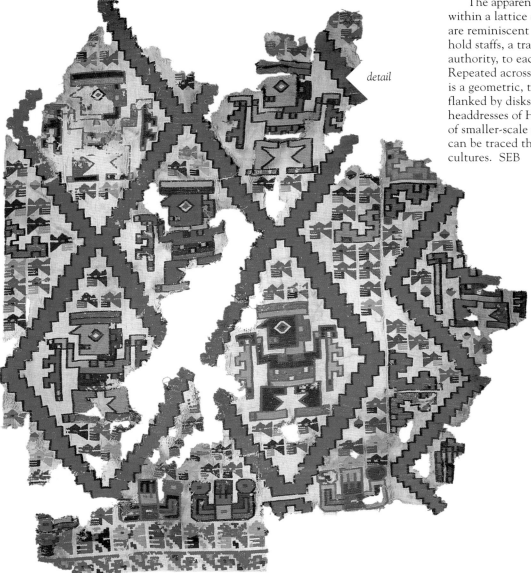

detail

111
CEREMONIAL MANTLE
Paracas, Early Horizon/Early Intermediate
Period, 100 B.C.–A.D. 200
Textile
164 cm x 307 cm (64½ x 118 in.)
XST-013-001

Between about 100 B.C. and A.D. 200, more than four hundred mummy bundles were buried at a place now called the Necrópolis (City of the Dead) on the Paracas Peninsula of Peru's southern desert coast. The most elaborate bundles consisted of a seated body wrapped in alternating layers of plain and lavishly decorated cloth, although black beans replaced human remains in one bundle (Daggett 1991: 48). More than one thousand decorated textiles were found in the bundles, along with other objects such as ceramics and gold ornaments (Paul 1990:1–46). The Necrópolis seems to have been used during a period of intense cultural interaction and transformation, as Paracas culture came to an end, Nasca society began to flower and a third group, the Topará, also was active. These three cultures each had related but distinct styles, all of which seem to be represented by either textiles or ceramics in the burials. This complex intermingling is very puzzling and raises many unanswered questions about the Necrópolis and about

chronological and cultural relationships among South Coast groups of the period (Silverman 1991).

Although most decorated textiles from the Necrópolis are in the form of garments, there is no agreement about whether they were worn in life or made especially for burial (see Paul 1990: 63–4). The most spectacular are the embroidered mantles, perhaps male garments worn about the shoulders. The theme of this stunning mantle is a schematic feline composed solely of multicolored lines; differently colored repeats are paired with one another and reproduced at different scales in the wide borders and the narrow, doubled bands that stripe the field. Abstract rendering makes it difficult to identify the type of cat represented; thus, its meaning is poorly understood.

The physical structure of yarns and of some fabrics may have carried some of the textiles' significance (Frame 1986). Because the complex processes of ordering required for textile manufacture were widely understood throughout the Andes,

textile structures may have served to encode and express larger conceptual categories. These categories may have underlain the organization of diverse aspects of ancient life, from botanical classification to social phenomena. SEB

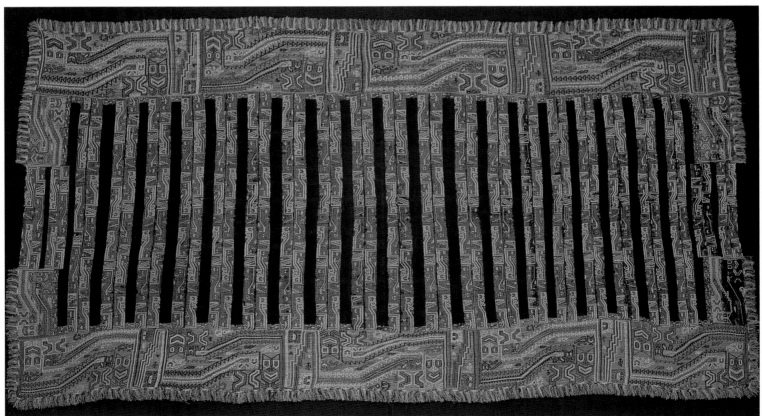

112
KILLER WHALE
Nasca, Early Intermediate Period,
A.D. 1–700
Ceramic
30 cm x 25.6 cm (11¾ x 10 in.)
XSC-034-005

The most powerful sea creature known to the ancient Nasca was the orca or killer whale, a predator of fish and seabirds as well as larger seals and sea lions. The being portrayed in this ceramic features the orca's blunt, toothy jaw, though the curving body and multiple dorsal and ventral fins may refer to other major marine predators such as a shark or snake mackerel (Peters 1991: 254–55, Proulx 1983a:96). That the creature is mythical is indicated by the representation of a human hand, which often clutches either a knife, as here, or a human trophy head; in this example, modeled feet are used as vessel supports and trophy heads are painted along the flanks of the body.

The notion of predation surely in part explains the constant association of the killer whale with the trophy head, which seems to have been an important aspect of religion on the South Coast. Elsewhere in Nasca art severed heads and plants often are shown together. This may be because the head was perceived as a locus of vitality and life force and the taking of heads, as a means of acquiring and redirecting that energy to the benefit of the possessor. The combined motif may also refer to interrelated cycles of death and regeneration.

The killer whale has a long history on the South Coast; it first appears in the ceramics of the Paracas culture (800 B.C.–1 A.D.), ancestor to the Nasca on the South Coast that made important contributions to the art of its successor. The creature continues through late Nasca phases, when it is reduced to a schematic head with a gaping mouth filled with blood. An enormous silhouette of the beast also is featured among the famous ground drawings on the Pampa Ingenio in the Nasca Valley. The lack of abstraction and use of incision, which emphasizes the voracious mouth, place this rendition in the earlier phases of the Nasca art style. SEB

113

DRUM
Nasca, Early Intermediate Period,
A.D. 1–700
Ceramic
44.6 cm x 27.2 cm (17½ x 10¾ in.)
XSc-31-1

Occasionally in other Nasca ceramics, figures are shown playing drums like this one—the drum lies on its side, its neck propped up by the musician, who strikes a skin stretched over the mouth of the instrument with a stick (see Musées royaux d'Art et d'Histoire 1990: Cat. no. 140). Life-sized ceramic drums with globular resonating chambers are relatively rare among ancient Andean instruments; many of the most elaborate examples were made by the Nasca (Jones 1987: 150). Several Nasca drums are anthropomorphized, as this one is: that is, the two-part chamber is worked as the head and corpulent body of a figure while the legs and feet are painted on the drum's neck (for exhibition purposes, the drum is turned over and rests on its mouth). The sound of the drum may have been conceived of as the figure's voice. An analogue for this notion may be found in effigy vessels of birds that have whistling spouts.

Though the figure's ornamentation is complex, its identity is not known. In each hand it clutches two small figures, the meaning of whose size and function are unknown. One is a human whose lower body is transformed into vegetal form; the other is a feline, with tongue extended. The feline may represent the pampas cat (*Lynchailurus colocolo*), a small spotted predator of the desert margins, which is shown in many other Nasca representations (Peters 191: 273–77). The feline is attached to the end of a spiked streamer that issues from the

figure's mouth. Similar serpentine steamers trail from the figure's head or headdress and those that spew form the mouth of the large eared head at the center of the figure's chest encircle the chamber of the drum and terminate in smaller versions of the same head. Streamers, which are common in Nasca art, correspond to no known object and instead may refer to an abstract concept of energy or animation (Martin 1991). SEB

The Nasca of the South Coast were contemporaries of the Moche. Their heartland is found in the Ica Valley and the drainage of the Nasca River, with its several tributaries. For the Nasca, like the Moche, the sea was a rich source both of food and mythology, and marine themes are common in their ceramics. This fisherman is shown carrying full nets over his shoulders and his simply rendered body is draped over the top of the vessel's white chamber, which some suggest represents an inflated, buoyant skin used as a boat (Proulx 1983a: 100; Sawyer 1975: 92). Although fisherman ceramics have been interpreted as scenes drawn from daily life (Sawyer 1975: 92), other quotidian

activities are rarely portrayed in Nasca art. It is likely that such figures were linked to legends and myths about the sea and its power.

In contrast to Moche ceramics, which emphasize modeled form and painting in a very reduced palette (white, red, and black), Nasca ceramics display a wider, more vivid range of colors and a flatter conception of form, even in sculptured ceramics, which are relatively uncommon. On the head of this fisherman, for example, only the simply modeled, wedgelike nose projects from the surface; other features are painted in vibrant, earth-toned slips that were applied before firing and burnished during the final stages of drying (Donnan 1992: 48), producing a lustrous, durable surface. SEB

115

SEATED FIGURE WITH DARTS
Nasca, Early Intermediate Period,
A.D. 1–700
16.6 cm x 13.4 cm (6½ x 5¼ in.)
XSC-042-001

Unlike the Moche, who favored the use of the mold, Nasca potters preferred coiling or drawing their ceramics (Carmichael 1986). In coiling, rolls of clay are laid in continuous spirals or individual rings. "Drawing" refers to squeezing, stretching, or pulling the clay. In vessel walls, these methods usually are used in combination, while the bases are formed by hand beating. A few vessels may be made of slabs of clay joined along the edges. After the initial formation, the vessel was paddled or scraped to thin the walls, further shape the vessel, and consolidate joins. Relief features are modeled or, occasionally, appliquéd. The tools required for ceramic production were simple: flattened sticks were used as paddles; water-washed river cobbles were used as anvils; and small fragments of shell, bone or other hard materials served as scraping instruments. One effigy vessel similar to this one has been analyzed; its chamber is drawn while the head is made of several coils and the face is modeled (Carmichael 1986:42, Fig. 9). This seated human figure, a hunter or warrior, holds darts and a dart-thrower; a sling, used for throwing stones, is wrapped around its head. SEB

116
SCENE WITH LLAMAS
Lima Culture, A.D. 200–600,
Early Intermediate Period
Ceramic
17.5 cm x 15.2 cm (11¾ x 10 in.)
XSc-034-005

This globular, double-spout-and-bridge vessel demonstrates characteristics of styles of both the North and South Coast. This merging of stylistic influences creates a high-relief scene reminiscent of North Coast pottery on a variant of the traditional South Coast vessel shape.

One side of the vessel depicts a llama herder guiding his unladen flock in a paired train, a method of transport common in Peru today. Llamas were the principal sacrificial animal in the ancient Andes, and this modeled scene may de-

pict events leading to their ritual use. The opposite side of the vessel portrays a spotted feline, similar in design to that on cat. no. 117, with its head lifted in relief. This jaguar rests on a concave surface that appears to represent a cave beneath the structure surmounting the vessel, which is guarded by a single figure dressed in hat and tunic. Elite residential compounds were similarly located on hilltops in the Lurin Valley (Moseley 1992:184). Such houses indicate sacred, ritual space in much Peruvian coastal art, however, lending credence to the interpretation of

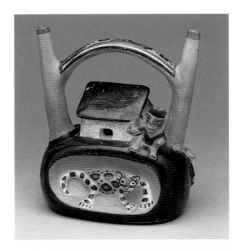

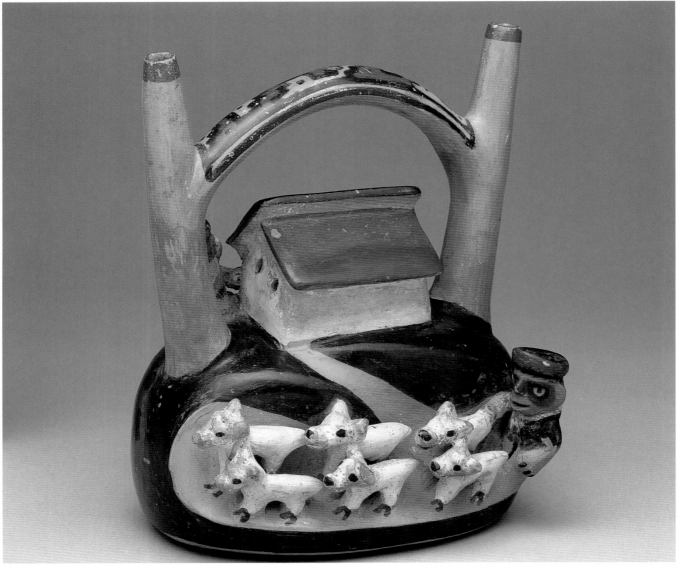

117
Two Jaguars
Lima, Early Intermediate Period,
A.D. 200-600
Ceramic
16.6 cm x 13.4 cm (6½ x 5¼ in.)
XSc-042-001

this piece as a ceremonial scene. Jaguars are also associated symbolically with sacrifice, and the figure depicted here may portray a priest or shaman preparing for ritual.

The Lima culture, which developed in the central Rimac Valley about A.D. 200, led to stronger settlement in this area and the monumental construction that underlies the modern city of Lima. The culture's influence extended from the site of Cerro Trinidad, in the northern Chancay region, to the Lurin Valley in the south, and may reflect loose political affiliations throughout the area at this time (Moseley 1992: 184).

Lima ceramic traditions adapted earlier white-on-red techniques, primarily utilizing black painting on a red slip surface, the style that is demonstrated in this double-spout-and-bridge vessel (Moseley 1992:184). Identical, spotted felines with heads in raised relief are depicted on both sides of this globular form. These cats are probably jaguars, animals widely associated with the underworld and sacrifice in pre-Hispanic cultures. The wide, dark-colored band beneath the jaguars may demarcate two distinct cosmological spaces on the vessel.

118, 119
FIGURES WITH TUNICS
Huari, Middle Horizon, A.D. 650–1000
Ceramic

14.2 cm x 12.2 cm (5½ x 6¼ in.)
XSc-019-008

12.8 cm x 19.2 cm (5 x 7½ in.)
XSc-019-009

During late Moche times, the Huari culture began to develop. The Huari capital was to the south of Moche territory, in the central highlands of Peru. Over a three-century span known as the Middle Horizon, from the time that Moche culture fell apart and before the Chimú asserted themselves on the north coast, the Huari established themselves as a dominant power and vigorously interacted with their contemporaries in far-flung areas of the Andes, from cultures in the highlands, such as the powerful Tiahuanaco in present-day Bolivia, to the Nasca and Pachacamac on the south and central coast of Peru. The nature of Huari's contact with other regions is still being debated but probably varied from armed conflict—one Huari fortification has been found inside Tiahuanaco territory—to peaceful, mutual beneficial exchange of goods, ideas, and technologies.

There is no single, homogeneous Huari style in ceramics. Instead, Huari pottery is found in a fairly wide range of local styles that feature certain similar imagery, often executed in polychrome slip painting that can be traced to Nasca ceramic technology (Menzel 1964; Proulx 1983b; Cook 1996). Vessel shapes sometimes also are alike. Double-chambered ceramics like these, for instance, are represented in several styles found during the second portion of the Middle Horizon: Viñaque, Pachacamac and, most commonly, Atarco (Menzel 1964: 41, 49,

57–8). In these vessels, the unmodeled back chamber is connected by a straplike bridge and a hollow tube to a second chamber, usually shaped as a human figure but also as various animals.

Huari imagery is very little studied and not much can be said about the identity or meaning of these two figures. They may represent living persons of rank or ancestors; the plump, compact bodies resemble the shape of mummy bundles characteristic of the Middle Horizon (see also Cook 1984–5). Ancestor veneration was an important part of Inca religious life and probably was also practiced among earlier cultures. The liquids that the vessels contained were likely an important part of their meaning, as was sound: vessels like these often have a whistle that piped as air was displaced by liquid in the chambers (Menzel 1964: 41, 49). Both figures seem to be dressed in a tunic (shirt), one ornamented with vertical stripes and the other with small rectangles, each with two dots at the top, arranged in a geometric pattern. The rectangles may represent shell or metal plackets that were sewn to garments. The facial decoration of one figure resembles a mustache and beard, which are shown occasionally on other Huari ceramics, while simple red semicircles are painted over the cheeks of the other figure. SEB

120

FOOT WITH *KERO*
Huari, Middle Horizon, A.D. 650–1000
Ceramic
13 cm x 12.2 cm (5 x 4¾ in.)
XSc-053-006

The rise of both Tiahuanaco and Huari cultures influenced politics and artistic traditions in Peru, marking a shift in power from the coast to the southern and south-central highlands (Morris 1995:97). Flared, tumbler-shaped vessels, called *keros*, became popular with the florescence of the great ceremonial center of Tiahuanaco in the Lake Titicaca basin and are considered characteristic of its culture. They were used by the Inca during Colonial times to drink *chicha*, a maize beer, for ceremonial and political events, and are still used in present-day Cuzco (Morris 1995:105).

This Huari version of the *kero* was probably produced on the South Coast. A foot forms its base, and part of the lower leg and ankle shape the body of the vessel. Bands of decoration around the upper portion of the cup incorporate a row of chevron patterns, distinctive of the Huari style, above panels of floral-like freer designs. Human sacrifice in the Andes often involved the offering of body parts, such as the head and limbs. These elements were commonly used as artistic motifs, as here and in Moche art (see cat. no. 99).

121

MONKEY
Huari, Middle Horizon, A.D. 650–1000
Ceramic
11.4 cm x 21.9 cm (4½ x 8½ in.)
XSc-037-008

The Huari people combined various coastal techniques, palettes, and iconography, creating a ceramic style that reflects those of the populations they conquered. Works characteristically display a complete slip in several colors, sharp outlining, and a burnished surface. Such bold hues, designs, and glossy surfaces helped to make the Huari style recognizable, enabling their makers to maintain a higher profile in the many regions they conquered (Stone-Miller 1995:149-50).

This unusual double vessel depicts a monkey seated between two small cups. While primates often appear as iconographic features on vessels, double-bowled cups were rare. Both of the cups in this piece are decorated in two distinct registers. The low, wide-mouthed cup in front is painted with circle and S motifs typical of the Huari style; the central image on the taller, rear cup may represent a schematic feline in profile. Because the North Coast was less rigidly controlled by the Huari than other areas they conquered, their traditions were blended with the more limited color scheme and production techniques of the Moche, as is demonstrated here.

122

FEATHER PANEL
Probably Huari, Middle Horizon,
A.D. 650–1000
Textile and feathers
100 cm x 241 cm (39½ x 95 in.)
XSc-029-001

This luxurious feathered panel probably was one of more than ninety similar panels found in a buried cache at Pampa Ocoña in the Churunga Valley on the South Coast of Peru. The cache was uncovered accidentally by workers and its exact configuration is unclear, but the panels are said to have been found rolled up and inside several fine, intact, portrait jars, each about three feet tall. Although an offering of Inca artifacts was found nearby, the portrait jars are in the earlier Huari style. Thus, the feather panels, too, may date to Huari rather than Inca times. The meaning of the cache is not known, though no human remains were found and, therefore, it seems to have been created for a votive rather than funerary purpose. It differs from several other Huari offerings, which include very large ceramics that were deliberately shattered in antiquity and buried without accompanying textiles (Cook and Conklin 1996: 417–18; Schreiber 1992: 111).

In Ocoña panels that have been technically documented, the feathers, from the blue-and-yellow macaw native to Amazonia, are tied onto strings that, in turn, are sewn to a base cloth of cotton. The stringing method and material differ according to feather color: yellow feathers are secured to cotton cords with one system of knots; blue feathers are attached to cords made of another plant fiber with a second set of knots (Greene 1991). It is likely that the contrast of materials, knots, and colors had meaning in antiquity. Though the panels sometimes are called mantles (shoulder garments), the cords attached to the top and at the back suggest that, instead, they were used as some sort of hanging (Cook and Conklin 1996: 418). SEB

123

SHIRT
Chimú, Late Intermediate Period,
A.D. 1000–1450
Textile
52.3 cm x 135 cm (20 ½ x 53 in.)
XST-020-001

LOINCLOTH
Chimú, Late Intermediate Period,
A.D. 1000–1450
Textile
100 cm x 111 cm (39 ½ x 43 ¾ in.)
XST-020-002

The Chimú, successors to the Moche on the North Coast of Peru, seem to have preferred matched sets of garments like the ensemble shown here, which includes a tunic (shirt) and loincloth, basic articles of male costume in the ancient Andes. Other common men's garments were the mantle (a shawl-like shoulder wrap) and headwear of several varieties (A. Rowe 1984: 28–9). The loincloth consists of a single, decorated panel, sometimes called a frontal, which undoubtedly hung at the front of the body and was visible beneath the tunic. This elaborate frontal is attached along its top to a simpler fabric, often extremely long, with ties at the end. The exact mechanics of how very long loincloths were arranged on the lower body, if they were actually worn, are not clear; the final appearance may have been that of a bulky, voluminous skirt.

Like most other Chimú textiles, the graphic vigor of these garments lies in the repetition of simple forms in several striking color combinations, here distributed along the diagonal. In both garments, a small, extremely geometricized figure with a cleft head and cross-shaped eyes is arranged in a continuous, unmarked grid against a red ground. The rectilinear arms of the figure curl upward from the shoulder, above a triangular body that, at the bottom, is ornamented with a striped, fringelike element.

In the border of each garment, against a gold ground, is a row of larger figures, completely bent over so that the feet and head rest on the same ground line; the hair or headdress flow upward, countering the direction of the upper body, and each has spindly arms and legs, often with two digits. This figure is known as the Anthropomorphized (Humanized) Wave, a creature that first appears in late Moche art and becomes common in later, Chimú representations (McClelland 1990). In late Moche examples, the body of the curving wave is edged with small volutes, perhaps representing splashes of water; later Chimú artisans translated this detail into geometric forms such as the serrated, spiky spine of the figures here. In some other Chimú representations of the creature, fish leap inside the body of the wave. The emergence of the Anthropomorphized Wave accompanies a general shift to maritime artistic themes in the art of the North Coast (McClelland 1990). Beyond signaling an increasing orientation to the sea, the meaning of the Anthropomorphized Wave is not yet well understood. SEB

PROCESSION WITH FIGURE ON LITTER
Lambayeque [Sicán] A.D. 900–1100
Ceramic
18.2 cm x 11.5 cm (7¼ x 4½ in.)
XXC-000-139

This ceramic double vessel from the Lambayeque region is Middle Sicán (or pre-Chimú) in style. It is composed of two boxlike chambers connected by a short tube. The rear chamber is surmounted by a conical spout with a narrow opening and is linked to the front chamber by an wide, flattened bridge. This spout-and-bridge form typifies the style found in the Lambayeque River drainage (Larco Hoyle 1949: 43). On the front chamber is a processional scene in which one figure is conveyed on a litter by four standing figures. All figures wear small colored hats and have the wide, comma-shaped eyes charac-teristic of the Lambayeque style (Cordy-Collins 1996:190).

Individuals of high status were often carried on litters in pre-Hispanic cultures. Evidence of their use has been found at the site of Batan Grande, the center of activity in the Lambayeque region during this period (Morris 1993: 127-8). Ceram-ics from this site depict a figure referred to as the Sicán lord riding a litter. Litters have also been excavated in other parts of this valley, and archaeologists believe the deceased were borne to the grave in this manner. Such litters may have been decorated with sheets of gold and silver.

Peruvian double vessels often produce a whistling sound as liquid pushed air through them. This basic whistling form demonstrates the Moche origins of later styles on the Peruvian North Coast such as Lambayeque and Chimú. The latter of these three styles are frequently confused because of their similar construction techniques.

125
VESSEL WITH FIGURES
Chimú, Late Intermediate Period,
A.D. 1000–1450
Ceramic
20 cm x 27.5 cm (8 x 10¾ in.)
Xsc-023-005

This double-chambered vessel consists of
a bottle with a tall neck and a low-relief,
press-molded design joined to a second,
rectangular chamber surmounted by a
group of modeled figures. The two chambers are also connected by a wide handle.
The design on the mold-made bottle
depicts an anthropomorphic figure wearing a tunic, round ear ornaments, and a
crescent headdress; arms are extended
and hands raised. This figure is flanked by
two profile avian figures, probably marine
birds, also wearing crescent headdresses.
Smooth figures stand out from the tex-

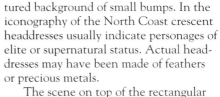

tured background of small bumps. In the
iconography of the North Coast crescent
headdresses usually indicate personages of
elite or supernatural status. Actual headdresses may have been made of feathers
or precious metals.

The scene on top of the rectangular
chamber shows a gathering of presumably
eleven individuals (two figures are missing). One individual is seated, cross-
legged with hands on knees, in the center
of the composition. He is surrounded by a
ring of standing figures, several of whom
are joined by their raised hands, perhaps
echoing the low-relief figure on the front
of the bottle. The seated figure is facing
two large jars, which were probably
meant to represent jars used for *chicha*
(maize beer), and a smaller, saucerlike
vessel. The largest figure, the one nearest
the handle, is distinguished by the crescent headdress, necklace, and ear ornaments, as well as by relative size. The
smaller figure to his left also wears a crescent headdress and necklace (although
no ear ornaments), but he seems to be a
secondary figure. Opposite the largest
figure are two musicians: one, with a fez-
type headdress, shakes a rattle; and the
other, wearing a hood, beats a small
drum suspended from the chest.
Three of the figures with upraised
arms and bands placed diagonally
across the chest may represent females; there is an indication of
breasts, and the costuming is not
the typical male tunic and
loincloth.

Chimú art is rarely
narrative: compositions
usually consist of patterns
of repeated geometric,
zoomorphic, and anthro-
pomorphic forms. As such,
Chimú imagery is more
ambiguous than Moche
art, which often conveys
much information through
the details of a scene. This
bottle is unusual in the
complexity of the iconog-
raphy, apparently referring
to a specific scene. The
association of the figures,
music, and drink may indicate some type
of ritual ceremony.   JP

126
MAN HOLDING SPONDYLUS SHELL
Chimú, Late Intermediate Period,
A.D. 1000–1450
Ceramic
22.8 cm x 18 cm (9 x 7 in.)
XSC-009-002

In the Late Intermediate Period, Chimú potters produced ceramic vessels on a large scale, aided by the use of press molds. Clay was pressed into mold negatives to create sections of the two halves of the vessel, and the resulting positives would be joined and smoothed over to complete the form. Finer ceramics such as this bottle were burnished to achieve a smooth, polished effect. The glossy grey-black surface is created in a smudging atmosphere during the firing process: at peak temperature, additional fuel is added, and the kiln is then buried, producing an intense smoke (Donnan 1992:20).

This vessel represents the continuation of a tradition of stirrup-spout bottles known from earlier periods on the North Coast of Peru. Chimú bottles often include small modeled animals, particularly monkeys and birds, at the juncture of the spout and the arch. In this example, a small monkey with a long curling tail clings to the spout. The chamber is molded in the shape of a man holding a relatively veristic depiction of a *Spondylus* shell. Traces of red pigment, referring to the bright coral red of the species *Spondylus princeps* Broderip or the red-purple of *Spondylus calcifer* Carpenter, are still on the shell. *Spondylus* sp., commonly known as the thorny oyster, is a tropical bivalve normally found in the warmer waters north of the Santa Elena Peninsula in Ecuador. It was highly valued in Peru, at considerable distances from its natural habitat (Pillsbury 1996). Of great importance in the ritual and economic life of the Chimú, *Spondylus* is found as whole shell in elite burials and offerings, as well as being cut into ornaments and inlays seen on elite goods. *Spondylus* was ground into dust as well: archaeological evidence provides support for a practice mentioned in a sixteenth-century chronicle of a courtier charged with scattering seashell dust where the king was to walk (Cordy-Collins 1990; Davidson 1980:10, 15–16, 54–55, Table 3). Although *Spondylus* was used by earlier cultures in Peru, its importation and distribution increased markedly in the Chimú period and may have played a key role in the development of the wealth of the Chimú empire. JP

127
VESSEL IN THE SHAPE OF A DOG
Chimú, Late Intermediate Period,
A.D. 1000–1450
Ceramic
15.5 cm x 18 cm (6 x 7 in.)
XXC-000-173

The chamber of this vessel is shaped in the form of a hairless dog, with its characteristic wrinkles represented by a modeled surface ribbing on the body and face. The spout extends from the lower back of the dog, and a wide, flat handle joins the spout to the back of the neck. The grey color of this smudge-fired vessel is close to the skin color of some species of hairless dogs known in Peru today.

Depictions of hairless dogs appear around A.D. 750 on Moche ceramic vessels and continue in later Andean ceramic traditions. Ceramic portrayals of hairless dogs occur earlier in western Mexico, however, and Alana Cordy-Collins (1994) has suggested that hairless dogs were introduced into Peru in the eighth century by maritime traders. In Mexico, such dogs were bred for food. While there is some evidence that dogs were eaten in northern Peru, the dogs may have also served a different role. Cordy-Collins has suggested that they may have been kept for perceived medicinal properties: a misconception that the body temperature of hairless dogs is higher (they seem warmer to the touch because of the lack of hair) has led to the belief that their warmth helps alleviate rheumatism. JP

128
SEATED FIGURE
Chimú, Late Intermediate Period,
A.D. 1000–1450
Wood, pigment, silver alloy
94 cm x 36 cm (37 x 14¼ in.)
XSc-059-001

129
STANDING FIGURE
Chimú, Late Intermediate Period,
A.D. 1000–1450
Wood, pigment
61 cm x 24 cm (24 x 9½ in.)
XSc-028-001

Chimú anthropomorphic wooden sculptures have been found in several contexts in the Moche Valley. Dozens of figures, in rigid, standardized poses, have been found in funerary contexts at the Huaca el Dragón and Huaca Tacaynamo, two platform structures located approximately three kilometers northeast from central Chan Chan, the Chimú capital. These figures may have been originally positioned in some sort of funerary tableaux and interred with the deceased (Jackson 1991).

The presence of bases and the larger size of these sculptures, however, suggest that they may have once served an architectural function. Kent Day excavated similar figures at the entrance to *ciudadela* Rivero, one of the nine monumental compounds at Chan Chan (Day 1973:140–147). The Rivero figures were each placed in their own niche, with the base below their feet serving as a stake to secure the figure in the floor. Although only two figures have survived *in situ* at Chan Chan, the other seven niches of the entryway probably also contained similar figures.

Both of these examples show individuals with trapezoidal headdresses, and at one time both had fringed loincloths and round ear ornaments (those of the seated figures are almost completely missing now, as is one arm). Both figures are shown grasping a cylindrical object, most likely a *kero* or ritual drinking vessel (see cat. nos. 134, 135). Such vessels were prominent during ritual and ceremonial occasions that undoubtedly were held in the large courts of the *ciudadelas* of Chan Chan.

Numerous layers of pale yellow pigment have been applied to the face of the standing figure. At one point the face appears to have been painted red; traces of this color are evident midway in the paint stratigraphy. Traces of red pigment are visible on the face of the seated

figure. The eyes and mouth of the standing figure are not painted; these areas may have been inlaid with other materials (the figures from Rivero, while missing the inlays, had a dark resin, probably an adhesive, in the eyes). The multiple paint layers on the face is similar to the treatment of a number of the architectural reliefs at Chan Chan, where the images, in generally good condition, appear to have been "ritually renewed," perhaps as part of a periodic ceremony carried out within the *ciudadelas* of Chan Chan (Pillsbury 1993:116–119).

An unusual feature of the seated figure is a series of small silver alloy pegs in exposed skin areas: the chest, back, legs, arms and hands of the figure. Parts of the body that were meant to be represented as covered, such as the face and the loincloth, do not have the pegs. It is unclear what function the pegs had: they may have been used for revetment or the attachment of some sort of ornament, although the wood now seems very worn.

Rectangular sections have been cut from the back of both sculptures: from the base of the seated figure and from the upper left section of the back of the standing figure. JP

130
PEDESTAL CUP
Chimú, Late Intermediate Period,
A.D. 1000–1450
Wood, gourd, fiber, shell
40 cm x 6.5 cm (15¾ x 6½ in.)
XSc-051-001

This elaborate, finely detailed vessel is composed of two parts: a gourd chamber, supported by an inlaid wooden figure carved in the shape of a feline. The two parts are attached by twine through the bottom of the gourd cup. Decorated gourds are one of the earliest art forms in ancient Peru; carved gourds were being used on the North Coast of Peru by 1950 B.C., before the appearance of pottery in this region (Bird 1963).

The gourd is engraved in panels, arranged in two bands below the rim of the vessel; thick dark borders mark the top and the bottom of the decorated bands (the dark areas are achieved by singeing the area with a hot tool). The upper band consists of a series of designs: one panel shows two birds; this alternates with two panels each containing one six-legged insect. The six-legged insect is repeated in one panel of the lower band, but most likely functions as a filler after the main panels were engraved. The panels of the lower band share similar imagery, yet no two panels are exactly alike, although portions of the images could have been created with the aid of templates. The majority of the figures are supernatural creatures, with zoomorphic bodies and some anthropomorphic characteristics, such as ear ornaments and headdresses. Each panel has one large figure on the left and a smaller one on the right, with birds occasionally used as filler elements where space permits. Three basic types of figures are repeated, although not always in the same position. All are variations of a zoomorphic figure shown in different positions, wearing different headdresses and other details. One figure is very similar to a creature repeated on a border of a relief at *ciudadela* Squier at Chan Chan (Pillsbury 1993: Fig. 161): the profile figure has a simple body, with a crescent headdress and a protruding tongue.

The wooden support is carved in the shape of a male jaguar, with its pelage markings indicated by circular shell inlays, including mother-of-pearl, and perhaps bone. The two remaining claws on the front paws appear to have been made from actual animals claws; the rear claws are made from shell. The eyes are created

131

Vessel in the Shape of a Snail
Inca, Late Horizon, A.D. 1450–1550
Ceramic
8.5 cm x 20 cm (3½ x 8 in.)
XSc-024-007

132

Vessel in the Form of a Mace
Inca, Late Horizon, A.D. 1450–1550
Ceramic
11.7 cm x 13.2 cm (4½ x 5¼ in.)
XSc-024-005

from mother-of-pearl and lapis lazuli inlays, and the ears, teeth, and whiskers are also inlaid with shell. Small fish forms are inlaid around the base on which the feline stands, and on the support that leads from the back of the feline neck. A single diamond-shaped element is inlaid on the lower portion of the base.

It is difficult to know with any certainty how this object was used. The iconography of the gourd is similar to that of a group of silver and gold goblets from Huaca la Misa, the funerary platform of *ciudadela* Rivero (Ríos and Retamozo 1982). As with the *keros* (cat. nos. 134, 135), such elaborate vessels were probably used in rituals and ceremonies carried out in the large courts of the *ciudadelas* of Chan Chan and elsewhere. Feasting was a critical aspect of Andean social and political relations, and such vessels were probably integral in the definition and reinforcement of status relations. The use of precious and exotic items, such as the inlays, and the amount of detail and quality of workmanship evident on the cup, all speak to the power of the individual who commissioned and owned the cup and his ability to marshal resources to create such a work. The iconography of the vessel undoubtedly underscored these references to wealth and rank. JP

Ceramic objects made and used in Cuzco, the capital of the Inca empire, and its vicinity, are known under the rubric of the Cuzco Inca style. This pottery was considered a prestige ware and was closely associated with the fine craftsmanship and status of the capital. Examples of this style are occasionally found in the provinces, presumably brought there as imperial gifts by Cuzco's ruling elite. Cuzco Inca style—particularly vessel shapes and design motifs—was also imitated in the provinces. Cuzco Inca pottery was handmade and often decorated with polychrome slips, particularly red and black on a buff-colored base. Ornamentation is usually based on the repetition of a limited number of geometric forms within bands.

This ceramic snail in the Cuzco Inca style is one of a pair; both have small openings at either end of the shell. It is possible that these served as *pacchas*, or ceremonial vessels used for pouring libations. *Pacchas*, which had openings at either end, were used as vessels through which offerings of *chicha* (maize beer) were poured on the earth to ensure continued growth and fertility. These specialized

vessels were used from the Early Intermediate Period onwards (Carrion Cachot 1955; Lothrop 1956). *Pacchas* are made in a variety of forms, commonly referring to agriculture, and in particular maize. Although this example is quite different from most vessels identifiable as *pacchas*, the snail form (probably a type of land snail) may have been important in beliefs about agricultural fertility and the land. A similar snail vessel, with a prominent spout on the shell, is now in the British Museum, Museum of Mankind (Joyce 1923: Fig. IX, 1).

Pacchas are often ceramic versions of utilitarian implements, such as foot plows. Foot plows, important tools in Inca agriculture, served as an apt vessel form for rituals designed to ensure the growth and fertility of crops. This ceramic mace may have also served as a *paccha*, as the hollow form has two perforations, which may have allowed for the passage of liquids. If this object was indeed used as a *paccha*, however, it is unclear what association may have been intended between the form and the ceremony. Maces were favored for hand-to-hand combat in Inca warfare. The wooden handles of actual maces were approximately eighty centimeters long and had stone or metal mace heads hafted to the shaft. In this ceramic example, the cord used to haft the mace head is carefully indicated in relief and with polychrome slip. JP

133
CUZCO BOTTLE
Inca, Late Horizon, A.D. 1450–1550
Ceramic
24.5 cm x 18.2 cm (9¾ x 7¼ in.)
XXC-000-172

Cuzco bottles (often called aryballoid vessels, because of similarities with the Greek form *aryballos*, or *urpu*, a Quechua name), are one of the most distinctive Inca ceramic objects, and a predominant form of the Cuzco Inca style. Cuzco bottles range in size from 8 to 100 cm, with most falling in two categories: the smaller ones, such as this example, are around 25 cm, with the average larger size vessels around 92 cm (Miller in Donnan 1992:110). The vessels have globular chambers with tall spouts and flaring rims. Small lugs, possibly used to secure a lid, are usually found just beneath the rim on either side of the spout. Strap handles, placed relatively low down on the chamber, allow for securing the large-size vessels on the backs of a porters: Inca effigy vessels on occasion show individuals carrying these vessels on their backs (Jones 1964: No. 45; Purin 1990: No. 243). In the present small example, the lug, modeled in the shape of a three-dimensional feline head, was probably ornamental. As the base is pointed, the large bottles may have been set into earthen floors; or on a flat floor, the bottles could be tipped forward to pour the contents of the vessel. Such vessels could be used to hold liquids such as *chicha* (maize beer) or other materials. The larger-size bottles would have been a focal point of the ritual feasting and drinking ceremonies in the Inca empire (see cat. nos. 134, 135).

Small versions of Cuzco bottles, such as this example, may have also been used to serve liquids, although they probably served a votive purpose as well. A number of Cuzco bottles smaller than this example (averaging around 17 cm) have been found in distant parts of the former Inca empire. On the Isla de la Plata off the coast of Ecuador, Dorsey found a suite of pairs of small ceramic objects, including a pair of Cuzco bottles, accompanying the burial of two individuals (Dorsey 1901; McEwan and van de Guchte 1992). More recently, a 17 cm high Cuzco bottle was found on the Ampato volcano, near Arequipa, Peru. The bottle, along with figurines and other objects, formed part of the assemblage accompanying the sacrifice of a young girl

(Reinhard 1996). Colin McEwan and Maarten van de Gutche (1992) have suggested that offerings such as these were part of the *capac hucha* ceremony, an important Inca ritual festival which culminated in the sacrifice of young children.

Both the large and small versions of the Cuzco bottles were usually embellished with polychrome slip designs. This example is one of the most finely painted examples known in the Cuzco Inca style, a prestige ware associated with the capital of the empire, and used as state gifts to

the outlying provinces. Most of the ornamentation on Inca ceramics is geometric; zoomorphic, anthropomorphic, and other motifs are rare, and tend to be found on fine Cuzco vessels. In this example, the front panel is divided into four bands, two of which depict a step design, and two of insect motifs, including dragonflys. The shoulder on the reverse side of the vessel (not shown) is ornamented with a geometric band, but the rest of the chamber is unadorned, as is typical of most Cuzco bottles. JP

134
KERO
Inca, Late Horizon, A.D. 1450–1550
Wood
27.8 cm x 21 cm (11 x 8¼ in.)
XSc-057-012

Keros, cylindrical cups with flaring rims, were used to consume *chicha* (maize beer) in the Middle Horizon and Late Horizon Periods. These ritual drinking vessels were of paramount importance in the maintenance of social and political relations in the Andes. During the Inca period, *keros* were typically made and used in pairs, as etiquette required that two individuals drink together. Cummins (1988) has argued that these vessels were integral to the consolidation of fundamental reciprocal relations between local communities and the Inca state. In ritual drinking ceremonies between Inca and non-Inca elites, pairs of *keros* would be exchanged in a series of toasts; *keros* were also given as gifts by the sovereign to the ruling *curacas*, or provincial nobility. The *keros* were an emblem of the Inca's benevolence towards a province, but also a reminder to subject lords of their responsibility to the Inca state.

Keros were also made of terra-cotta, silver, and gold; the material used probably corresponded to social rank. Cummins notes that gold *keros* would be used by *curacas* with ten thousand followers; while wooden *keros* would have been for *curacas* with only a hundred (1988:250–251). Pre-Hispanic examples are decorated with incised geometric designs, typical of the Inca aesthetic. As with other Inca objects created under state administration, the *keros* are highly standardized, showing uniformity in size and ornamentation.

The design of this *kero* is divided into two registers: the lower level consists of vertical bands of incised chevrons separated by plain bands; the upper register is divided by a horizontal zigzag, separating the grid pattern incisions from the simple vertical lines. The three-dimensional zoomorph placed perpendicular to the rim is a hybrid, with attributes of a reptile and a puma, which may represent the mythical beings called *katari*. Such creatures are found on what Cummins has called *katari kero*. Cummins suggests that these creatures were emblematic of Inca rulers, and served to remind the viewer of the power of the sovereign (1988:219–222). JP

135
KERO
Inca, Colonial Period, A.D. 1550–?
Wood with pigments
20.7 cm x 17 cm (8 x 6¾ in.)
XXC-00K-00

Keros, or wooden ritual drinking vessels, continued to be made and used in the colonial period. Whereas the pre-Hispanic examples are generally austere, monochrome compositions of geometric patterning, the colonial examples are brightly painted and lacquered vessels with detailed figural compositions. As seen in this colonial example, the paint is often inlaid: the principal forms are shallowly carved from the vessel and the resin-based pigment is added to these depressions. As Cummins (1988) has shown, while there continued to be a need for *keros* in the colonial period, the decorative form of the vessel changed considerably to meet the needs of the changing social conditions. There was new interest in "representation" in a Western sense, so that the cups would be understood within what was becoming a largely figural tradition. Thus, in the Colonial period the cups are pictorial, with narrative depictions of native life and ritual.

The painting on this *kero* is divided into three registers: the upper register; with a figural composition; a middle band of repeating geometric motifs, similar to the pre-Hispanic tradition of *tocapu* (geometric design squares); and a lower band of repeating floral elements. The imagery of colonial *keros* is standardized, with most of the known painted examples falling into a few categories of representation (Cummins 1988:29ff) with specific iconographic clusters repeated over and over again. The upper register of this *kero* shows the Inca-Colloa agricultural scene, a composition of an anthropomorphized sun flanked by twin stylized mountains, with leaping animals on their slopes. On either side of the mountains are profile figures seated on a low stool, raising a *kero* in their hands. Behind these figures are storage jars (see cat. no. 133), from which their *keros* were probably filled. Female figures with *keros* are behind the storage vessels of the Cuzco bottle type. Additional figures carry staves, agricultural implements, and lances; one figure holds a *pututu*, or conch shell trumpet. The figures on the viewer's left side of the composition are dressed in traditional Inca attire. The seated figure on the right wears a turban-shaped headdress with a crescent, identifying the individual as a *curaca* (noble) of the Colloa, an ethnic group from the region near Lake Titicaca. This scene may relate to the myth of Incari and Collari (Cummins 1988:418–426). Still common in the southern Andes, the myth centers on a series of contests between the rulers of these two competing ethnic groups, which the Inca ruler invariably wins. JP

136
QUIPU
Inca, Late Horizon, A.D. 1450–1550
Fiber
75 cm x 58 cm (29½ x 22¾ in.)
XST-035-001

The Inca called their principal recording device a *quipu*, a Quechua word for knot. Administrative data and imperial histories were recorded and recalled by a system of colored and knotted cords. Data were indicated by the position and type of knot, as well as the position and color of the string. *Quipus* are known from the Middle Horizon period, but most date to the Late Horizon period and are closely associated with the complex administration of the Inca empire. This *quipu* system proved to be highly effective and an easily portable method of recording data. A few hundred of them probably survive in museum and private collections.

Guaman Poma, an Andean writing in the late sixteenth to early seventeenth century, illustrates a *quipucamayo* (a specialist charged with the care and interpretation of *quipus*) fingering the cords of a *quipu*, apparently taking stock of the holdings of the immense storage facilities or *collca* of the Inca (Guaman Poma 1980:309, folio 335 [337]). The *quipu* consists of a center string, which is held horizontally, with sometimes hundreds of pendant strings hanging down vertically from this stem. Tertiary strings are attached to these pendant cords. Numbers were recorded using a base-ten positional system, with sums of the values of the pendant cords recorded in an upper cord. When not being used, the *quipu* is rolled and bundled up for safekeeping. JP

137

PLAQUE WITH INCISED DECORATION
Chavín, Early Horizon, 400–200 B.C.
Gold
18 cm x 44 cm (7 x 17¼ in.)
XSB-003-013

The creation of large precious-metal artifacts appears to have been stimulated by the spread of the Chavín cult in the middle of the first millennium B.C. In a search for technologies to convey the otherwordly power of the cult, new methods and materials were introduced to produce symbols of the religious system and create costume elements worn by the leaders associated with the cult. Crowns showing the primary deity, like the Larco piece, were not only worn by individuals but were also buried with them. These burials present convincing evidence for emerging inequality during the Early Horizon and attest to the central role that religious ideology played in this fundamental sociocultural transformation.

This large, horizontal gold object is decorated with the main deity of the Chavín cult, flanked by its avian supernatural attendants. It is made of thin metal sheet, which was produced by the cold-hammering of native gold with fine-grained hammer stones. The embossed relief images were made from the back using tracing tools, then the surface was burnished to eliminate tool marks. The numerous, small sunken areas on the artifact, many of which correspond in position to eyes of the figures, were probably prepared for inlays. Although no trace of such inlays remain on this piece, looted Chavín-style gold objects with semiprecious stone and shell encrustation's still intact have been documented (Alva 1992). While lacking provenance, this remarkable gold object resembles the crowns and other gold objects recovered from Early Horizon sites in the coastal valleys of Lambayeque and Zaña and in the highland environments of the Jequetepeque and Mosna drainages (Alva 1992; Burger 1992, 1996). The shape of the piece is similar to that of the gold crowns recovered from Chongoyape and Kuntur Wasi, and, as in these other pieces, the pairs of small holes punched in its sides may have been used to secure the decorated gold sheet into the desired cylindrical form.

The central anthropomorphic figure is shown frontally, a stance associated solely with the main deity in the Chavín art style. The conventionalized bilobed ears and simplified snake heads (in which the eyes, nose, and mouth have been conflated) indicate that this piece dates from the end of the Chavín sequence. Indeed, there are strong similarities between the iconography

on this piece and the famous Raimondi Stone, the polished granite sculpture from Chavín de Huántar depicting the latest known representation of Chavín's main deity. Because the deity is shown holding a staff of authority in each hand, the term "Staff God" has been applied to this representation (Rowe 1967). The Larco piece shows the deity wearing a relatively simple headdress with pairs of serpents projecting from its sides. Also typical of this deity are the collar or tippet around its neck and sash or breechcloth, whose ends are shown as snakes. Both the hands and feet are shown with claws or talons, more avian than human or feline. Like the representation in the Raimondi Stone, the deity's mouth has rounded corners and turns downwards, with interlocking canine teeth extruding from

the mouth and overlapping the lips. With no primary or secondary sexual characteristics shown, the deity's gender is left unspecified, potentially incorporating both male and female elements. The incorporation of feline, avian, and human elements in the main deity likewise conveys its transcendent nature.

While representations of Chavín's main deity are rare on stone sculpture, they are relatively common on precious metal and other portable objects. A distinctive, but generally similar, representation of the main deity occurs on a gold crown from Chongoyape and on two smaller plaques possibly from the same site (Burger 1996: 47–52). While the Larco piece is in classic late Chavín style and conforms the rough bilateral symmetry characteristic of it, the

image on it relies less heavily on metaphorical substitution than most other examples, and as a result, it is easier to understand the imagery at first glance than is generally possible.

What distinguishes the Larco piece from other representations of the main deity in gold or stone is the inclusion of secondary figures, whose profile poses and positioning on either side of the central axis expresses their lesser status. If this piece is a crown, only the main deity would have been visible from the front when it was worn. Their powerful beaks and taloned claws represent raptorial attributes, but the fanged feline mouths, headdresses with serpents, tippets, and the jaws substituted at the waists of the figures attest to their supernatural characters. Serpents extrude from the chests of each avian supernatural, perhaps representing feathers, and the legs of the creature are bent backwards emerging from the jaws as if mimicking the position of tail feathers (compare the supernatural avians from the Carwa textiles [Burger 1993: Fig. 7d]). Instead of wings, however, these secondary figures have human arms ending in braceleted bird claws.

John Rowe (1967) suggested that these figures represent attendant angels to the principal deity and linked them to the low-relief sculptural renderings on the columns of Chavín de Huántar's New Temple. Flanking the main axis of this section of the site, a supernatural hawk and harpy eagle face inward and each holds a staff, as on the Larco specimen, but an unusual feature of the Larco crown is that the four staffs are positioned diagonally: on the Raimondi Stone they are positioned vertically, while on the columnar avians from Chavín de Huántar, the staffs are horizontal. On the Larco crown, this change of angle appears to link the staffs of the main deity and the secondary figures into a continuous guilloche or braid and situate the three figures in the open interstices of this geometric form. The use of the guilloche and related netlike patterns was particularly popular in classic Cupisnique art and its introduction on this piece (as on one of the Kuntur Wasi crowns) reflects the influence of art of the North Coast on Early Horizon iconography (see Burger 1992: 205–207, 1996: 82–84). RLB

138
MASK OF A FANGED DEITY
Moche III-V, A.D. 200–700
Copper and bone
17.5 cm x 23.5 cm (7 x 9¼ in.)
XSB-001-001

The Moche people who ruled over much of Peru's North Coast during the first half of the first millennium A.D. were among the most skilled and innovative metalsmiths in the Americas. At the time this mask was made, they had developed most of the metalworking techniques ever used by ancient American metalworkers, including hammering, lost-wax casting, embossing, gilding, and silvering. Although gold was undoubtedly the most prestigious metal in ancient Peruvian cultures in terms of its symbolic content and cultural value, the Moche valued copper highly and placed large numbers of copper objects into important burials as evidenced by the recently excavated tombs at the site of Sipán (Alva and Donnan 1993).

This life-size mask depicts the face of the fanged god, a supreme Moche deity well known from countless renditions in sculpted and painted ceramic works. The hammered face still has the original inlaid eyes and three of four fangs in a white material, perhaps shell. The pupils are inlaid with a darker material, probably mussel. Although the inlays give the face a certain amount of life, the expression on the face is still remote and detached, a quality that is present in many depictions of this deity. Round embossed ornaments are worn in the ears. Along the top of the forehead are a number of holes suggesting that the mask may have been attached to a backing, perhaps a mummy bundle or statuary. The corroded copper shows textile impressions indicating that the mask was in contact with fabrics during burial. HK

139
HEADDRESS ORNAMENTS WITH FELINE FACE
Moche III-V, A.D. 200–700
Gold
24 cm x 28 cm (9½ x 11 in.)
XSB-004-029

140
HEADDRESS ORNAMENT WITH HUMAN FACE
Moche III-V, A.D. 200–700
Gold
27 cm x 29.6 cm (10½ x 11¾ in.)
XSB-007-010

141
HEADDRESS ORNAMENT WITH FANNED PLUME
Moche III-V, A.D. 200–700
Gold
24.2 cm x 27.3 cm (9½ x 10¾ in.)
XSB-006-005

Headdresses were an important part of ancient Peruvian costume. The numerous depictions of headgear on Moche painted and sculpted ceramics show great diversity of form and type. Styles ranged from simple caps and headbands made of fiber

or basketry wound around the head to elaborate multipiece complex arrangements made of a variety of materials. These three embossed sheet-gold ornaments were probably once part of such headdress assemblages worn by important personages in Moche society. The paired holes under the chins and above the heads of the faces suggest they were attached as frontals to a turban or cap.

Each ornament is decorated with a large frontal repoussé face in the center; one of the faces is feline (cat. no. 139), one is human (cat. no. 140), and one is a combination of the two (cat. no. 141). Two of the frontals (cat. nos. 139, 140) have a rounded shape with cutout upside-down animal figures on either side of the faces, which fit well into the circular outline. The third ornament (cat. no. 141) is tall and elongated with flared side elements and a separately attached center piece. The big open mouth of the feline face (cat. no. 139) has bared teeth and fangs, exhibit a great deal of aggression; it is flanked by upside-down profile birds with prominent curved beaks. (A virtually identical headdress ornament is in the collection of The Metropolitan Museum of Art, New York.) The birds have been identified as condors, however, they lack the caruncles on the top of their beaks, which usually are shown in Moche iconography. The human face (cat. no. 140), by contrast, is serene and devoid of expression; it, too, is flanked by upside-down profile creatures, which have been variously interpreted as jaguars, sky-pumas, or moon-monsters. They have large heads with fanged mouths, spiked backs, and long tails arching over their backs to end in spirals behind their heads. An interesting feature on this frontal, said to have been found in a tomb near the sand dune of El Purpur in the Virú Valley (Jones 1979), are the profile legs and feet that appear on either side of the chin, yet there is no body. Between the legs is a zigzag line, which may be a reference to a tunic border. The upper part of these two frontals is in the shape of a fanned plume, which is a separate element in the case of the third headdress (cat. no. 141). It has a repoussé design along the top. Unlike the face on the two round frontals, the human fanged face on the elongated frontal has concave eyes, which were originally inlaid with another material, probably shell; one of the inlays is still in place. HK

142
Pectoral
Cupisnique?, 1200–200 B.C.
Snail shell and turquoise
35.5 cm x 43.3 cm (14 x 17 in.)
XSB-006-009

143
Pectoral
Moche III-V, A.D. 200–700
Gold and turquoise
21 cm x 50 cm (8¼ x 19¾ in.)
XSB-006-006

Collars or bibs made of colorful stone and shell beads are known from many coastal cultures in Peru from the early periods to the last few centuries before the conquest. They seem to have been particularly lavish ornaments worn by important people in ancient Peruvian societies. In the recently discovered tomb of a Moche dignitary at the site of Sipán, the lord was bedecked with several such splendid pectorals made of thousands of individually cut beads threaded to create appealing patterns (Alva and Donnan 1993).

The shell collar is made of numerous flat and elongated links cut from shell, each with a row of four pierced turquoise disks set into circular depressions. Shells and other products of the sea were highly symbolic materials in ancient Andean cultures and played a major role in myth and religion. They were often included in articles of adornment and symbols of rank. The *Spondylus* shell in particular was highly prized, probably because of its brilliant red color. Unavailable from the cold waters off the Peruvian coastal desert, it became a major item of trade from the warm Ecuadorian waters to the north. Among the Inca it was believed to bring rain, probably because it came from the sea, the source of all rain. It was also considered the favorite food of the gods and was offered in rituals in many forms: whole, cracked, and ground into powder. The importance of the *Spondylus* shell in Andean ritual life is evidenced by its many depictions in the ceramic medium as well as in metal works. *Spondylus* shells were also often placed in burials of important individuals.

In similar necklaces the links of the collar have drill holes for stringing along their long sides; here, the links are arranged raylike in four concentric semicircles. Along the outer edge of the collar is a row of profile animal heads, also sculpted in shell. Their eyes are inlaid with small perforated turquoise disks. Near the center at the bottom of the collar the faces change direction so that

when the collar is seen from the front, they face in opposite directions. The stringing is modern.

The Moche turquoise collar is made of countless very tiny drilled turquoise beads. In its current configuration, it has a semicircular stepped shape with seven

segments created by long spacer beads, which hold the many strings of small stone beads in place. Eight small embossed gold ornaments in form of human figures hang from the bottom of the spacer beads. The collar is outlined on all sides by a row of tiny gold balls. HK

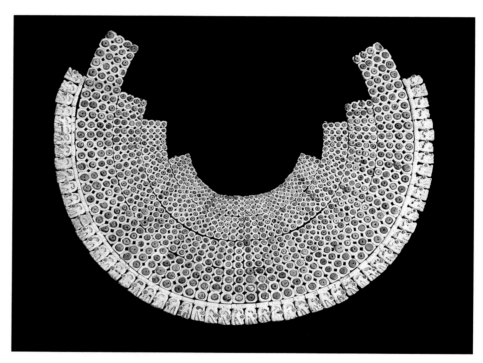

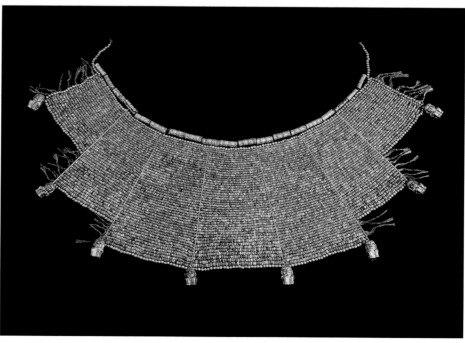

144
Nose Ornament
Moche III-V, A.D. 200–700
Gold
6 cm x 6 cm (2⅜ x 2⅜ in.)
XSB-008-006

145
Necklace with Frogs
Moche III-V, A.D. 200–700
Gold
61.5 cm (24¼ in.)
XSB-009-011

Ornaments made to be worn in the nose are among the earliest jewelry forms in pre-Hispanic America. They were a favorite item of facial adornment in the early cultures of ancient Peru. Those worn by high-ranking individuals were made of gold and silver, materials that were rare and symbolically meaningful.

Moche burials have yielded numerous examples of magnificent nose ornaments, sometimes several in the same tomb. Invariably Moche nose ornaments are made of hammered sheet metal; the mid-section is often plain and semicircular in shape with a small round hole and narrow opening for the septum. When worn the ornament would have covered the wearer's mouth. This fancy example shows dense surface designs of embossed and cutout animal forms, which were created with chasing tools and sharp chisels while the sheet rested on a resilient surface such as leather or sand. On either side of the plain mid-section are two fanged animals in profile, probably serpents, arranged as though whiskers; they have spiked and spotted spiral bodies to which dangles are attached with staples. Below them are two creatures in profile, possibly felines, with big round eyes, fangs, massive paws, spotted bodies, and curled noses and tails. Along the bottom of the ornaments are free hanging dangles, each separately attached with two strip metal rings. When the nose ornament was worn, the dangles would have been in constant movement, creating a delicate ringing sound and catching the bright glitter of the sun.

Fanged creatures are very common in Moche iconography and are often difficult to interpret. The fangs may refer to a variety of species which were symbolically meaningful. Serpents, for example, shed their skin regularly and are therefore linked to ideas of renewal, rebirth, regeneration, growth, and fertility. Felines are animals much feared and admired because of their speed and aggression. They are skillful hunters and able to move in different realms: in water, on land, and in trees. They are therefore considered excellent intermediaries between the world of the living and the spirit world. HK

The ancient Peruvians seldom cast gold or silver although they had developed the technology to do so. They collected gold primarily from placer deposits in rivers, but also mined the precious metal from auriferous quartz veins. In pre-Hispanic America gold was used exclusively for ostentatious display, mostly items of personal adornment, and, to a lesser degree, ritual objects such as beakers and rattles (Lechtman 1979, 1980, 1984).

The Peruvians had a clear preference for the hammering process when working with gold or silver. It has been suggested that the use of sheet metal fashioned from ingots with stone hammers and anvils was culturally meaningful to the people because this tradition lasted from the early beginnings of gold working in the second millennium B.C. to the time of the conquest in the sixteenth century (Lechtman 1984a). The hammering tradition was so strong that even three-dimensional objects, which elsewhere in the pre-Hispanic world would have been cast, were constructed of several separately shaped pieces of sheet and joined by tabs or staples or by soldering. Such a process was used in this case: the little frogs that are part of the necklace were made of separately shaped parts, which were then joined by soldering. The pierced nose holes and eyes inlaid with perforated turquoise disks give them a lifelike look. The arrangement of the frogs, alternating with tubular and round beads, as well as the stringing, are modern.

Frogs occur frequently in the iconography of Moche art. As water and land animals that mutate from eggs to tadpoles to frogs, they are associated with ideas of transformation, growth, and fertility. HK

146
NECKLACE
Moche III-V, A.D. 200–700
Rock crystal
25.5 cm x 10.3 cm (10 x 14¼ in.)
XSB-016-004

147
SPEAR-THROWER WITH BIRD
Moche III-V, A.D. 200–700
Gold and lapis lazuli
65 cm (25½ in.)
XSB-006-003

Semiprecious stones of various kinds and colors were highly valued in many cultures in pre-Hispanic America from early on. They were widely traded and worked into jewelry items for the elite and, to a lesser degree, into ritual objects.

The ancient Americans did not manufacture glass. The transparent, brilliant rock crystal, which could be worked into glistening artifacts, must have been a particularly valued material. Rock crystal beads are attributed to a number of early Peruvian cultures. Since iron tools to work hard stones like rock crystal were unknown, the method of shaping was percussion with hammer stones, abrading with stone files or grinding stones, and drilling with hardwood or stone drills. The holes of the beads were usually drilled from both sides. The stringing is modern. HK

Spear-throwers were widely used in pre-Hispanic America by hunters and warriors alike. Their purpose was to lengthen the throwing arm so that the projectile, attached to one end of the thrower would travel over a longer distance. The throwers were secured in the hand by finials, or finger grips (see cat. nos. 101, 102), which were often in the form of intriguing miniature sculptures. The importance of this weapon is emphasized by the great care taken to adorn the finger grips and by the choice of precious materials they are made of. The function of the elaborate ones is not clear; they may have been for ritual display.

In this example the hook is topped by a small golden condor identified by the caruncle on its forehead (Schaffer 1983). Sitting on a small wooden platform, the

bird appears to be feeding on a human corpse lying on its back with outstretched arms. The bird is constructed of many individually shaped pieces of sheet, which were then soldered into place. Its eyes are inlaid with lapis lazuli. Carrion eaters, condors are often shown in Moche art, in the ceramic and metal mediums, pecking at human and animal heads and bodies. They were, perhaps, associated, in ancient Peruvian thought with predation, death, and sacrifice. HK

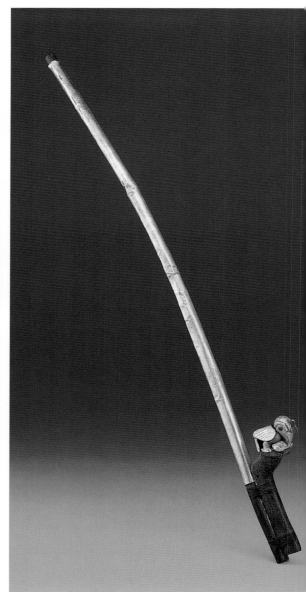

148
Pair of Mosaic Earplugs
Moche III-V, A.D. 200–700
Gold, turquoise, chrysocolla, quartz,
Spondylus shell, pyrite, gypsum, soapstone
9.4 cm x 10.1 cm (3¾ x 4 in.)
XSB-006-001/002

149
Pair of Mosaic Earplugs
Moche III-V, A.D. 200–700
Gold, turquoise, snail shell
8.4 cm x 7.8 cm (3⅜ x 3 in.)
XSB-008-C04/C05

Large ear ornaments with circular frontals and long tubular shafts in back, which counterbalanced the weight of the frontals, were common personal adornments of prominent individuals on Peru's North Coast for at least a millennium. They were a symbol of their wealth and power.

Among the most elaborate earplugs created by the Moche are the ones decorated on their frontals with brilliantly colored stone and shell mosaic. The materials used in the mosaics include turquoise, chrysocolla, quartz, and other semiprecious stones as well as *Spondylus* shell. In recent years, at the site of Sipán in the Moche heartland on Peru's North Coast, archaeologists uncovered the undisturbed tomb of an important ruler who had been laid to rest in great splendor. Among the countless items of personal finery interred with this ruler were three sets of ear ornaments similar in concept and craftsmanship to the present examples.

One of the pairs shown here (cat. no. 148) features mythological bird-headed warrior figures, with gold-tipped beaks. In their outstretched hands each holds a war club with a circular shield and a sling with a round projectile made of gold. The warriors have golden eyes and wear round golden earplugs and headdresses with plumes and appendages ending in a small animal head with a golden eye. The three tassels at the bottom of their belts are also made of gold.

The frontals of the second pair (cat. no. 149) are divided into eight wedge-shaped segments of alternating blue and white color. The design is simple and easy to read; it consists of lizards, their tails meeting in the center. Details like eyes are inlaid in a contrasting color. The outer rim of both pairs of frontals is surrounded by hollow gold balls. Both pairs of ear plugs are said to have come from a grave in the vicinity of the great sand dune of El Purpur in the Virú Valley (Jones 1979). HK

150
Long Ear Ornament Frontals
Chimú, Late Intermediate Period,
A.D. 1000–1450
Gold
22 cm x 7.8 cm (8¾ x 3 in.)
XSB-005-002/010

These ear ornaments are similar in configuration and surface design to a very elaborate pair in the Dumbarton Oaks Collection in Washington, D.C. According to the catalogue (Lothrop 1957) the Dumbarton Oaks ornaments were found together with a mask and grand breastplate in a tomb of the Chimú period near the coastal site of Huarmey, about 160 miles north of Lima. Lothrop believes that these objects constituted the adornments of the outer wrappings of a mummy bundle and calls them "some of the most complex objects from Peru," which must have "appeared sumptuous even in the eyes of a people well-accustomed to seeing ornaments of gold" (1957: 274).

In the last few centuries before the Spanish conquest, the rulers of the Chimú empire on Peru's North Coast had become very powerful and amassed great wealth from all parts of their realm. The royal tombs contained in the imposing high-walled adobe compounds at the capital city of Chan Chan in the Moche Valley are said to have been filled with hoards of precious objects in valued materials. The tombs have been exploited by treasure hunters from early colonial times to the present.

These ear ornaments may have once been part of a set similar to the one in the Dumbarton Oaks collection. They consist of disks embossed with a step-fret pattern. In the center of each disk, set in a sheet-gold socket, is a hollow rod; it is covered with a gold cap and surrounded by six plain semicircular danglers. From each disk hangs a gold plaque embossed with the same pattern as the disks. Suspended from the plaques by pairs of gold wire are six serpents with zigzag bodies and embossed faces. Attached to their mouths are gold rings holding danglers. The many articulated parts of the ornaments would have been set in motion with each step of the wearer and the slightest movement of the head to create a dazzling visual and auditory effect. The ornaments were probably attached to a backing, which has since been lost. HK

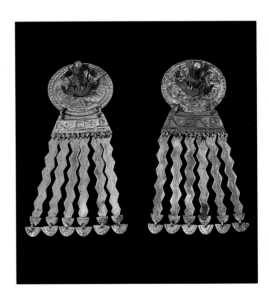

151
BROOCH
Chimú, Late Intermediate Period,
A.D. 1000–1450
Silver alloy
8.3 cm x 8.8 (3¼ x 3½ in.)
XSB-020-C05

152
BROOCH
Chimú, Late Intermediate Period,
A.D. 1000–1450
Silver alloy
10.9 cm x 10.7 cm (4¼ x 4¼ in)
XSB-020-003

These ornaments, cut from a sheet of
silver alloy, may have once served as
embellishments on high-status Chimú
textiles or on some other type of backing.
Geometric and zoomorphic forms were
sewn onto finely woven garments, adding
bright, glittering details to the costumes
of the nobility. As with many Chimú
metal objects, the small dangles at the
bottom of the ornaments enliven the
imagery with movement.

In both ornaments, the compositions
are articulated below a tripartite bar. On
cat. no. 151, the frame of this bar continues along the sides and bottom of the
ornament, circumscribing the figures
within it. On cat. no. 152, two profile
monkeys with long, curling tails hold a
crescent-shaped object. Two smaller profile monkeys sit in the center of the composition; their paws reach upwards, and
their heads are turned outward to face the
monkeys holding the crescent shape. The
crescent shape may represent a tule boat,
a light watercraft still used for fishing in
some areas along the North Coast of Peru
(Cordy-Collins 1977).

The first ornament shows a frontal
figure with ear ornaments, a crescent
headdress, and two appendages terminat-
ing in tassels. A bird with a fish in its beak
is perched at the ends of both tassels. The
figure wears the traditional male attire of a
tunic and loincloth, but the arms of the
figure terminate in zoomorphic profile
heads with protruding tongues that extend
up and around the muzzle to touch their
ears. Two small profile anthropomorphic
figures are located between the arms and
the body of the larger figure. Figures with
similar peaked caps are occasionally seen in
representations of divers and other individuals associated with the sea (Cordy-
Collins 1990; Martínez Compañón 1978:
E125). As with much of Chimú art, these
compositions reiterate a maritime theme:
from the wave form of the headdress appendages to the surrounding creatures, a
watery realm is suggested. JP

153 >

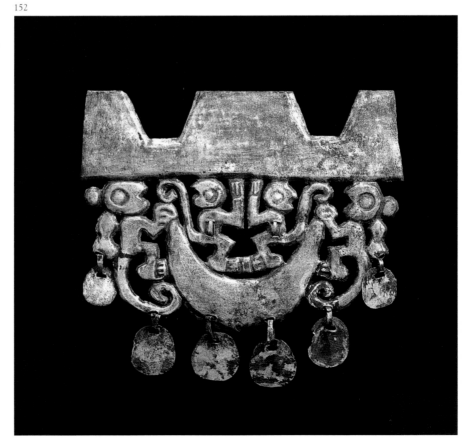

153
SET OF ORNAMENTS
Chimú, Late Intermediate Period,
A.D. 1000–1450
Gold

PECTORAL
20 cm x 49 cm (7⅞ x19¼ in.)
XSB-011-007

CROWN
16 cm x 22 cm (6¼ x 8¾ in.)
XSB-011-001

FOUR FEATHER PLUMES FOR CROWN
27 cm (10½ in.)
XSB-011-001

HOMBRERA
8.8 cm x 18 cm (7 in.)
XSB-011-006

HOMBRERA
8.8 cm x 18 cm (7 in.)
XSB-011-010

EARPLUG
12.5 cm (5 in.)
XSB-011-005

EARPLUG
12.5 cm (5 in.)
XSB-011-009

NECKLACE
5 cm x 41.5 cm (16¼ in.)
XSB-011-008

Elite costume ornaments, these objects would have served to differentiate individuals of high status in the Chimú period. This set includes a headdress, ear ornaments, a necklace and bracelet of hollow gold beads, a pair of ear ornaments, and a pectoral. Presumably these objects all came from the same grave lot and were all associated with a specific nobleman in his lifetime, and then buried with him upon his death.

Very few silver and gold Chimú objects have been excavated scientifically, limiting our understanding of the cultural associations of these works. In the early colonial period, individuals were given what amounted to mining rights to plunder Chimú burial structures (Zevallos 1994). This set of ornaments provides a rare glimpse of the type of regalia probably worn by the Chimú nobility. The only other comparable set, also thought to be a grave lot, is now at Dumbarton Oaks (Boone 1996:225, plates 55–65).

The headdress is composed of a plain cylinder form with a flaring base and top,

surmounted by four projecting elements, representing golden feathers. Under the striations at the top of these plumes are embossed borders, which consist of a repetition of a profile anthropomorphic figure wearing a crescent headdress and an appendage hanging down the back, which terminates in a profile zoomorphic head. Some of the figures hold a circular object.

Large ear ornaments were an important part of the regalia of Andean noblemen. The disks are backed by thick tubes, which would have been inserted through the ear lobe. In the sixteenth century members of the Inca nobility were called *orejones* (long ears) by the Spaniards, referring to the distended character of their ear lobes. These ear ornaments have a central boss around which are repeated anthropomorphic heads, also wearing ear ornaments.

The necklace is made up of nine hollow gold spheres. The hollow beads are formed by creating two hemispheres from sheet metal, either by shaping the sheet metal over a wooden mold, or perhaps by pressing the sheet metal into a hemisphere-shaped depression. The two halves are then joined together. Usually the original cords used to string the beads do not survive, and most of these necklaces are restrung on new cords in modern times. This configuration may be original, however, as similar short choker-style bead necklaces are seen on wooden sculptures from the same time period and region (see for example American Museum of Natural History 41.0/7359, Morris and von Hagen, 1993:125, Fig. 114).

The pectoral is semicircular, with the two end panels hinged onto the main section, perhaps lying across the shoulders when worn, as epaulets, while the rest of the collar lies on the chest. Thirty gold tabs or pendants form the lower border. The main portion of the pectoral is filled with embossed profile figures, wearing crescent headdresses and carrying circular objects, similar to the figures on the headdress feathers of this set. The repetition and similarity of the forms on the pectoral suggest that they were made with the aid of a mold or template.

The end panels of the pectoral have a design that is distinctive from the main area of the pectoral, but perhaps related to

the ear ornaments. Both panels are divided into three sections with borders created by a wave pattern. Each of the three sections contains a figure: all are shown in frontal view and wear regalia similar to this set: ear ornaments, necklace, and headdress, in addition to a tunic. The figures grasp what are likely representations of trophy heads, perhaps the decapitated bounty of war, in each hand. The trophy heads themselves wear ear ornaments, suggesting that the victims were of high status. The trophy heads look very similar to the heads depicted on the ear ornaments of this set, perhaps indicating that the ear ornaments too refer to a practice of war captives or sacrificial victims. JP

154

PAIR OF FACE BEAKERS
Lambayeque, Late Intermediate Period,
A.D. 800–1150
Gold
21.6 cm x 17 cm (8½ x 6¾ in.)
XSB-101-011

20.3 cm x 18 cm (8 x 7 in.)
XSB-010-010

After the decline of the Moche culture in the eighth century A.D., the Lambayeque culture (also called Sicán) emerged as a strong force on Peru's North Coast. The royal tombs discovered in the Batán Grande region in the Lambayeque Valley contained some of the largest and most ostentatious objects ever created in gold in pre-Hispanic America. Among them are beakers of the kind illustrated here. One of the richest Sicán tombs, discovered in the late 1950s by local people, is said to have contained more than 170 gold and silver beakers of various sizes grouped in stacks, often as many as ten to a stack (Carcedo and Shimada 1985). The beakers may have been used during the lifetime of the owner and in funerary rituals before interment.

Technologically the beakers represent remarkable achievements by master metalworkers who had a profound under-standing of the material with which they were working. Production began by consistently striking an ingot of metal with a domed hammer stone on a stone anvil to stretch the material. Frequent annealing was required to avoid stress fractures. Eventually the sheet was hammered over different types of wooden molds to raise the walls of the beakers and to create designs (Easby 1956).

A frequent theme on Lambayeque beakers, which usually have flat bases and flaring sides, is a broad frontal repoussé face with comma-shaped eyes and a straight nose with flaring nostrils. Many beakers have faces that are upright when the beaker itself is upside-down. It is only on such beakers that the mouths are fanged and perhaps have tongues protruding over the lower lips (Jones 1995). The ears are worked as raised ovals that constrict near the bottom where round ear ornaments are indicated. The faces are topped by caps with a raised band above the short, straight-sided foreheads. Be-neath the faces is a relief collarlike molding. It has been suggested that this face, which appears on many objects from the period, is that of the Sicán deity (Shimada 1997).

The reddish color over much of the surface of the beakers is the result of oxidation and corrosion of copper and silver in the gold alloy. Laboratory test of Lambayeque gold objects have often shown low gold contents in the copper-silver alloys despite a golden surface color. The surfaces of those pieces were enriched through the depletion gilding process (Lechtman 1984b).

In a series of extensive studies Heather Lechtman (1974, 1979, 1984) has discussed the evolution of the use of alloys in Andean metallurgy. She suggests a close association between technology and idea systems and stresses the importance of working processes and essence of materials in objects in ancient Peruvian cultures. HK

155, 156

MINIATURE OBJECTS
Chimú, Late Intermediate Period,
A.D. 1000–1450
Silver, copper alloy

BOX
12 cm x 27 cm (4¾ x 10 ⅝ in.)
XSB-018-C16

CIRCLE
11.3 cm (4½ in.)

TABLE
4.9 cm x 8.3 cm (3¼ in.)

BED
.6 cm x 8.5 cm (3¼ in.)
XSB-018-B21

STIRRUP-SPOUT VESSEL
5.2 cm x 2.8 cm (2 in.)

OVEN
4.5 cm x 3.5 cm (1¾ in.)

SET OF NEEDLES
8.4 cm x 2.5 cm (3¼ in.)

KERO
10 cm x 4.1 cm (4 in.)

This box was reportedly found together with these seven miniature silver objects in the grave of a young girl. As with much of Chimú art, the design of this metal box is marked by an emphasis on geometric borders. The composition of the lid and the sides of the box is essentially the same: two central panels, each consisting of a figure

wearing a crescent headdress flanked by two profile anthropomorphic figures; this group is surrounded by a step-motif border. On the front and back of the box, two profile birds divide the two sets of figures. The two end panels have the crescent headdress figure and a single, profile anthropomorphic figure. Three strips of metal hinge the lid to the box. Impressions evident on the surface corrosion suggest that the box may have been covered by a textile at one point.

A common interpretation of miniature objects is that they are toys, an interpretation reinforced by the reported context for this box. Miniature objects in the Andean world, however, often served a votive purpose, and these miniature objects may have been sacred offerings. At Pacatnamu, a Late Intermediate Period site on the North Coast of Peru, numerous miniature textiles were associated with burials of young females. Bruce (1986) has suggested that the burials were dedicatory offerings, and the miniature textiles substituted for full-size textiles that accompany more elaborate burials.

Chimú wooden boxes of similar size and composition are known (Purin 1990: nos. 302, 303), but none has been reported with contents. Miniature silver objects have reportedly been found in several tombs in the Chancay Valley (A. Rowe 1984:155–157; see also Purin 1990: nos.

357, 358, 359). The Chancay miniature objects consist of a double-spout vessel, musical instruments, and other implements.

The miniature objects illustrated here include a bed, a disk, a box with four supports, and a *kero* (ritual drinking vessel), among others. The bed, the disk, and the box with four supports repeat the step-motif border found on the large box, suggesting that these objects and the box were intended as a set. A miniature stirrup-spout vessel, a typical North Coast vessel shape, is also in this set; as with larger examples, the vessel was made in pieces and soldered together. JP

157

BOWL WITH EMBOSSED BIRDS
Chimú, Late Intermediate Period,
A.D. 1000–1450
Silver alloy
5.1 cm x 16.7 cm (1⅞ x 6½ in.)
XSB-019-C06

The city of Chan Chan was notable for its dedication to craft production; Chimú artisans were clustered in *barrios* (or neighborhoods), where they produced finely woven textiles, inlaid wooden sculptures, and other items. Particularly in the later history of Chan Chan, the scale of manufacturing at the site included as many as twelve thousand full-time artisans living and working in the city (J. Topic 1990:149). Chimú artisans were renown in the Inca period; Cieza de León (1959 [1553]:241) notes that Chimú metalsmiths were taken to Cuzco by the Inca as their work was considered to be superior.

This low-wall, silver-alloy bowl was created by shaping and joining two pieces of sheet metal to form the interior and exterior surfaces. The relatively thick rim has a squared indentation on one side, which perhaps functioned as a spout. Embossed birds cover the bowl's

surface; these forms were probably created with the aid of a wooden template or mold, over which the sheet metal was pressed. The birds are arranged in circular bands radiating out from the central roundel, which encircles a single bird. The bands of birds face alternating directions, with a final band occurring at the bowl rim.

The bird depicted is most likely a maritime species that inhabits the guano islands and littoral near Chan Chan, perhaps a cormorant. Such seabirds are a prominent motif in the architectural reliefs at Chan Chan, where many compositions include framing bands of birds and fish. In some reliefs at Chan Chan, the marine birds are depicted simply, such as in this example, while others are shown wearing crescent headdresses and carrying implements, suggesting mythic or metaphorical associations. JP

158

INCISED BOWL
Chimú, Late Intermediate Period,
A.D. 1000–1450
Silver
4.5 cm x 13.8 cm (1¾ x 5½ in.)
XSB-019-B15

This small bowl was probably made from a single, relatively thick sheet of silver, which was hammered into this shape. The designs were created by incising the imagery on the surface with a sharp instrument. Faint traces of the imagery on the exterior of the bowl can be seen in the interior, which is otherwise plain. Figure definition in the composition is emphasized by the crosshatching seen in the background. The imagery centers on a roundel enclosing an anthropomorphic figure with a crescent headdress. Radiating outward from the roundel are three large figures, also with crescent headdresses, each holding what appears to be a cord encircling two smaller profile anthropomorphic figures, which are shown with the knees up, touching their elbows. Crescent-headdressed figures similar to the one in the central roundel are found at the interstices of the principal trio. Smaller profile figures holding trefoil elements representing *Spondylus* (a marine bivalve of great ritual importance in the Andes) shells are found near the feet and above the trio. At the top of the composition, along the bowl rim, is a band of similar elements.

The trio of figures probably represents *Spondylus* shell divers, with the divers' cords extended from the hand of the main figure and encircling the profile diving figure. This theme is found both on portable objects from the Late Intermediate period and on architectural reliefs at Chan Chan (Cordy-Collins 1990; Pillsbury 1996). Under normal conditions, *Spondylus* is harvested from the warmer tropical waters off the coast of Ecuador (or farther north) at a depth of between fifteen and fifty meters. The difficulty of procurement was undoubtedly part of its attractiveness as an exotic, elite material in the central Andean region of Peru (see cat. no. 126). The depiction of its acquisition may refer not so much to its actual harvesting, but to myths or legendary histories which feature supernaturals and *Spondylus*, and serve to reinforce the economic position of this important valuable in Chimú society.

Such bowls were probably used by the Chimú elite, and possibly interred with them upon their death. In some respects, this bowl is similar to a remark-

159

INCISED BOWL
Chimú, Late Intermediate Period,
A.D. 1000–1450
Gold and silver
10 cm x 10 cm (4 x 4 in.)
XSB-011-003

able set of silver and gold objects found in the Huaca la Misa, the funerary platform of *ciudadela* Rivero at Chan Chan (Ríos and Retamozo 1982). The Huaca la Misa set primarily consists of drinking goblets, but the imagery and incision seen on this bowl is similar to a number of those goblets. Both this bowl and the Huaca de la Misa set probably were made relatively late in the Chimú sequence, perhaps in the late fourteenth to early fifteenth century. JP

This small bowl was created by joining and shaping two equal-size pieces of gold and silver sheet metal. An incised design covers the entire exterior surface, with the line separating gold and silver halves running through a central figure incised on the bottom of the bowl. This frontal anthropomorphic figure wears circular ear ornaments and an elaborate headdress. The headdress is a complex affair, depicting two step elements from which a crescent form emerges, the ends of which terminate in profile zoomorphic heads. These zoomorphic creatures also wear headdresses and have protruding tongues and rounded ears. The appendages of the frontal anthropomorphic figure terminate in similar profile zoomorphic heads as well. Circling this figure are profile zoomorphic forms with tails and a serrated crest on the back. The complex central figure is also repeated on the sides of the bowl. Interspersed between these central figures are serpent forms, rendered as if from a dorsal view, *Spondylus* shells, and other motifs. A band of repeating profile

zoomorphs with tassels occurs at the bottom and rim of the bowl. As with cat. no. 158, the background of the composition is crosshatched to emphasize the images.

Bimetallic objects—and even buildings created by joining two different materials or materials of two different colors—have attracted much interest in Andean studies because of their possible reference to bilateral social and conceptual divisions. Calancha (1977[1638], libro II, capítulo XIX:934–935) records a myth common on the coast of Peru which states that humans were created from three eggs: the *curacas* and other male members of the nobility were created from a golden egg, their wives from silver eggs, and commoners from copper eggs. Bimetallic works are not common on the North Coast, but a few notable examples are known from the Moche culture, particularly the gold and silver backflap and other objects excavated at the royal tombs of Sipán (Alva and Donnan 1993:154, Fig. 166). JP

160

Zoomorphic vessel
Chimú, Late Intermediate Period,
A.D. 1000–1450
Silver
18.7 cm x 15.8 cm (7¼ x 6¼ in.)
XSB 019 B14

The body of this silver vessel is shaped
into two rounded chambers, the top one
partially serving as the body of a quadru-
ped, probably an armadillo. Although
certain characteristics of the animal are
suggested in this rendering, such as the
triangular muzzle, prominent oval ears,
and hinged bands of the carapace, it
seems that the artist was not entirely
familiar with armadillos, as the legs,
claws, and tail of the real creature are
substantially different from this portrayal.
Hunted for food, these nocturnal animals
may also have been important in beliefs
about death and regeneration, given that
they live underground.

Each chamber of the vessel includes a
band of incised decoration. Both show
similar imagery consisting of a repetition
of two sets of figures. One is an anthropomorphic figure with a bundle slung over
his back; seen in profile is an anthropomorphic figure perched on the bundle.
These figures alternate with a seated
profile anthropomorphic figure with a
monkey with a long curling tail, standing
on his shoulder and arching over his head
(in some instances the figure and the
monkey hold an object between them).
Other small figures, some with a long cap
with a tassel, are interspersed between
these two sets of figures in the lower band;
in the band on the upper (animal) chamber, a diving bird is placed between the
figure with the bundle and the figure with
the monkey. A band of a repeated step
design is found above the incised imagery
on the bottom chamber, and below the
incised imagery of the upper chamber.

A trefoil element, representing a
Spondylus shell (see cat. no. 126), is
shown in front of some of the figures
carrying bundles. A similar figure with a
bundle and a *Spondylus* shell is found on a
relief at *ciudadela* Uhle at Chan Chan
(Pillsbury 1993:Fig. 39). The figure at
Chan Chan is also shown with a parrot,
suggesting that these figures with
bundles, if not representing long-distance
traders, at least were surrounded by valuable items closely associated with elite
status, such as exotic shells and feathers.

The neck of this vessel has been bro-
ken and restored, and the incision around
the spout may have been reconstructed in
modern times. JP

Bibliography

General sources

Adorno, R. *Guaman Poma: Writing and Resistance in Colonial Peru*. Latin American Monographs, no. 68. Austin: University of Texas Press, 1986.

Anton, Ferdinand. *The Art of Ancient Peru*. New York: G. P. Putnam's Sons, 1972.

Arriaga, Pablo José de. *Extirpacion de la idolatria del Piru* [1621]. Biblioteca de Autores Españoles. Vol. 209. Madrid: Atlas, 1968.

———— *The Extirpation of Idolatry in Peru*. Trans. L. C. Keating. Lexington: University of Kentucky Press, 1968.

Baessler, Adolf. *Ancient Peruvian Art*. Trans. A. H. Keene. New York: Dodd, Mead and Co.; Berlin: A. Asher, 1902-1903.

Benson, Elizabeth P., ed.. *Death and the Afterlife in Pre-Columbian America*. Washington, D.C.: Dumbarton Oaks Research Library and Collections, 1975.

———— "Art, Agriculture, Warfare and the Guano Islands." *Andean Art: Visual Expression and its Relation to Andean Beliefs and Values*, ed. Penny Dransart. Worldwide Archaeology Series 13. Avebury and Aldershot, England, 1995.

———— *Precolumbian Metallurgy of South America*. Washington, D.C.: Dumbarton Oaks, 1979.

Bonavia, Duccio. *Mural Painting in Ancient Peru*. Trans. Patricia J. Lyon. Bloomington: University of Indiana Press, 1985.

Boone, Elizabeth Hill, ed. *Andean Art at Dumbarton Oaks*. 2 vols. Washington, D.C.: Dumbarton Oaks Research Library and Collections, 1996.

Bridges, Marilyn. *Planet Peru: An Aerial Journey through a Timeless Land*. Photography Division of Eastman Kodak, 1991.

Bruhn, Karen Olsen. *Ancient South America*. Cambridge and New York: Cambridge UP, 1994.

Carerra, Fernando de la. *Arte de la Lengua Yunga de los valles del Obispado de Truxillo del Peru, con un confessionario y todas las oraciones traducidas en la lengua y otras cosas*. Lima: José Contreras, 1644.

Cieza de León, Pedro. *La Crónica del Peru*. Madrid: Calpe, 1922.

Cordy-Collins, Alana, and Jean Stern, eds. *Pre-Columbian Art History: Selected Readings*. Palo Alto, Calif.: Peek Publications, 1977.

D'Harnoncourt, Rene. "Introduction." In *Ancient Arts of the Andes*, W. Bennett, 1954.

Dillehay, Tom D. *Tombs for the Living: Andean Mortuary Practices*. Washington, D.C.: Dumbarton Oaks Research Library and Collections, 1995.

Donnan, Christopher. *Ceramics of Ancient Peru*. Los Angeles: Fowler Museum of Cultural History, UCLA, 1992.

Duviols, Pierre. "Un inédit de Cristóbal de Albornoz: La instrucción para descubrir las Guacas del Piru y sus camayos de haziendas." *Journal de la Société des Americanistes* (Paris) LXVI, no. 1 (1967).

Easby, Dudley T. "Ancient American Goldsmiths." *Natural History* (New York) LXV, no. 8 (1956).

Frame, Mary. "Visual Images of Fabric Structures in Ancient Peruvian Art." In *The Junius B. Bird Conference on Andean Textiles*, ed. A. Rowe, 1986.

Gayton, Anna H. "The Cultural Significance of Peruvian Textiles: Production, Function, Aesthetics." *Kroeber Anthropological Society Papers* 25 (1961): 111–128.

Greene, Virginia. "An Ancient Andean Feathered Headdress." In *The Gift of Birds: Featherworking of Native South America Peoples*, ed. R. Reina and K. Kensinger. Monograph 75. Philadelphia: University Museum, 1991.

Gombrich, Ernst. *Art and Illusion*. Princeton, N.J.: Princeton University Press, 1960.

Gonzales Holguin, Diego. *Vocabulario de la Lengua General de todo el Peru, Llamada Quechua* [1608]. Lima: Instituto de Historia, Universidad Nacional Mayor de San Marcos, 1952.

Gonzalez la Rosa, M. "Estudio de las antiguedades peruanas halladas bajo el guano." *Revista Historica* 3 (1908). Lima.

J. Haas, T. and S. Pozorski, eds. *Origins and Development of the Andean State*. Cambridge: Cambridge University Press, 1987.

Jones, Julie, ed. *The Art of Pre-Columbian Gold: the Jan Mitchell Collection*. New York: The Metropolitan Museum of Art, 1985.

Joralemon, Donald and Douglas Sharon. *Sorcery and Shamanism: Curanderos and Clients in Northern Peru*. Salt Lake City: University of Utah Press, 1993.

Julien, Catherine J. "Guano and Resource Control in Sixteenth Century Arequipa." In *Andean Ecology and Civilization: an Interdisciplinary Perspective on Andean Ecological Complementarity*, ed. Shozo Masuda, Izumi Shimada, and Craig Morris. Tokyo: University of Tokyo Press, 1985.

Katz, Lois, ed. *Art of the Andes: Pre-Columbian Sculptured and Painted Ceramics from the Arthur M. Sackler Collection*. Washington, D.C.: The Arthur M. Sackler Foundation and The AMS Foundation for the Arts, Sciences and Humanities, 1983.

Kubler, George. *Art and Architecture of Ancient America*, 3rd ed. Harmondsworth and New York: Penguin Publishing, 1984.

———— Towards Absolute Time: Guano Archaeology." A Reappraisal of Peruvian Archaeology, ed. Wendell C. Bennett, *Memoirs of the Society for American Archaeology* (Salt Lake City and Menasha, Wisc.), no. 4 (1948).

Larco Herrera, Rafael. "Some exponents of Chimu ceramics." *Art and Archaeology* (Washington, D. C.) 30, no. 4 (1930): 121–127.

Larco Hoyle, Rafael. *Los Cupisniques*. Lima, 1941.

———— *La Cultura Salinar*. Buenos Aires: Sociedad Geográfica Americana, 1944.

———— *Los Cupisniques*. Buenos Aires: Sociedad Geográfica Americana, 1945.

———— *Cronología Arqueología del Norte del Peru*. Buenos Aires: Sociedad Geográfica Americana, 1948.

———— *Las Epocas Peruanas*. Published by the author, Lima, 1963.

Lavalle, José Antonio de. *Culturas Precolombinas: Chimú*. Colección Arte y Tesoros del Perú, Lima: Banco de Crédito del Perú, 1988.

————, ed. *Oro del Antiguo Perú*. Lima: Banco de Crédito, 1992.

Lechtman, Heather N. "Issues in Andean Metallurgy." In *Precolumbian Metallurgy of South America*, ed. E.P. Benson, 1979.

———— "The Central Andes." In *The Coming of Age of Iron*, ed. T. A. Wertime and J.D. Muhly. New Haven: Yale University Press, 1980.

———— "Andean Value Systems and the Development of Prehistoric Metallurgy." *Tecnhology and Culture* 25, 1(1984): 1–36, Chicago.

———— "Precolumbian Surface Metallurgy." *Scientific American* 250, no. 6 (1984).

Lippard, Lucy. *Overlay, Contemporary Art and the Art of Prehistory*. New York: Pantheon Books, 1983.

Lothrop, Samuel K., W.F. Foshag, and Joy Mahler. *Pre-Columbian Art, Robert Woods Bliss Collection*. London: Phaidon Press, 1957.

Lumbreras, Luis. *The Peoples and Cultures of Ancient Peru*. Washington, D.C.; Smithsonian Institution Press, 1989.

Martínez Compañón y Bujanda, Baltasar Jaime. *La Obra del Obispo Martínez Compañón sobre Trujillo del Perú; Siglo XVIII* [c. 1782-1789]. 9 volumes.

Madrid: Ediciones Cultura Hispánica del Centro Iberoamericano de Cooperación, 1978-1991.

Menzel, Dorothy. "Style and Time in the Middle Horizon." *Nawpa Pacha* 2(1964): 1–106.

Millones, Luis, and Yoshio Onuki, eds. *El Mundo Ceremonial Andino.* Lima: Editorial Horizonte, 1994.

Morris, Craig, and Adriana von Hagen. *The Inka Empire and its Andean Origins.* New York: Abbeville Press, 1993.

Moseley, Michael E. *The Incas and their Ancestors.* London and New York: Thames and Hudson, 1992.

Phipps, Elena. "Discontinuous Warp Textiles in Pre-Columbian Weaving Tradition." Master's thesis, Columbia University, 1982.

Rostworowski de diez Canseco, María. *Estructuras Andinas del Poder. Ideología religiosa y politica.* Lima: Instituo de Estudios Peruanos, 1983.

——— *Estructuras Andinas del Poder,* 4th ed. Lima: Instituto de Estudios Peruanos, 1996.

——— "Costa Peruana Prehispanica." rev. ed. Lima: Instituto de Estudios Peruanos, 1989. Reprint, Lima: Instituto de Estudios Peruanos, 1996

Rowe, Ann P. *Costumes and Featherwork of the Lords of Chimor: Textiles from Peru's North Coast.* Feather identification by John P. O'Neill. Washington, D.C.: The Textile Museum, 1984.

——— "The Art of Peruvian Textiles." In *Andean Art at Dumbarton Oaks,* ed. Elizabeth Hill Boone, 1996.

——— ed. *The Junius B. Bird Conference on Andean Textiles, April 7th and 8th, 1984.* Washington, D.C.: The Textile Museum, 1986.

——— Elizabeth Benson, and Anne-Louise Schaffer, eds. *The Junius B. Bird Pre-Columbian Textile Conference.* Washington, D.C.: The Textile Museum and Dumbarton Oaks Research Library and Collections, 1979.

Rowe, John H., and Dorothy Menzel. *Peruvian Archaeology: Selected Readings.* Palo Alto, Calif.: Peek Publications, 1967.

Sawyer, Alan R. *Ancient Andean Arts in the Collections of the Krannert Art Museum.* Urbana-Champaign: University of Illinois, 1975.

Santo Tomas, Fray Domingo de. *Lexicon* [1563], Facsimile ed. Lima: Instituto de Historia, Universidad Nacional Mayor de San Marcos, 1951.

Shimada, Izumi. "Temples of Time." *Archaeology* (New York) 34, no. 5 (1981).

——— "Das Grab von Huaca Loro und die Sicán-Kultur." In *Sicán–Ein Fürstengrab in Alt-Peru.* Exh. cat. Zurich: Museum Rietberg, 1997.

Speltz, Alexander. *The History of Ornament.* Leipzig, 1915. Reprint. New York, 1989.

Steward, J., ed. *Handbook of South American Indians.* Bureau of American Ethnology, Bulletin 143. Washington, D.C.: Smithsonian Institution Press, 1946.

Stone-Miller, Rebecca, ed. *To Weave for the Sun: Ancient Andean Textiles.* London and New York: Thames and Hudson, 1994.

Strong, William Duncan, and Clifford Evans, Jr. *Cultural Stratigraphy in the Viru Valley, Northern Peru.* Columbia Studies in Archaeology and Ethnology IV. New York, 1952.

Taylor, Gerald. *Ritos y Tradiciones de Huarochiri.* Lima: Instituto de Estudios Peruanos, 1987.

Tello, Julio C. "Arte Antiguo Peruano, I." *Inca,* vol. II (1938).

Towle, Margaret A. *The Ethnobotany of Pre-Columbian Peru.* Chicago: Aldine Publishing Company, 1961.

Townsend, Richard F., ed. *The Ancient Americas: Art from Sacred Landscapes,* exh. cat. Chicago: Prestel in association with The Art Institute of Chicago, 1992.

Ubelohde Doering, Heinrich. *The Art of Ancient Peru.* New York: Frederick A. Praeger, 1954.

Early Horizon

Alva, Walter. *Cerámica Temprano en el Valle de Jequetepeque, Norte del Perú.* Materialen zur Allgemeinen und Vergleichenden Archaudologie Band 32, Munchen: Verlag C.H. Beck, 1986.

——— "Ofebrería del Formativo." In *Oro del Antiguo Perú, ed.* José Antonio de Lavalle, 1992.

Benson, Elizabeth P., ed. *Dumbarton Oaks Conference on Chavín.* Washington, D.C.: Dumbarton Oaks Research Library and Collection, 1971.

Burger, Richard L. *The Prehistoric Occupation of Chavin de Huantar, Peru.* University of California Publications in Anthropology. Vol. 14. Berkeley: University of Calfiornia Press, 1984.

——— *Chavín and the Origins of Andean Civilization.* London and New York: Thames and Hudson, 1992.

——— "The Chavin Horizon: Stylistic Chimera or Socioeconomic Metamorphisis." In *Latin American Horizons,* ed. Don Rice. Washington, D.C.: Dumbarton Oaks Research Library and Collections, 1993.

——— "Chavin." In *Andean Art at Dumbarton Oaks,* ed. Elizabeth Hill Boone, 1996.

Burger, Richard L. and Lucy Salazar-Burger. "Recent Investigations at the Initial

Period Center of Cardal, Lurin Valley." *Journal of Field Archaeology* 18 (1991): 275–296.

——— "La Organización Dual en el Ceremonial Andino Temprano: Un Repaso Comparativo." In *El Mundo Ceremonial Andino,* ed. Luis Millones and Yoshio Onuki, 1994.

Carrión Cachot, Rebeca. *Los Ultimos Descubrimientos en Chavin-La Serpiente Símbolo las Lluvias y la Fecundidad.* Actas del 33 Congreso Internacional de Americanistas. San Jose, Costa Rica, 1958.

Cordy-Collins, Alana. "Cotton and the Staff God: Analysis of an Ancient Chavin Textile." In ed. A. Rowe, E. Benson, and A-L. Schaffer, 1973.

Donnan, Christopher, ed. *Early Ceremonial Architecture in the Andes.* Washington, D.C.: Dumbarton Oaks Research Library and Collections, 1985.

Elera, Carlos. *Investigaciones sobre patrones funerarios en el sitio formativo del Morro de Eten, Valle de Lambayeque, costa norte del Perú.* PUC: Memoria de Bachiller, 1986.

——— "El Complejo Cultural Cupisnique: Anecedentes y Desarrollo de su Ideología Religiosa." In *El Mundo Ceremonial Andino,* ed. Luis Millones and Yoshio Onuki, 1994.

Elera, Carlos, Jose Pinilla and Victor Vazquez. "Bioindicadores a zoologicos de eventos ENSO para el Formativo Medio y Tardío de Puémape-Perú." *Pachacamac* 1, no. 1 (1992): 9–19.

Grieder, Terence. *The Art and Archaeology of Pashash.* Austin: University of Texas Press, 1978.

Lumbrereras, Luis G. *The Peoples and Cultures of Ancient Peru.* Washington, D.C.: Smithsonian Institution Press, 1974.

Reichel-Dolmatoff, G. *The Shaman and the Jaguar: A Study of Narcotic Drugs Among the Indians of Colombia.* Philadelphia: Temple University Press, 1975.

Roe, Peter. *A Further Exploration of the Rowe Chavin Seriation and its Implications for North Central Coast Chronology.* Studies in Pre-Columbian Art and Archaeology, no. 13. Washington, D.C.: Dumbarton Oaks Research Library and Collections, 1974.

Rowe, John H. *Chavín Art: an Inquiry into its Form and Meaning.* New York: The Museum of Primitive Art, 1962.

——— "Form and Meaning in Chavin Art." In *Peruvian Archaeology,* ed. J.H. Rowe and D. Menzel, 1967.

——— "The Influence of Chavín Art on Later Styles." In ed. E. P. Benson, 1971.

Salazar-Burger, Lucy and Richard L. Burger. "La Araña en la Iconografía del

Horizonte Temprano en la Costa Norte del Perú." *Beitrage zur Allgemeinen und Vergleichenden Archaologie Band* 4(1983): 213–253.

———— "Cupisnique." In *Andean Art at Dumbarton Oaks*, ed. Elizabeth Hill Boone, 1996.

Stone, Rebecca. "Possible Uses, Roles and Meanings of Chavín-style Painted Textiles of South Coast Peru." In *Investigations of the Andean Past*, ed. D. Sandweiss. Ithaca, New York, 1983.

Tello, Julio C. l923 "Wirakocha." *Inca* I(1923): 93–320, 583–606.

———— *Chavin: Cultura Matriz de la Civilización Andina.* Lima: UNMSM, 1960.

Ulbert, Cornelius. *Die Keramik der Forativzeitlichen Siedlund Montegrande, Jequetepequetal, Nord-Peru.* Komission fur Allgemeine und Vergleichende Archaologie Band 52. Mainz am Rhein, 1994.

Watanabe, Luis. "Sitios Tempranos en el Valle de Moche, Costa Norte del Perú." Ph.d. dissertation, UNMSM, 1976.

Willey, Gordon. *Prehistoric Settlement Patterns in the Viru Valley, Peru.* Smithsonian Institution Bureau of American Ethnology Bulletin 155. Washington, D.C.: US Government Printing Office, 1953.

Paracas and Nasca

Aveni, A., ed. *The Lines of Nazca.* Philadelphia: The American Philosophical Society, 1990.

Carmichael, Patrick H. "Nasca Pottery Construction." *Nawpa Pacha* 24(1986): 31–48.

Daggett, Richard E. "Paracas: Discovery and Controversy." In *Paracas Art and Architecture*, ed. A. Paul, 1991.

Jones, Julie. "Nasca Drum (1978.412.111)." In *The Pacific Islands, Africa, and the Americas.* New York: The Metropolitan Museum of Art, 1987.

Morrison, Tony. *Pathways to the Gods: The Mystery of the Andes Lines.* Harper and Row, 1978.

Paul, Anne and S. Niles. "Identifying Hands at Work on a Paracas Mantle." *The Textile Museum Journal* 23 (1985).

Paul, Anne, ed. *Paracas Art and Architecture: Objects and Context in South Coastal Peru.* Iowa City: University of Iowa Press, 1991.

———— "Procedures, Patterns, and Deviations in Paracas Embroidered Textiles." In *To Weave for the Sun*, ed. R. Stone-Miller, 1994.

———— *Paracas Ritual Attire: Symbols of Authority in Ancient Peru.* Norman, Okla.: University of Oklahoma Press, 1990.

Peters, Ann H. "Ecology and Society in Embroidered Images from the Paracas Necrópolis." In *Paracas Art and Architecture*, ed. A. Paul, 1991.

Proulx, Donald A. "The Nasca Style." In *Art of the Andes*, ed. L. Katz, 1983.

———— "Tiahuanaco and Huari." In *Art of the Andes*, ed. L. Katz, 1983.

Reinhard, Johan. "Interpreting the Nazca Lines." In *The Ancient Americas*, ed. R. Townsend, 1992.

Silverman, Helaine. "The Early Nasca Pilgrimage Center of Cahuachi and the Nasca Lines: Anthropological and Archaeological Perspectives." In *The Lines of Nazca*, ed. A. Aveni, 1990.

———— "The Paracas Problem: Archaeological Perspectives." In *Paracas Art and Architecture*, ed. A. Paul, 1991.

Yacovleff, Eugenio. "La deidad primitiva de los Nasca." *Revista del Museo Nacional* (Lima) 1, no. 2 (1932).

Moche

Alva, Walter. "Into the Tomb of a Moche Lord." *National Geographic*, 174, no. 4 (1988): 516–549.

———— *Sipan.* Lima: Backus y Johnston en la cultura y artes del Peru, 1994.

Alva, Walter, and Christopher B. Donnan. *Royal Tombs of Sipan.* Los Angeles: University of California, Fowler Museum of Culteral History, 1993.

Arsenault, Daniel. "El personaje del pie amputado en la cultura mochica del Peru: Un ensayo sobre la arqueología del poder." *Latin American Antiquity* 4, no. 3 (1993): 225–245.

Benson, Elizabeth P. *The Mochica: A Culture of Peru.* New York: Praeger, 1972.

———— "A Man and a Feline in Mochica Art." *Studies in Pre-Columbian Art and Archaeology* 14. Washington, D.C.: Dumbarton Oaks, 1974.

———— "Death-associated Figures on Mochica Pottery." In *Death and the Afterlife in Pre-Columbian America*, ed. E. P. Benson, 1975.

———— "The Bag with the Ruffled Top: Some Problems of Identification in Moche Art." *Journal of Latin American Lore* 4, no. 1. Los Angeles: University of California, Latin American Center, 1978.

———— "The Well-Dressed Captives: Some Observations on Moche Iconography." *Baessler-Archiv* N.F. XXX(1982): 181–222.

———— "A Moche 'Spatula'." *The Metropolitan Museum Journal* 18(1984): 39–52.

———— "The Moche Moon." In *Recent Studies in Andean Prehistory and Protohistory*, ed. D. P. Kvietok and D. H. Sandweiss. Ithaca, New York:

Cornell University, Latin American Studies Program, 1985.

———— "Bats in South American Iconography." *Andean Past* I (1987): 165-190. Ithaca: Cornell University, latin American Studies Program.

———— "Women in Mochica Art." In *The Role of Gender in Pre-Columbian Art and Archaeology*, ed. Virginia E. Miller. Lanham, Maryland: University Press of America, 1988.

———— "The Chthonic Canine." *Latin American Indian Languages Journal* 7, no. 1(1991): 95–107.

———— "The World of Moche." In *The Ancient Americas*, ed. R. Townsend, 1992.

Berezkin, Yuri. "An identification of anthropomorphic mythological personages in Moche representations." *Nawpa Pacha* 18(1980-81): 1–26.

Bergh, Susan E. "Death and Renewal in Moche Phallic-Spouted Vessels." *RES: Anthropology and Aesthetics* (1993): 78–94.

Bourget, Steve. "El mar y la muerte en la iconografía moche." In *Moche: Propuestas y perspectivas*, ed. S. Uceda and E. Mujica, 1994.

———— "Los Sacerdotes a la Sombra del Cerro Blanco y del Arco Bicéfalo." *Revista del Museo de Arqueología, Antropología e Historia* 5. Trujillo: Universidad Nacional de Trujillo, 1994.

Castillo Butters, Jaime Luis. *Personajes míticos, escenas y narraciones en la iconografía mochica.* Lima: Pontificia Universidad Católica del Péru, 1989.

———— *Treasures of Sacred Civilizations: Life and Art in Ancient Peru.* Lima: Promperú, 1994.

Classen, Constance. *Inca Cosmology and the Human Body.* Salt Lake City: University of Utah Press, 1993.

Coe, Sophie D. *America's First Cuisine.* Austin: University of Texas Press, 1994.

Conklin, William J. "Moche Textile Structures." In *The Junius B. Bird Pre-Columbian Textile Conference*, ed. A. Rowe, E. Benson, and A-L. Schaffer, 1979.

Donnan, Christopher. *Moche Art of Peru.* Los Angeles: Fowler Museum of Cultural History, UCLA, 1978.

———— "Moche Ceramic Technology." *Nawpa Pacha* 3 (1965): 115–135.

———— *Moche Art and Iconography.* Los Angeles: University of California Latin American Center Publications, 1976.

———— "Dance in Moche Art." *Nawpa Pacha* 20 (1982): 97–120.

———— *Ceramics of Ancient Peru.* Los Angeles: University of California, Fowler Museum of Cultural History, 1992.

————. "Moche Funerary Practice." In ed. T. D. Dillehay, 1995.

———— and D. McClelland. "The Burial Theme in Moche Iconography." *Studies in Pre-Columbian Art and Archaeology*, no. 21. Washington, D.C.: Dumbarton Oaks Research Library and Collection, and Trustees for Harvard University, 1979.

———— and L. J. Castillo. "Finding the Tomb of a Moche Priestess." *Archaeology* 45, 6 (1992).

———— and W. Alva. *The Royal Tombs of Sipán.* Los Angeles: Fowler Museum of Cultural History, UCLA, 1993.

———— and Carol J. Mackey. *Ancient Burial Patterns of the Moche Valley, Peru.* Austin and London: University of Texas Press, 1978.

Gillin, John. *Moche: A Peruvian Coastal Community.* Institute of Social Anthropology Publication 3. Washington, D.C.: Smithsonian Institution, 1945.

Hocquenghem, Anne Marie. *Iconografía Mochica.* Lima: Pontificia Universidad Católica del Perú, 1987.

Jones, Julie. "Mochica Works of Art in Metal." In *Precolumbian Metallurgy of South America*, ed. E.P. Benson, 1979.

Kutscher, Gerdt. *Nordperuanische Gefässmalereien des Moche-Stils.* Materialien zur Allgemeinen und Vergleichenden Archäologie 18, ed. Ulf Bankmann. Munich: Verlag C. H. Beck, 1983.

Larco Hoyle, Rafael. See p. 19, this volume.

Lechtman, Heather. "New Perspectives on Moche Metallugry: Techniques of Gilding Copper at Loma Negra, Northern Peru." *American Antiquity* 47, no. 1(1982): 3–30.

Pozorski, Shelia Griffis. "Prehistoric Subsistence Patterns and Site Economics in the Moche Valley, Peru." Ph.D. dissertation, University of Texas, 1976.

Quilter, Jeffrey. "The Moche Revolt of the Objects." *Latin American Antiquity* 1, no. 1(1990): 42–65.

Schaffer, Ann-Louise. "Cathartidae in Moche Art and Culture." In *Flora and Fauna Imagery in Precolumbian Cultures: Iconography and Function.* BAR International Series 171. Oxford, 1983.

Shimada, Izumi. *Pampa Grande and the Mochica Culture.* Austin: University of Texas Press, 1994.

Shimada, Melody. "Paleoethnozoological/ botanical Analysis of Moche V Economy at Pampa Grande, Peru." Master's thesis, Princeton University, 1979.

Uceda, Santiago and Ricardo Morales. "Informe Cuarta Temporada, 1995." Proyecto Arqueológico Huaca de la Luna, Universidad Nacional de Trujillo, Facultad de Ciencias Sociales, 1996.

Uceda, Santiago, and Elias Mujica, eds. *Moche: Propuestas y perspectivas.* Trujillo: Universidad Nacional de La Libertad, 1994.

Uceda, Santiago, Ricardo Morales, and Elias Mujica. *Huacas del Sol y de la Luna.* Trujillo: Universidad Nacional de La Libertad, Archaeological Project Huaca de la Luna, 1996.

Wassén, S. Henry. "Ulluchu in Moche Iconography and Blood Ceremonies: the Search for Identification." *Göteborgs Etnografiska Museum Arstryck Annals* (1985–86): 59–85.

Late Intermediate Period

Bennett, Wendell C. *Ancient Arts of the Andes.* New York: Museum of Modern Art, 1954.

Bird, Junius B. "Pre-Ceramic Art from Huaca Prieta, Chicama Valley." *Nawpa Pacha* 1(1963): 29–34.

Bruce, Susan Lee. "Textile Miniatures from Pacatnamu, Peru." In ed. Ann P. Rowe, 1986.

Calancha, Antonio de la. *Coronica Moralizada del Orden de San Augustín en el Peru* [1638]. 6 vols. Trans. Ignacio Prado Pastor. Lima: Published privately, 1977.

Carrion Cachot, Rebeca. "El Culto al Agua en el Antiguo Peru, La Paccha Elemento cultural Pan-andino." *Revista del Museo Nacional de Antropología y Arqueología* 2, no. 2 (1955): 7–100.

Cordy-Collins, Alana. "The Moon is a Boat!: A Study in Iconographic Methodology." In *Pre-Columbian Art History*, eds. Alana Cordy-Collins and Jean Stern, 1977.

———— "Fonga Sigde, Shell Purveyor to the Chimu Kings." In *The Northern Dynasties*, eds. M. Moseley and A. Cordy-Collins, 1990.

————"An Unshaggy Dog Story." *Natural History* 103, no. 2(1994): 34–41.

Cummins, Thomas B. F. "Abstraction to Narration: Kero Imagery of Peru and the Colonial Alteration of Native Identity." Ph.D. dissertation, UCLA, 1988.

Davidson, Judith R. "The Spondylus Shell in Chimu Iconography." Master's thesis, California State University, 1980.

Day, Kent C. "Architecture of Ciudadela Rivero, Chan Chan, Peru." Ph.D. dissertation, Harvard University, 1973.

Deletaille, Emile, and Lin Deletaille, coordinators. *Trésors du Noveau Monde.* Brussels: Musées Royaux d'Art et d'Histoire, 1992.

Dorsey, George A. *Archaeological Excavations on the Island of La Plata, Ecuador.* Field Columbian Museum Publication 56, Anthropological Series 2 (5), Chicago, 1901.

Jackson, Margaret. "A Passion Play Revisited: Cultural Continuity and Political Legitimation in Chimu Wooden Sculpture from the Moche Valley, Peru." Master's thesis, UCLA, 1991.

Lothrop, Samuel J. "Peruvian Pacchas and Keros." *American Antiquity* 21(1956): 233–243.

Mackey, Carol. "The Southern Frontier of the Chimu Empire." In *The Northern Dynasties*, eds. M. Moseley and A. Cordy-Collins, 1990.

———— "Chimu Administration in the Provinces." In *Origins and Development of the Andean State*, eds. J. Haas, T. and S. Pozorski, 1987.

Martínez Compañón y Bujanda, Baltasar Jaime. *La Obra del Obispo Martínez Compañón sobre Trujillo del Perú; Siglo XVIII.* 9 vols. Madrid: Ediciones Cultura Hispánica del Centro Iberoamericano de Cooperación, 1978-1991.

McClelland, Donna. "A Maritime Passage from Moche to Chimu." In *The Northern Dynasties*, eds. M. Moseley and A. Cordy-Collins, 1990.

Moseley, M. and A. Cordy-Collins, eds. *The Northern Dynasties: Kingship and Statecraft in Chimor.* Washington, D.C.: Dumbarton Oaks Research Library and Collection, 1990.

Moseley, M. and K. Day, eds. *Chan Chan: Andean Desert City.* Albuquerque: University of New Mexico Press, 1982.

Muelle, Jorge and Robert Wells. *Las Pinturas del Templo de Pachacamac.* Revista del Museo Nacional, vol. VIII, no. 3, Lima, 1939.

Pillsbury, Joanne. "Sculpted Friezes of the Empire of Chimor." Ph.D. dissertation, Columbia University, 1993.

———— "The Thorny Oyster and the Origins of Empire: Implications of Recently Uncovered *Spondylus* Imagery from Chan Chan, Peru." *Latin American Antiquity* 7, no. 4(1996): 313–340.

Ríos, Marcela and Enrique Retamozo. *Vasos Ceremoniales de Chan Chan.* Lima: Instituto Cultural Peruano Norteamericano, 1982.

Rostworowski, Maria. *Pachacamac y el Señor de los Milagros.* Lima: Instituto de Estudios Peruanos, 1992.

Shimada, Izumi and J. A. Griffin. "Precious Metal Objects of the Middle Sicán." *Scientific American* 270, no. 4 (1994).

Shimada, Izumi. "Behind the Golden Mask: Sicán Gold Artifacts from Batán Grande, Peru." In *The Art of Pre-Columbian Gold*, ed. J. Jones, 1985.

Topic, John R. "Craft Production in the Kingdom of Chimor." In *The Northern Dynasties*, eds. M. Moseley and A. Cordy-Collins, 1990.

Young-Sanchez, Margaret. "Textile Traditions of the Late Intermediate Period."

In *To Weave for the Sun*, ed. R. Stone-Miller, 1994.

Zevallos Quiñones, Jorge. *Huacas y Huaqueros en Trujillo durante el Virreynato (1535-1835)*. Trujillo: Normas Legales, 1994.

Huari and Tiahuanaco

Browman, D. "New Light on Andean Tiwanaku." *American Scientist* 69, no. 4 (1981).

Cook, Anita G. "The Middle Horizon Ceramic Offerings from Conchopata." *Nawpa Pacha* 22-23(1984-85): 49–90.

——— "Huari." In *Andean Art at Dumbarton Oaks*, ed. Elizabeth Hill Boone, 1996.

Cook, Anita G. and William J. Conklin. "Blue and Yellow Panel (B-522)." In *Andean Art at Dumbarton Oaks*, ed. Elizabeth Hill Boone, 1996.

Cordy-Collins, Alana. "Lambayeque." In *Andean Art at Dumbarton Oaks*, ed. Elizabeth Hill Boone, 1996.

Isbell, W. and G. McEwan, eds. *Huari Administrative Structure: Prehistoric Monumental Architecture and State Government*. Washington, D.C.: Dumbarton Oaks, 1991.

Kolata, Alan and C. Ponce Sangines. "Tiwanaku: the City at the Center." In *The Ancient Americas*, ed. R. Townsend, 1992.

Prümers, Heiko. *Der Fundort "El Castillo" im Huarmeytal, Peru. Ein Beitrag zum Problem des Moche-Huari Textilstils*. Berlin: Holos Verlag, 1990.

Schreiber, Katharina J. *Huari Imperialism in Middle Horizon Peru*. Anthropological Papers 87. Ann Arbor: Museum of Anthropology, University of Michigan, 1992.

Stone, R. "Color Patterning and the Huari Artist: the 'Lima Tapestry' Revisited." In ed. Ann P. Rowe, 1986.

Stone-Miller, Rebecca. *Art of the Andes from Chavín to Inca*. London: Thames & Hudson, 1995.

——— "Camelids and Chaos in Huari and Tiwanaku." In *The Ancient Americas*, ed. R. Townsend, 1992.

Stone-Miller, R., and G. McEwan. "The Representation of the Huari State in Stone and Thread: A Comparison of Architecture and Tapestry Tunics." *RES: Anthropology and Aesthetics* 19 (1990).

Inca

Ascher, Marcia, and Robert Ascher. *The Code of the Quipu: A Study in Media, Mathematics, and Culture*. Ann Arbor: University of Michigan Press, 1981.

Cieza de León, Pedro. *The Incas* [1553].
Trans. Harriet de Onis. Norman: University of Oklahoma Press, 1959.

Classen, Constance. *Inca Cosmology and the Human Body*. Salt Lake City: University of Utah Press, 1993.

Cobo, Bernabé. *Historia del Nuevo Mundo*. 4 vols. Ed. Marcos Jimenez de la Espada. Seville: Sociedad de Bibliofilos Andaluces, 1890-1895.

——— *History of the Inca Empire* [1653]. Trans./ed. Roland Hamilton. Austin: University of Texas Press, 1983.

——— *Inca Religion and Customs* [1653]. Trans./ed. Roland Hamilton. Austin: University of Texas Press, 1990.

Garcilaso de la Vega. *Primera Parte de los Commentarios Reales*, 2nd ed., Madrid, 1923.

Gasparini, Graziano and Luis Margolis. *Inca Architecture*. Bloomington: Indiana University Press, 1980.

Guaman Poma de Ayala, Felipe. *El Primer Nueva Corónica y Buen Gobierno*. ed. J. Murra and R. Adorno. Trans. Jorge J. L. Urioste. 3 vols. Mexico: Siglo Veintiuno, 1980.

Hyslop, John. *The Inka Road System*. New York: Academic Press, 1984.

——— *Inka Settlement Planning*. Austin: University of Texas Press, 1990.

Jones, Julie. *Art of Empire: the Inca of Peru*. Greenwich, New York: The Museum of Primitive Art and New York Graphic Society, 1964.

Joyce, T. A. "Pakcha." *Inca*. 1, 4(1923): 761–778.

Lunt, Sarah. "The Manufacture of the Inca Aryballus." In *Recent Studies in Pre-Columbian Archaeology*, eds. Nicholas J. Saunders and Olivier de Montmollin, BAR International Series 421 (ii), Oxford, 1988.

Mackey, Carol, Hugo Pereyra, Carlos Radicati, Humberto Rodriguez, and Oscar Valverde. *Quipu y Yupana: Colección de Escritos*. Lima: Consejo Nacional de Ciencia y Tecnología, Ministerio de la Presidencia, 1990.

McEwan, Colin, and Maarten van de Guchte. "Ancestral Time and Sacred Space in Inca State Ritual." In *The Ancient Americas*, ed. R. Townsend, 1992.

Morris, Craig and Adriana von Hagen. *The Inka Empire and its Andean Origins*. New York: The American Museum of Natural History and Abbeville Press, 1993.

Morris, Craig and Donald Thompson. *Huánuco Pampa: An Inca City and its Hinterland*. London and New York: Thames and Hudson, 1985.

Moseley, Michael E. *The Incas and Their Ancestors*. London: Thames & Hudson, 1992.

Murra, John. "Cloth and its Functions in the Inca State." *American Anthropologist* 64, no. 4(1962): 710–28.

Niles, Susan. "Artists and Empire in Inca and Colonial Textiles." In *To Weave for the Sun*, ed. R. Stone-Miller, 1994.

Paternosto, Cesar. *Piedra abstracta, le escultura Inca: una vision contemporana*. Mexico: Fondo de Cultura Economica, 1989.

Protzen, Jean-Pierre. *Inka Architecture and Construction at Ollantaytambo*. Oxford and New York: Oxford UP, 1993.

——— "Inca Stonemasonry." *Scientific American* 254, no. 2 (1986).

Purin, Sergio, ed. *Inca - Perú, 3000 Ans d'Histoire: Musées Royaux d'Art et d'Histoire, Bruxelles, 21.9 - 30.12.1990*. 2 vols. Ghent: Imschoot, 1990.

Ranney, Edward and John Hemming. *Monuments of the Incas*. Boston, 1982; Albuquerque: University of New Mexico Press, 1990.

Reinhard, Johan. "Peru's Ice Maidens: Unwrapping the Secrets." *National Geographic* 189, 6(1996): 62–81.

Rowe, Ann P. "Technical Features of Inca Tapestry Tunics." *The Textile Museum Journal* 17 (1978).

Rowe, John. "Inca Culture at the Time of the Spanish Conquest." In *Handbook of South American Indians*, ed. J. Steward, 1946.

——— "Standardization in Inca Tapestry Tunics." In *The Junius B. Bird Pre-Columbian Textile Conference*, ed. A. Rowe, E. Benson, and A-L. Schaffer, 1979.

Zuidema, R. Tom. *Inca Civilization in Cuzco*. Austin: University of Texas Press, 1990.

——— *The Ceque System of Cuzco*. Leyden: 1964.

Index

Page numbers in **boldface** type refer to principal catalogue descriptions.

ILLUSTRATION CREDITS

ACCOMPANYING THE ESSAYS:

PREFACE: Daniel Giannoni

BERRIN: Fig. I Courtesy Museo Arqueológico Rafael Larco Herrera; Fig. 2 Kathleen Berrin; Fig. 3 Carlos Rojas Vila; Fig. 4 Charles M. Rick, Jr.; Fig. 5 Courtesy of the University of Texas Press

EVANS: Figs. 1–5 Courtesy of the Museo Arqueológico Rafael Larco Herrera

BURGER: Fig. 1 After Pulgar Vidal 1972; Figs. 2–5 Richard L. Burger; Fig. 6 Drawing by Richard L. Burger and Luis Caballero

ROSTWOROWSKI: Figs. 1–2 John W. Rick; Fig. 3 Elizabeth P. Benson

BENSON: Fig. 1 Kathleen Berrin; Figs.2, 3 Elizabeth P. Benson; Fig. 4 Kutscher 1983: Abb. 316B; Fig. 5. Baessler 1902–3, pl. 93

DONNAN: Fig. 1 Daniel Giannoni; Fig. 2 Robert Easley; Fig. 3, 4, 6–12, 14 Drawings by Donna McClelland

PASZTORY: Fig. 1 Esther Pasztory; Fig. 2 Courtesy of The Art Institute of Chicago; Fig. 3 Drawing by Janice Robertson; Fig. 4 Copyright © Philadelphia Museum of Art; Fig.5 Ivam Centro Julio Gonzalez Institut Valencia d'Arte Moderna 1992, p1. 127; Fig. 6 Courtesy Museo Arqueológico Rafael Larco Herrera; Fig. 7 Drawings by Janice Robertson; Fig. 9 Copyright © Museum of Modern Art, New York

IN THE CATALOGUE OF OBJECTS:

All photographs by Carlos Rojas Vila except cat. nos. 15, 34, 73, 86, 94, 104, 119, 121, 130, 145, ‖146, 148, 157, 158, 160, which are by Daniel Giannoni.

THE SPIRIT OF ANCIENT PERU
Treasures from the Museo Arqueológico Rafael Larco Herrera

is produced by the Publications Department of the
Fine Arts Museums of San Francisco

Ann Heath Karlstrom, Director of Publications and Graphic Design
Karen Kevorkian, Managing Editor

Book design by Dana Levy, Perpetua Press, Los Angeles
Copyediting by Tish O'Connor, Perpetua Press, and Brenda Johnson-Grau
Type composed on a Macintosh Computer in Goudy and Weiss fonts

Printed and bound by C&C Offset Printing Co., Hong Kong